Clean Code in Python

Second Edition

Develop maintainable and efficient code

Mariano Anaya

BIRMINGHAM - MUMBAI

Clean Code in Python
Second Edition

Copyright © 2020 Packt Publishing

All rights reserved. No part of this book may be reproduced, stored in a retrieval system, or transmitted in any form or by any means, without the prior written permission of the publisher, except in the case of brief quotations embedded in critical articles or reviews.

Every effort has been made in the preparation of this book to ensure the accuracy of the information presented. However, the information contained in this book is sold without warranty, either express or implied. Neither the author, nor Packt Publishing or its dealers and distributors, will be held liable for any damages caused or alleged to have been caused directly or indirectly by this book.

Packt Publishing has endeavored to provide trademark information about all of the companies and products mentioned in this book by the appropriate use of capitals. However, Packt Publishing cannot guarantee the accuracy of this information.

Producers: Tushar Gupta
Acquisition Editor – Peer Reviews: Divya Mudaliar
Content Development Editor: Bhavesh Amin
Technical Editor: Karan Sonawane
Project Editor: Mrunal Dave
Copy Editor: Safis Editing
Proofreader: Safis Editing
Indexer: Tejal Soni
Presentation Designer: Ganesh Bhadwalkar

First published: August 2018
Second Edition: December 2020

Production reference: 2281220

Published by Packt Publishing Ltd.
Livery Place
35 Livery Street
Birmingham B3 2PB, UK.

ISBN 978-1-80056-021-5

www.packt.com

packt.com

Subscribe to our online digital library for full access to over 7,000 books and videos, as well as industry leading tools to help you plan your personal development and advance your career. For more information, please visit our website.

Why subscribe?

- Spend less time learning and more time coding with practical eBooks and Videos from over 4,000 industry professionals
- Learn better with Skill Plans built especially for you
- Get a free eBook or video every month
- Fully searchable for easy access to vital information
- Copy and paste, print, and bookmark content

Did you know that Packt offers eBook versions of every book published, with PDF and ePub files available? You can upgrade to the eBook version at www.Packt.com and as a print book customer, you are entitled to a discount on the eBook copy. Get in touch with us at customercare@packtpub.com for more details.

At www.Packt.com, you can also read a collection of free technical articles, sign up for a range of free newsletters, and receive exclusive discounts and offers on Packt books and eBooks.

Contributors

About the author

Mariano Anaya is a software engineer who spends most of his time creating software and mentoring fellow programmers. Mariano's primary areas of interest are software architecture, functional programming, and distributed systems. He was a speaker at *Euro Python* in 2016 and 2017, and *FOSDEM* 2019. To find out more about him, you can refer to his GitHub account with the username `rmariano`.

Dedicated to my family and friends, for their unconditional support.

About the reviewer

Tarek Ziadé has been a Python developer for a long time. Back in the old days, he founded the French Python User group (AFPY) and was involved in the language development around packaging. He has written books about Python in both French (his native language) and English.

Tarek worked at Mozilla for over a decade, building tools and services, leveraging Python's awesomeness in projects at scale. He now works as a principal engineer at Elastic.

Table of Contents

Preface

Who this book is for?

This book is suitable for all software engineering practitioners who are interested in software design or learning more about Python. It is assumed that the reader is already familiar with the principles of object-oriented software design and has experience writing code.

It will appeal to team leads, software architects and senior software engineers who want to learn good Python coding techniques to create projects from scratch or work on their legacy systems to save costs and improve efficiency.

The book is organized in such a way that the content is in increasing order of complexity. The first chapters cover the basics of Python, which is a good way to learn the main idioms, functions, and utilities available in the language. The idea is not just to solve some problems with Python, but to do so in an idiomatic way.

Experienced programmers will also benefit from the topics in this book, as some sections cover advanced topics in Python, such as decorators, descriptors, and an introduction to asynchronous programming. It will help the reader discover more about Python because some of the cases are analyzed from the internals of the language itself.

Scientists using Python for data processing can also benefit from the content of this book, and to that end, several parts of the book are dedicated to setting up projects from the ground up, in terms of tools, configuration of environments, and good practices to release software.

It is worth emphasizing the word "practitioners" in the first sentence of this section. This is a book that takes a pragmatic approach. Examples are limited to what the case study requires but are also intended to resemble the context of a real software project. It is not an academic book, and as such the definitions made, the remarks made, and the recommendations are to be taken with caution. The reader is expected to examine these recommendations critically and pragmatically rather than dogmatically. After all, practicality beats purity.

What this book covers

Chapter 1, Introduction, Code Formatting, and Tools, is an introduction to the main tools the reader needs to set up a development environment in Python. We cover the basics a Python developer is recommended to know to start working with the language effectively. It also includes some guidelines for maintaining readable code in the project, such as tools for static analysis, documentation, type checking, and code formatting. Having a common understanding of coding standards is a good thing but relying on good intentions only doesn't scale. That's why the chapter concludes by discussing tools to work more effectively.

Chapter 2, Pythonic Code, looks at the first idioms in Python, which we will continue to use in the following chapters. We cover the particular features of Python, how they are meant to be used, and in this chapter, we start building knowledge around the idea that Pythonic code is in general of much better quality.

Chapter 3, General Traits of Good Code, reviews general principles of software engineering making the focus on writing more maintainable code. With the knowledge gained from the previous chapter, we take a look at general clean design ideas, and how they can be implemented in Python.

Chapter 4, The SOLID Principles, covers a set of design principles for object-oriented software design. This acronym is part of the language or jargon of software engineering, and we see how each one of them can be applied to Python. In particular, the reader will learn how dependency injection makes the code more maintainable, a concept that will be very useful in the next chapters.

Chapter 5, Using Decorators to Improve Our Code, looks at one of the greatest features of Python. After understanding how to create decorators (for functions and classes), we put them in action for reusing code, separating responsibilities, and creating more granular functions. Another interesting learning point from this chapter is how to use decorators to our advantage to simplify complex and repetitive function signatures.

Chapter 6, Getting More Out of Our Objects with Descriptors, explores descriptors in Python, which take object-oriented design to a new level. While this is a feature more related to frameworks and tools, we can see how to improve the readability of our code with descriptors, and also reuse code. The content revisited in this chapter will make the reader achieve a higher level of understanding of Python.

Chapter 7, Generators, Iterators, and Asynchronous Programming, starts by showing how generators are a fantastic feature of Python. The fact that iteration is a core component of Python could make us think that it leads to a new programming model. By using generators and iterators in general, we can think differently about the way we write our programs. With the lessons learned from generators, we go further and learn about coroutines in Python and the basics of asynchronous programming. This chapter wraps up by explaining the new syntax (and new magic methods!) for asynchronous programming and asynchronous iteration.

Chapter 8, Unit Testing and Refactoring, discusses the importance of unit tests in any codebase that claims to be maintainable. We discuss refactoring as a pre-requisite to evolve and maintain a code base, and how unit tests are critical for this. All of this, with the support of the proper tools (mainly the `unittest` and `pytest` modules). Finally, we learn how the secret for good testing lies not so much on the tests themselves, but on having testable code.

Chapter 9, Common Design Patterns, reviews how to implement the most common design patterns in Python, not from the point of view of solving a problem, but by examining how they solve problems by leveraging a better and more maintainable solution. The chapter mentions the peculiarities of Python that have made some of the design patterns invisible and takes a pragmatic approach to implement some of them. We discuss other (not so "conventional") patterns that are Python-specific.

Chapter 10, Clean Architecture, focuses on the idea that clean code is the base of good architecture. All those details we mentioned in the first chapter, and everything else revisited along the way, will play a critical role in the entire design when the system is deployed.

To get the most out of this book

The reader is expected to have some degree of programming experience and be somehow familiarized with the basics of Python's syntax. Also, basic programming knowledge, like structured programming, and knowledge of object-oriented design is assumed.

To test the code, you need to have Python installed, which can be downloaded from `https://www.python.org/downloads/`. The code runs with Python 3.9+, and the creation of a virtual environment is highly recommended. Alternative, the code can be tested in a Docker image.

Download the example code files

The code bundle for the book is hosted on GitHub at `https://github.com/PacktPublishing/Clean-Code-in-Python-Second-Edition`. We also have other code bundles from our rich catalog of books and videos available at `https://github.com/PacktPublishing/`. Check them out!

Download the color images

We also provide a PDF file that has color images of the screenshots/diagrams used in this book. You can download it here: `https://static.packt-cdn.com/downloads/9781800560215_ColorImages.pdf`

Conventions used

There are a number of text conventions used throughout this book.

`CodeInText`: Indicates code words in text, database table names, folder names, filenames, file extensions, pathnames, dummy URLs, user input, and Twitter handles. For example; "Then, just running the `pylint` command is enough to check it in the code."

A block of code is set as follows:

```
@dataclass
class Point:
    lat: float
    long: float
```

When we wish to draw your attention to a particular part of a code block, the relevant lines or items are set in bold:

```
setup(
    name="apptool",
    description="Description of the intention of the package",
    long_description=long_description,
)
```

Any command-line input or output is written as follows:

```
>>> locate.__annotations__
{'latitude': float, 'longitue': float, 'return': __main__.Point}
```

Bold: Indicates a new term, an important word, or words that you see on the screen, for example, in menus or dialog boxes, also appear in the text like this. For example: "We would like a design with a better **separation of concerns**."

Warnings or important notes appear like this.

Tips and tricks appear like this.

Get in touch

Feedback from our readers is always welcome.

General feedback: Email feedback@packtpub.com and mention the book's title in the subject of your message. If you have questions about any aspect of this book, please email us at questions@packtpub.com.

Errata: Although we have taken every care to ensure the accuracy of our content, mistakes do happen. If you have found a mistake in this book, we would be grateful if you would report this to us. Please visit, http://www.packtpub.com/submit-errata, selecting your book, clicking on the Errata Submission Form link, and entering the details.

Piracy: If you come across any illegal copies of our works in any form on the Internet, we would be grateful if you would provide us with the location address or website name. Please contact us at copyright@packtpub.com with a link to the material.

If you are interested in becoming an author: If there is a topic that you have expertise in and you are interested in either writing or contributing to a book, please visit http://authors.packtpub.com.

Reviews

Please leave a review. Once you have read and used this book, why not leave a review on the site that you purchased it from? Potential readers can then see and use your unbiased opinion to make purchase decisions, we at Packt can understand what you think about our products, and our authors can see your feedback on their book. Thank you!

For more information about Packt, please visit packtpub.com.

1

Introduction, Code Formatting, and Tools

In this chapter, we will explore the first concepts related to clean code, starting with what it is and what it means. The main goal of the chapter is to understand that clean code is not just a nice thing to have or a luxury in software projects. It's a necessity. Without quality code, the project will face the perils of failing due to an accumulation of technical debt (*technical debt* is something we'll discuss at length later in the chapter, so don't worry if you haven't heard the term before).

Along the same lines, but going into a bit more detail, are the concepts of formatting and documenting the code. These also might sound like superfluous requirements or tasks, but again, we will discover that they play a fundamental role in keeping the code base maintainable and workable.

We will analyze the importance of adopting a good coding guideline for this project. Realizing that maintaining the code aligned to a reference is a continuous task, we will see how we can get help from automated tools that will ease our work. For this reason, we'll discuss how to configure tools that will automatically run on the project as part of the build.

The goal of this chapter is to have an idea of what clean code is, why it is important, why formatting and documenting the code are crucial tasks, and how to automate this process. From this, you should acquire a mindset for quickly organizing the structure of a new project, aiming for good code quality.

After reading this chapter, you will have learned the following:

- That clean code really means something far more important than formatting
- That having standard formatting is a key component in a software project for the sake of its maintainability
- How to make the code self-documenting by using the features that Python provides
- How to configure tools to automate static verifications on the code

Introduction

We'll start first by understanding what clean code is, and why this is important for a software engineering project for it to be successful. In the first two sections, we will learn how important it is to maintain good code quality in order to work efficiently.

Then we'll discuss some exceptions to these rules: that is, situations in which it might even be cost-effective to not refactor our code to pay off all its technical debt. After all, we cannot simply expect general rules to apply everywhere, as we know there are exceptions. The important bit here is to properly understand why we would be willing to make an exception and identify these kinds of situations properly. We wouldn't want to mislead ourselves into thinking something shouldn't be improved when in fact it should.

The meaning of clean code

There is no sole or strict definition of clean code. Moreover, there is probably no way of formally measuring clean code, so you cannot run a tool on a repository that will tell you how good, bad, or maintainable that code is. Sure, you can run tools such as `checkers`, `linters`, `static analyzers`, and so on, and those tools are of much help. They are necessary, but not sufficient. Clean code is not something a machine or script can recognize (so far) but rather something that we, as professionals, can decide.

For decades of using the term programming languages, we thought that they were meant to communicate our ideas to machines so they can run our programs. We were wrong. That's not the truth, but part of the truth. The real meaning of the "language" part of "programming languages" is to communicate our ideas to other developers.

Here is where the true nature of clean code lies. It depends on other engineers to be able to read and maintain the code. Therefore, we, as professionals, are the only ones who can judge this. Think about it; as developers, we spend much more time reading code than actually writing it. Every time we want to make a change or add a new feature, we first have to read all the surroundings of the code we have to modify or extend. The language (Python) is what we use to communicate among ourselves.

So, instead of giving you a definition (or my definition) of clean code, I invite you to go through the book, read all about idiomatic Python, see the difference between good and bad code, identify traits of good code and good architecture, and then come up with your own definition. After reading this book, you will be able to judge and analyze code for yourself, and you will have a clearer understanding of clean code. You will know what it is and what it means, regardless of any definition given to you.

The importance of having clean code

There are a huge number of reasons why clean code is important. Most of them revolve around the ideas of maintainability, reducing technical debt, working effectively with agile development, and managing a successful project.

The first idea I would like to explore is with regard to agile development and continuous delivery. If we want our project to successfully deliver features constantly at a steady and predictable pace, then having a good and maintainable code base is a must.

Imagine you are driving a car on a road towards a destination you want to reach at a certain point in time. You have to estimate your arrival time so that you can tell the person who is waiting for you. If the car works fine, and the road is flat and perfect, then I do not see why you would miss your estimation by a large margin. However, if the road is in poor condition and you have to step out to move rocks out of the way, or avoid cracks, stop to check the engine every few kilometers, then it is very unlikely that you will know for sure when you are going to arrive (or if you will arrive). I think the analogy is clear; the road is the code. If you want to move at a steady, constant, and predictable pace, the code needs to be maintainable and readable. If it is not, every time product management asks for a new feature, you will have to stop to refactor and fix the technical debt.

Technical debt refers to the concept of problems in the software as a result of a compromise or a bad decision being made. It's possible to think about technical debt in two ways. From the present to the past: what if the problems we are currently facing are the result of previously written bad code? And, from the present to the future: if we decide to take a shortcut now, instead of investing time in a proper solution, what problems are we creating for ourselves further down the line?

The word *debt* is a good choice. It's debt because the code will be harder to change in the future than it would be to change it now. That incurred cost is the interest of the debt. Incurring technical debt means that tomorrow, the code will be harder and more expensive to change (it would even be possible to measure this) than it is today, and even more expensive the day after, and so on.

Every time the team cannot deliver something on time and has to stop to fix and refactor the code, it is paying the price of technical debt.

One could even argue that a team that owns a code base with technical debt is not doing agile software development. Because, what's the opposite of agile? Rigid. If the code is riddled with code smells, then it can't be easily changed, so there's no way the team would be able to quickly react to changes in requirements and deliver continuously.

The worst thing about technical debt is that it represents a long-term and underlying problem. It is not something that raises an alarm. Instead, it is a silent problem, scattered across all parts of the project, that one day, at one particular time, will wake up and become a show-stopper.

In some more alarming cases, "technical debt" is even an understatement, because the problem is much worse. In the previous paragraphs, I referred to scenarios in which technical debt makes things harder for the team in the future, but what if the reality is much more dangerous? Imagine taking a shortcut that leaves the code in a fragile position (one simple example could be a mutable default argument in a function that causes a memory leak, as we'll see in later chapters). You could deploy your code and it would work fine for quite some time (for as long as that defect doesn't manifest itself). But it's actually a crash waiting to happen: one day, when least expected, a certain condition in the code will be met that will cause a runtime problem with the application, like a time-bomb inside the code that at a random time goes off.

We clearly would like to avoid scenarios like the aforementioned one. Not everything can be caught by automated tools, but whenever it's possible, it's a good investment. The rest relies on good, thorough code reviews, and good automated testing.

Software is only useful to the degree to which it can be easily changed. Think about it. We create software to respond to some needs (whether it is purchasing a plane ticket, shopping online, or listening to music, just to name a few examples). These requirements are rarely frozen, meaning the software will have to be updated as soon as something in the context that led to that software being written in the first place changes. If the code can't be changed (and we know reality does change), then it's useless. Having a clean code base is an absolute requirement for it to be modified, hence the importance of clean code.

Some exceptions

In the previous section, we explored the critical role a clean code base plays in the success of a software project. That said, remember that this is a book for practitioners, so a pragmatic reader might rightfully point out that this begs the question: "Are there legitimate exceptions to this?"

And of course, this wouldn't be a truly pragmatic book if it didn't allow the reader to challenge some of its assumptions.

Indeed, there are some cases in which you might want to think of relaxing some of the constraints of having a pristine code base. What follows is a list (by no means exhaustive) of situations that might justify skipping some of the quality checks:

- Hackathons
- If you're writing a simple script for a one-off task
- Code competitions
- When developing a proof of concept
- When developing a prototype (as long as you make sure it's indeed a prototype that will be thrown away)
- When you're working with a legacy project that will be deprecated, and it's only in maintenance mode for a fixed, short-lived period of time (and again, provided this is assured)

In these cases, common sense applies. For example, if you just arrived at a project that will be live only for the next few months until it gets decommissioned, then it's probably not worth going through all the trouble of fixing all of its inherited technical debt, and waiting for it to be archived might be a better option.

Notice how these examples all have in common that they assume the code can afford not being written under good quality standards is also code that we will never have to look at again. This is coherent with what was previously exposed and can be thought of as the counter-proposal of our original premise: that we write clean code because we want to achieve high maintainability. If there's no need to maintain that code, then we can skip the effort of maintaining high-quality standards on it.

Remember that we write clean code so we can maintain a project. That means to be able to modify that code ourselves in the future, or, if we're transitioning the ownership of that code to another team in the company, to make this transition (and the lives of the future maintainers) easier. That means, that if a project is in maintenance mode only, but it's not going to be deprecated, then it might still be a good investment to pay off its technical debt. This is because at some point (and usually when least expected), there will be a bug that will have to be fixed, and it would be beneficial for the code to be as readable as possible.

Code formatting

Is clean code only about formatting and structuring the code? The short answer is no.

There are some coding standards like PEP-8 (`https://www.python.org/dev/peps/pep-0008/`) that state how the code should be written and formatted. In Python, PEP-8 is the most well-known standard, and that document provides guidelines on how we should write our programs, in terms of spacing, naming convention, line length, and more.

However, clean code is something else that goes far beyond coding standards, formatting, linting tools, and other checks regarding the layout of the code. Clean code is about achieving quality software and building a system that is robust and maintainable. A piece of code or an entire software component can be 100% compliant with PEP-8 (or any other guideline) and still not satisfy these requirements.

Even though formatting is not our main goal, not paying attention to the code structure has some perils. For this reason, we will first analyze the problems with a bad code structure and how to address them. After that, we will see how to configure and use tools for Python projects to automatically check the most common problems.

To sum this up, we can say that clean code has nothing to do with things like PEP-8 or coding styles. It goes way beyond that, and it's something more meaningful to the maintainability of the code and the quality of the software. However, as we will see, formatting code correctly is important to work efficiently.

Adhering to a coding style guide on your project

A coding guideline is a bare minimum a project should have to be considered being developed under quality standards. In this section, we will explore the reasons behind this. In the following sections, we can start looking at ways to enforce this automatically by using tools.

The first thing that comes to my mind when I try to find good traits in a code layout is consistency. I would expect the code to be consistently structured so that it is easy to read and follow. If the code is not correct nor consistently structured, and everyone on the team is doing things in their own way, then we will end up with code that will require extra effort and concentration to be understood. It will be error-prone, misleading, and bugs or subtleties might slip through easily.

We want to avoid that. What we want is exactly the opposite of that—code that we can read and understand as quickly as possible at a single glance.

If all members of the development team agree on a standardized way of structuring the code, the resulting code will look much more familiar. As a result of that, you will quickly identify patterns (more about this in a second), and with these patterns in mind, it will be much easier to understand things and detect errors. For example, when something is amiss, you will notice that, somehow, there is something odd in the patterns you are used to seeing, which will catch your attention. You will take a closer look, and you will more than likely spot the mistake!

As stated in the classical book, *Code Complete*, an interesting analysis of this was done in the paper titled *Perceptions in Chess* (1973), where an experiment was conducted to identify how different people can understand or memorize different chess positions. The experiment was conducted on players of all levels (novices, intermediate, and chess masters), and with different chess positions on the board. They found out that when the position was random, the novices did as well as the chess masters; it was just a memorization exercise that anyone could do at reasonably the same level. When the positions followed a logical sequence that might occur in a real game (again, consistency, adhering to a pattern), then the chess masters performed exceedingly better than the rest.

Now imagine this same situation applied to software. We, as the software engineer experts in Python, are like the chess masters in the previous example. When the code is structured randomly, without following any logic, or adhering to any standard, then it would be as difficult for us to spot mistakes as a novice developer. On the other hand, if we are used to reading code in a structured fashion, and we have learned to get ideas quickly from the code by following patterns, then we are at a considerable advantage.

In particular, for Python, the sort of coding style you should follow is PEP-8. You can extend it or adopt some of its parts to the particularities of the project you are working on (for example, the length of the line, the notes about strings, and so on).

If you realize the project you're working on doesn't adhere to any coding standard, push for the adoption of PEP-8 in that code base. Ideally, there should be a written document for the company or team you're working in that explains the coding standard that's expected to be followed. These coding guidelines can be an adaptation of PEP-8.

 If you notice there's not an alignment in your team with the code style, and there are several discussions about this during code reviews, it's probably a good idea to revisit the coding guidelines and invest in automatic verification tools.

In particular, PEP-8 touches on some important points for quality traits that you don't want to miss in your project; some of them are:

- **Searchability**: This refers to the ability to identify tokens in the code at a glance; that is, to search in certain files (and in which part of those files) for the particular string we are looking for. One key point of PEP-8 is that it differentiates the way of writing the assignment of values to variables, from the keyword arguments being passed to functions. To see this better, let's use an example. Let's say we are debugging, and we need to find where the value to a parameter named location is being passed. We can run the following grep command, and the result will tell us the file and the line we are looking for:

```
$ grep -nr "location=" .
./core.py:13:    location=current_location,
```

  Now, we want to know where this variable is being assigned this value, and the following command will also give us the information we are looking for:

```
$ grep -nr "location =" .
./core.py:10:    current_location = get_location()
```

  PEP-8 establishes the convention that, when passing arguments by keyword to a function, we don't use spaces, but we do when we set values to variables. For that reason, we can adapt our search criteria (no spaces around the = in the first example, and one space in the second) and be more efficient in our search. That is one of the advantages of following a convention.

- **Consistency**: If the code has a uniform format, the reading of it will be much easier. This is particularly important for onboarding, if you want to welcome new developers to your project, or even hire new (and probably less experienced) programmers on your team, and they need to become familiar with the code (which might even consist of several repositories). It will make their lives much easier if the code layout, documentation, naming convention, and such is identical across all files they open, in all repositories.

- **Better error handling**: One of the suggestions made in PEP-8 is to limit the amount of code inside a try/except block to the minimum possible. This reduces the error surface, in the sense that it reduces the likelihood of accidentally swallowing an exception and masking a bug. This is, arguably, perhaps hard to enforce by automatic checks, but nonetheless something worth keeping an eye on while performing code reviews.

- **Code quality**: By looking at the code in a structured fashion, you will become more proficient at understanding it at a glance (again, like in *Perception in Chess*), and you will spot bugs and mistakes more easily. In addition to that, tools that check the quality of the code will also hint at potential bugs. Static analysis of the code might help to reduce the ratio of bugs per line of code.

As I mentioned in the introduction, formatting is a necessary part of clean code, but it doesn't end there. There are more considerations to take into account, such as documenting design decisions in the code and using tools to leverage automatic quality checks as much as possible. In the next section, we start with the first one.

Documentation

This section is about documenting code in Python, from within the code. Good code is self-explanatory but is also well-documented. It is a good idea to explain what it is supposed to do (not how).

One important distinction: documenting code is not the same as adding comments to it. This section intends to explore docstrings and annotations because they're the tools in Python used to document code. That said, parenthetically, I will briefly touch on the subject of code comments, just to establish some points that will make a clearer distinction.

Code documentation is important in Python, because being dynamically typed, it might be easy to get lost in the values of variables or objects across functions and methods. For this reason, stating this information will make it easier for future readers of the code.

There is another reason that specifically relates to annotations. They can also help in running some automatic checks, such as type hinting, through tools such as mypy (http://mypy-lang.org/) or pytype (https://google.github.io/pytype/). We will find that, in the end, adding annotations pays off.

Code comments

As a general rule, we should *aim to have as few code comments as possible*. That is because our code should be self-documenting. This means that if we make an effort to use the right abstractions (like dividing the responsibilities in the code throughout meaningful functions or objects), and we name things clearly, then comments shouldn't be needed.

Before writing a comment, try to see if you can express the same meaning using only code (that is, by adding a new function, or using better variable names).

The opinion stated in this book about comments agrees pretty much with the rest of the literature on software engineering: comments in code are a symptom of our inability to express our code correctly.

However, in some cases, it's impossible to avoid adding a comment in code, and not doing so would be dangerous. This is typically the case when something in the code must be done for a particular technical nuance that's not trivial at first glance (for example, if there's a bug in an underlying external function and we need to pass a special parameter to circumvent the issue). In that case, our mission is to be as concise as possible and explain in the best possible way what the problem is, and why we're taking this specific path in the code so that the reader can understand the situation.

Lastly, there's another kind of comment in code that is definitely bad, and there's just no way to justify it: commented out code. This code must be deleted mercilessly. Remember that code is a communication language among developers and is the ultimate expression of the design. Code is knowledge. Commented out code brings chaos (and most likely contradictions) that will pollute that knowledge.

There's just no good reason, especially now, with modern version control systems, to leave commented out code that can be simply deleted (or stashed elsewhere).

To sum up: code comments are evil. Sometimes a necessary evil, but nonetheless something we should try to avoid as much as possible. Documentation on code, on the other hand, is something different. That refers to documenting the design or architecture within the code itself, to make it clear, and that's a positive force (and also the topic of the next section, in which we discuss docstrings).

Docstrings

In simple terms, we can say that docstrings are **documentation** embedded in the source code. A **docstring** is basically a literal string, placed somewhere in the code to document that part of the logic.

Notice the emphasis on the word **documentation**. This is important because it's meant to represent explanation, not justification. Docstrings are not comments; they are documentation.

Docstrings are intended to provide documentation for a particular component (a `module`, `class`, `method`, or `function`) in the code that will be useful for other developers. The idea is that when other engineers want to use the component you're writing, they'll most likely take a look at the docstring to understand how it's supposed to work, what the expected inputs and outputs are, and so on. For this reason, it is a good practice to add docstrings whenever possible.

Docstrings are also useful to document design and architecture decisions. It's probably a good idea to add a docstring to the most important Python modules, functions, and classes in order to hint to the reader how that component fits in the overall architecture.

The reason they are a good thing to have in code (or maybe even required, depending on the standards of your project) is that Python is dynamically typed. This means that, for example, a function can take anything as the value for any of its parameters. Python will not enforce, nor check, anything like this. So, imagine that you find a function in the code that you know you will have to modify. You are even lucky enough that the function has a descriptive name, and that its parameters do as well. It might still not be quite clear what types you should pass to it. Even if this is the case, how are they expected to be used?

Here is where a good docstring might be of help. Documenting the expected input and output of a function is a good practice that will help the readers of that function understand how it is supposed to work.

 To run the following code you'll need an `IPython` (https:// ipython.org/) interactive shell with the version of Python set according to the requirements of this book. If you don't have an `IPython` shell, you can still run the same commands in a normal `Python` `shell`, by replacing the `<function>??` with `help(<function>)`.

Consider this good example from the standard library:

```
Type: method_descriptor
```

Here, the docstring for the `update` method on dictionaries gives us useful information, and it is telling us that we can use it in different ways:

1. We can pass something with a `.keys()` method (for example, another dictionary), and it will update the original dictionary with the keys from the object passed per parameter:

```
>>> d = {}
>>> d.update({1: "one", 2: "two"})
>>> d
{1: "one", 2: 'two'}
```

2. We can pass an iterable of pairs of keys and values, and we will unpack them to update:

```
>>> d.update([(3, "three"), (4, "four")])
>>> d
{1: 'one', 2: 'two', 3: 'three', 4: 'four'}
```

3. It's also telling us that we can update the dictionary with values taken from keyword arguments:

```
>>> d.update(five=5)
>>> d
{1: 'one', 2: 'two', 3: 'three', 4: 'four', 'five': 5}
```

(Note that in this form, the keyword arguments are strings, so we cannot set something in the form 5="five" as it'd be incorrect.)

This information is crucial for someone who wants to learn and understand how a new function works, and how they can take advantage of it.

Notice that in the first example, we obtained the docstring of the function by using the double question mark on it (dict.update??). This is a feature of the IPython interactive interpreter (https://ipython.org/). When this is called, it will print the docstring of the object you are expecting. Now, imagine that in the same way, we obtained help from this function of the standard library; how much easier could you make the lives of your readers (the users of your code), if you place docstrings on the functions you write so that others can understand their workings in the same way?

The docstring is not something separated or isolated from the code. It becomes part of the code, and you can access it. When an object has a docstring defined, this becomes part of it via its __doc__ attribute:

```
>>> def my_function():
        """Run some computation"""
        return None
    ...
>>> my_function.__doc__  # or help(my_function)
'Run some computation'
```

This means that it is even possible to access it at runtime and even generate or compile documentation from the source code. In fact, there are tools for that. If you run Sphinx, it will create the basic scaffold for the documentation of your project. With the autodoc extension (sphinx.ext.autodoc) in particular, the tool will take the docstrings from the code and place them in the pages that document the function.

Once you have the tools in place to build the documentation, make it public so that it becomes part of the project itself. For open source projects, you can use read the docs (https://readthedocs.org/), which will generate the documentation automatically per branch or version (configurable). For companies or projects, you can have the same tools or configure these services on-premise, but regardless of this decision, the important part is that the documentation should be ready and available to all members of the team.

There is, unfortunately, one downside to docstrings, and it is that, as happens with all documentation, it requires manual and constant maintenance. As the code changes, it will have to be updated. Another problem is that for docstrings to be really useful, they have to be detailed, which requires multiple lines. Taking into account these two considerations, if the function you're writing is really simple, and self-explanatory, it's probably better to avoid adding a redundant docstring that will require maintenance later on.

Maintaining proper documentation is a software engineering challenge that we cannot escape from. It also makes sense for it to be like this. If you think about it, the reason for documentation to be manually written is because it is intended to be read by other humans. If it were automated, it would probably not be of much use. For the documentation to be of any value, everyone on the team must agree that it is something that requires manual intervention, hence the effort required. The key is to understand that software is not just about code. The documentation that comes with it is also part of the deliverable. Therefore, when someone is making a change on a function, it is equally important to also update the corresponding part of the documentation to the code that was just changed, regardless of whether it's a wiki, a user manual, a README file, or several docstrings.

Annotations

PEP-3107 introduced the concept of annotations. The basic idea of them is to hint to the readers of the code about what to expect as values of arguments in functions. The use of the word **hint** is not casual; annotations enable type hinting, which we will discuss later on in this chapter, after the first introduction to annotations.

Annotations let you specify the expected type of some variables that have been defined. It is actually not only about the types, but any kind of metadata that can help you get a better idea of what that variable actually represents.

Consider the following example:

```
@dataclass
class Point
    lat: float
    long: float



def locate(latitude: float, longitude: float) -> Point:
    """Find an object in the map by its coordinates"""
```

Here, we use `float` to indicate the expected types of `latitude` and `longitude`. This is merely informative for the reader of the function so that they can get an idea of these expected types. Python will not check these types nor enforce them.

We can also specify the expected type of the returned value of the function. In this case, `Point` is a user-defined class, so it will mean that whatever is returned will be an instance of `Point`.

However, types or built-ins are not the only kind of thing we can use as annotations. Basically, everything that is valid in the scope of the current Python interpreter could be placed there. For example, a string explaining the intention of the variable, a callable to be used as a callback or validation function, and so on.

We can leverage annotations to make our code more expressive. Consider the following example for a function that is supposed to launch a task, but that also accepts a parameter to defer the execution:

```
def launch_task(delay_in_seconds):
    ...
```

Here, the name of the argument `delay_in_seconds` seems quite verbose, but despite that fact, it still doesn't provide much information. What constitutes acceptable good values for seconds? Does it consider fractions?

How about we answer those questions in the code?

```
Seconds = float
def launch_task(delay: Seconds):
    ...
```

Now the code speaks for itself. Moreover, we can argue that with the introduction of the `Seconds` annotation, we have created a small abstraction around how we interpret time in our code, and we can reuse this abstraction in more parts of our code base. If we later decide to change the underlying abstraction for seconds (let's say that from now on, only integers are allowed), we can make that change in a single place.

With the introduction of annotations, a new special attribute is also included, and it is __annotations__. This will give us access to a dictionary that maps the name of the annotations (as keys in the dictionary) with their corresponding values, which are those we have defined for them. In our example, this will look like the following:

```
>>> locate.__annotations__
{'latitude': <class 'float'>, 'longitude': <class 'float'>, 'return':
<class 'Point'>}
```

We could use this to generate documentation, run validations, or enforce checks in our code if we think we have to.

Speaking of checking the code through annotations, this is when PEP-484 comes into play. This PEP specifies the basics of type hinting; the idea of checking the types of our functions via annotations. Just to be clear again, and quoting PEP-484 itself:

> *"Python will remain a dynamically typed language, and the authors have no desire to ever make type hints mandatory, even by convention."*

The idea of type hinting is to have extra tools (independent from the interpreter) to check the correct use of types throughout the code and to hint to the user if any incompatibilities are detected. There are useful tools that run checks around the data types and how they're used in our code, in order to find potential problems. Some example tools, such as mypy and pytype, are explained in more detail in the *Tooling section*, where we will talk about using and configuring the tools for the project. For now, you can think of it as a sort of linter that will check the semantics of the types used in code. For this reason, it is a good idea to configure mypy or pytype on the project and use it at the same level as the rest of the tools for static analysis.

However, type hinting means more than just a tool for checking the types in our code. Following up from our previous example, we can create meaningful names and abstractions for types in our code. Consider the following case for a function that processes a list of clients. In its simplest form, it can be annotated just using a generic list:

```
def process_clients(clients: list):
    ...
```

We can add a bit more detail if we know that in our current modeling of the data, clients are represented as tuples of integers and text:

```
def process_clients(clients: list[tuple[int, str]]):
    ...
```

But that still doesn't give us enough information, so it's better to be explicit and have a name for that alias, so we don't have to infer what that type means:

```
from typing import Tuple
Client = Tuple[int, str]
def process_clients(clients: list[Client]):
    ...
```

In this case, the meaning is clearer, and it supports evolving datatypes. Perhaps a tuple is the minimal data structure that fits the problem to represent a client correctly, but later on, we will want to change it for another object or create a specific class. And in this case, the annotation will remain correct, and so will all other type verifications.

The basic idea behind this is that now the semantics extend to more meaningful concepts, making it even easier for us (humans) to understand what the code means, or what is expected at a given point.

There is an added benefit that annotations bring. With the introduction of PEP-526 and PEP-557, there is a convenient way of writing classes in a compact way and defining small container objects. The idea is to just declare attributes in a class, and use annotations to set their type, and with the help of the @dataclass decorator, they will be handled as instance attributes without having to explicitly declare it in the __init__ method and set values to them:

```
from dataclasses import dataclass

@dataclass
class Point:
    lat: float
    long: float
```

```
>>> Point.__annotations__
{'lat': <class 'float'>, 'long': <class 'float'>}
>>> Point(1, 2)
Point(lat=1, long=2)
```

Later in the book, we'll explore other important uses of annotations, more related to the design of the code. When we explore good practices for object-oriented design, we might want to use concepts like dependency injection, in which we design our code to depend on interfaces that declare a contract. And probably the best way to declare that code relies on a particular interface is to make use of annotations. More to the point, there are tools that specifically make use of Python annotations to automatically provide support for dependency injection.

In design patterns, we usually also want to decouple parts of our code from specific implementations and rely on abstract interfaces or contracts, to make our code more flexible and extensible. In addition, design patterns usually solve problems by creating the proper abstractions needed (which usually means having new classes that encapsulate part of the logic). In both these scenarios, annotating our code will be of extra help.

Do annotations replace docstrings?

This is a valid question, since in older versions of Python, long before annotations were introduced, the way to document the types of the parameters of functions or attributes was to put docstrings on them. There are even some conventions for formats on how to structure docstrings to include the basic information for a function, including types and the meaning of each parameter, the return value, and possible exceptions that the function might raise.

Most of this has been addressed already in a more compact way by means of annotations, so one might wonder if it is really worth having docstrings as well. The answer is yes, and this is because they complement each other.

It is true that a part of the information previously contained in the docstring can now be moved to the annotations (there's no longer the need to indicate the types of the parameters in the docstrings as we can use annotations). But this should only leave more room for better documentation on the docstring. In particular, for dynamic and nested data types, it is always a good idea to provide examples of the expected data so that we can get a better idea of what we are dealing with.

Consider the following example. Let's say we have a function that expects a dictionary to validate some data:

```
def data_from_response(response: dict) -> dict:
    if response["status"] != 200:
        raise ValueError
    return {"data": response["payload"]}
```

Here, we can see a function that takes a dictionary and returns another dictionary. Potentially, it could raise an exception if the value under the key "status" is not the expected one. However, we do not have much more information about it. For example, what does a correct instance of a response object look like? What would an instance of result look like? To answer both of these questions, it would be a good idea to document examples of the data that is expected to be passed in by a parameter and returned by this function.

Let's see if we can explain this better with the help of a docstring:

```python
def data_from_response(response: dict) -> dict:
    """If the response is OK, return its payload.

    - response: A dict like::

    {
        "status": 200, # <int>
        "timestamp": "....", # ISO format string of the current
        date time
        "payload": { ... } # dict with the returned data
    }

    - Returns a dictionary like::

    {"data": { .. } }

    - Raises:
    - ValueError if the HTTP status is != 200
    """
    if response["status"] != 200:
        raise ValueError
    return {"data": response["payload"]}
```

Now, we have a better idea of what is expected to be received and returned by this function. The documentation serves as valuable input, not only for understanding and getting an idea of what is being passed around but also as a valuable source for unit tests. We can derive data like this to use as input, and we know what would be the correct and incorrect values to use on the tests. Actually, the tests also work as actionable documentation for our code, but this will be explained in more detail later on in the book.

The benefit is that now we know what the possible values of the keys are, as well as their types, and we have a more concrete interpretation of what the data looks like. The cost is that, as we mentioned earlier, it takes up a lot of lines, and it needs to be verbose and detailed to be effective.

Tooling

In this section, we will explore how to configure some basic tools and automatically run checks on code, with the goal of leveraging part of the repetitive verification checks.

This is an important point: remember that code is for us, people, to understand, so only we can determine what is good or bad code. We should invest time in code reviews, thinking about what is good code, and how readable and understandable it is. When looking at the code written by a peer, you should ask such questions as:

- Is this code easy to understand and follow to a fellow programmer?
- Does it speak in terms of the domain of the problem?
- Would a new person joining the team be able to understand it, and work with it effectively?

As we saw previously, code formatting, consistent layout, and proper indentation are required but not sufficient traits to have in a code base. Moreover, these are things that we, as engineers with a high sense of quality, would take for granted, so we would read and write code far beyond the basic concepts of its layout. Therefore, we are not willing to waste time reviewing these kinds of items, so we can invest our time more effectively by looking at actual patterns in the code in order to understand its true meaning and provide valuable results.

All of these checks should be automated. They should be part of the tests or checklist, and this, in turn, should be part of the continuous integration build. If these checks do not pass, make the build fail. This is the only way to actually ensure the continuity of the structure of the code at all times. It also serves as an objective parameter for the team to have as a reference. Instead of having some engineers or the leader of the team always having to point out the same comments about PEP-8 on code reviews, the build will automatically fail, making it something objective.

The tools presented in this section will give you an idea of checks you could automatically perform on the code. These tools should enforce some standards. Generally, they're configurable, and it would be perfectly fine for each repository to have its own configuration.

The idea of using tools is to have a *repeatable* and automatic way of running certain checks. That means that every engineer should be able to run the tools on their local development environment and reach the same results as any other member of the team. And also, that these tools should be configured as part of the **Continuous Integration (CI)** build.

Checking type consistency

Type consistency is one of the main things we would like to check automatically. Python is dynamically typed, but we can still add type annotations to hint to the readers (and tools) about what to expect in different parts of the code. Even though annotations are optional, as we have seen, adding them is a good idea not only because it makes the code more readable, but also because we can then use annotations along with some tooling to automatically check for some common errors that are most likely bugs.

Since type hinting was introduced in Python, many tools for checking type consistency have been developed. In this section, we'll take a look at two of them: mypy (https://github.com/python/mypy), and pytype (https://github.com/google/pytype). There are multiple tools, and you might even choose to use a different one, but in general, the same principles apply regardless of the specific tool: the important part is to have an automatic way of validating changes, and adding these validations as part of the CI build. mypy is the main tool for optional static type checking in Python. The idea is that, once you install it, it will analyze all of the files in your project, checking for inconsistencies in the use of types. This is useful since, most of the time, it will detect actual bugs early, but sometimes it can give false positives.

You can install it with pip, and it is recommended to include it as a dependency for the project on the setup file:

```
$ pip install mypy
```

Once it is installed in the virtual environment, you just have to run the preceding command and it will report all of the findings on the type checks. Try to adhere to its report as much as possible, because most of the time, the insights provided by it help to avoid errors that might otherwise slip into production. However, the tool is not perfect, so if you think it is reporting a false positive, you can ignore that line with the following marker as a comment:

```
type_to_ignore = "something" # type: ignore
```

It's important to note that for this or any tool to be useful, we have to be careful with the type annotations we declare in the code. If we're too generic with the types set, we might miss some cases in which the tool could report legitimate problems.

In the following example, there's a function that is intended to receive a parameter to be iterated over. Originally, any iterable would work, so we want to take advantage of Python's dynamic typing capabilities and allow a function that can use passing lists, tuples, keys of dictionaries, sets, or pretty much anything that supports a for loop:

```
def broadcast_notification(
    message: str,
    relevant_user_emails: Iterable[str]
):
    for email in relevant_user_emails:
        logger.info("Sending %r to %r", message, email)
```

The problem is that if some part of the code passes these parameters by mistake, `mypy` won't report an error:

```
broadcast_notification("welcome", "user1@domain.com")
```

And of course, this is not a valid instance because it will iterate every character in the string, and try to use it as an email.

If instead, we're more restrictive with the types set for that parameter (let's say to accept only lists or tuples of strings), then running `mypy` does identify this erroneous scenario:

```
$ mypy <file-name>
error: Argument 2 to "broadcast_notification" has incompatible type
"str"; expected "Union[List[str], Tuple[str]]"
```

Similarly, `pytype` is also configurable and works in a similar fashion, so you can adapt both tools to the specific context of your project. We can see how the error reported by this tool is very similar to the previous case:

```
File "...", line 22, in <module>: Function broadcast_notification was
called with the wrong arguments [wrong-arg-types]
        Expected: (message, relevant_user_emails: Union[List[str],
Tuple[str]])
  Actually passed: (message, relevant_user_emails: str)
```

One key difference that pytype has though, is that it won't just check the definitions against the arguments, but try to interpret if the code at runtime will be correct, and report on what would be runtime errors. For example, if one of the type definitions is temporarily violated, this won't be considered an issue as long as the end result complies with the type that was declared. While this is a nice trait, in general, I would recommend that you try not to break the invariants you set in the code, and avoid intermediate invalid states as much as possible because that will make your code easier to reason about and rely on fewer side-effects.

Generic validations in code

Besides using tools like the ones introduced in the previous section, to check for errors on the type management of our program, we can use other tools that will provide validations against a wider range of parameters.

There are many tools for checking the structure of code (basically, this is compliance with PEP-8) in Python, such as pycodestyle (formerly known as pep8 in PyPi), flake8, and many more. They are all configurable and are as easy to use as running the command they provide.

These tools are programs that run over a set of Python files, and check the compliance of the code against the PEP-8 standard, reporting every line that is in violation and the indicative error of the rule that got broken.

There are other tools that provide more complete checks so that instead of just validating the compliance with PEP-8, they also include extra checks for more complicated situations that exceed PEP-8 (remember, code can still be utterly compliant with PEP-8 and still not be of good quality).

For example, PEP-8 is mostly about styling and structuring our code, but it doesn't enforce us to put a docstring on every public method, class, or module. It also doesn't say anything about a function that takes too many parameters (something we'll identify as a bad trait later on in the book).

One example of such a tool is pylint. This is one of the most complete and strict tools there is to validate Python projects, and it's also configurable. As before, to use it, you just have to install it in the virtual environment with pip:

```
$ pip install pylint
```

Then, just running the pylint command would be enough to check it in the code.

It is possible to configure pylint via a configuration file named pylintrc. In this file, you can decide the rules you would like to enable or disable, and parametrize others (for example, to change the maximum length of the column). For example, as we have just discussed, we might not want every single function to have a docstring, as forcing this might be counterproductive. However, by default, pylint will impose this restriction, but we can overrule it in the configuration file by declaring it:

```
[DESIGN]
disable=missing-function-docstring
```

Once this configuration file has reached a stable state (meaning that it is aligned with the coding guidelines and doesn't require much further tuning), then it can be copied to the rest of the repositories, where it should also be under version control.

 Document the coding standards agreed by the development team, and then enforce them in configuration files for the tools that will run automatically in the repository.

Finally, there's another tool I would like to mention, and that is `Coala` (`https://github.com/coala/coala`). `Coala` is a bit more generic (meaning it supports multiple languages, not just Python), but the idea is similar to the one before: it takes a configuration file, and then it presents a command-line tool that will run some checks on the code. When running, if the tool detects some errors while scanning the files, it might prompt the user about them, and it will suggest automatically applying a fixing patch, when applicable.

But what if I have a use case that's not covered by the default rules of the tools? Both `pylint` and `Coala` come with lots of predefined rules that cover the most common scenarios, but you might still detect in your organization some pattern that it was found to led to errors.

If you detect a recurrent pattern in the code that is error-prone, I suggest investing some time in defining your own rules. Both these tools are extensible: in the case of `pylint`, there are multiple plugins available, and you can write your own. In the case of `Coala`, you can write your own validation modules to run right alongside the regular checks.

Automatic formatting

As mentioned at the beginning of the chapter, it would be wise for the team to agree on a writing convention for the code, to avoid discussing personal preferences on pull requests, and focus on the essence of the code. But the agreement would only get you so far, and if these rules aren't enforced, they'll get lost over time.

Besides just checking for adherence to standards by means of tooling, it would be useful to automatically format the code directly.

There are multiple tools that automatically format Python code (for example, most of the tools that validate PEP-8, like `flake8`, also have a mode to rewrite the code and make it PEP-8 compliant), and they're also configurable and adaptable to each specific project. Among those, and perhaps because of just the opposite of full flexibility and configuration, is one that I would like to highlight: `black`.

`black` (`https://github.com/psf/black`) has a peculiarity that formats code in a unique and deterministic way, without allowing any parameters (except perhaps, the length of the lines).

One example of this is that `black` will always format strings using double-quotes, and the order of the parameters will always follow the same structure. This might sound rigid, but it's the only way to ensure the differences in the code are kept to a minimum. If the code always respects the same structure, changes in the code will only show up in pull requests with the actual changes that were made, and no extra cosmetic modifications. It's more restrictive than PEP-8, but it's also convenient because, by formatting the code directly through a tool, we don't have to actually worry about that, and we can focus on the crux of the problem at hand.

It's also the reason `black` exists. PEP-8 defines some guidelines to structure our code, but there are multiple ways of having code that is compliant with PEP-8, so there's still the problem of finding style differences. The way `black` formats code is by moving it to a stricter subset of PEP-8 that is always deterministic.

As an example, see that the following code is PEP-8 compliant, but it doesn't follow the conventions of `black`:

```
def my_function(name):
    """
    >>> my_function('black')
    'received Black'
    """
    return 'received {0}'.format(name.title())
```

Now, we can run the following command to format the file:

```
black -l 79 *.py
```

And we can see what the tool has written:

```
def my_function(name):
    """
    >>> my_function('black')
    'received Black'
    """
    return "received {0}".format(name.title())
```

On more complex code, a lot more would have changed (trailing commas, and more), but the idea can be seen clearly. Again, it's opinionated, but it's also a good idea to have a tool that takes care of details for us.

It's also something that the Golang community learned a long time ago, to the point that there is a standard tool library, go fmt, that automatically formats the code according to the conventions of the language. It's good that Python has something like this now.

When installed, the 'black' command, by default, will attempt to format the code, but it also has a '--check' option that will validate the file against the standard, and fail the process if it doesn't pass the validation. This command is a good candidate to have as part of the automatic checks and CI process.

It's worth mentioning that black will format a file thoroughly, and it doesn't support partial formatting (as opposed to other tools). This might be an issue for legacy projects that already have code with a different style because if you want to adopt black as the formatting standard in your project, you'll most likely have to accept one of these two scenarios:

1. Creating a milestone pull request that will apply the black format to all Python files in the repository. This has the disadvantages of adding a lot of noise and polluting the version control history of the repo. In some cases, your team might decide to accept the risk (depending on how much you rely on the git history).

2. Alternatively, you can rewrite the history with the changes in the code with the black format applied. In git, it's possible to rewrite the commits (from the very beginning), by applying some commands on each commit. In this case, we can rewrite each commit after the 'black' formatting has been applied. In the end, it would look like the project has been in the new form from the very beginning, but there are some caveats. For starters, the history of the project was rewritten, so everyone will have to refresh their local copies of the repository. And secondly, depending on the history of your repository, if there are a lot of commits, this process can take a while.

In cases where formatting in the "all-or-nothing" fashion is not acceptable, we can use yapf (https://github.com/google/yapf), which is another tool that has many differences with respect to black: it's highly customizable, and it also accepts partial formatting (applying the formatting to only certain regions of the file).

yapf accepts an argument to specify the range of the lines to apply the formatting to. With this, you can configure your editor or IDE (or better yet, set up a git pre-commit hook), to automatically format the code only on the regions of the code that were just changed. This way, the project can get aligned to the coding standards, at staged intervals, as changes are being made.

To conclude this section on tools that format the code automatically, we can say that black is a great tool that will push the code toward a canonical standard, and for this reason, you should try to use it in your repositories. There's absolutely no friction with using black on new repositories that are created, but it's also understandable that for legacy repositories this might become an obstacle. If the team decides that it is just too cumbersome to adopt black in a legacy repository, then tools such as yapf could be more suitable.

Setup for automatic checks

In Unix development environments, the most common way of working is through Makefiles. Makefiles are powerful tools that let us configure commands to be run in the project, mostly for compiling, running, and so on. Besides this, we can use a Makefile in the root of our project, with some commands configured to run checks on the formatting and conventions of the code, automatically.

A good approach for this would be to have targets for the tests, and each particular test, and then have another one that runs altogether; for example:

```
.PHONY: typehint
typehint:
	mypy --ignore-missing-imports src/

.PHONY: test
test:
	pytest tests/

.PHONY: lint
lint:
	pylint src/

.PHONY: checklist
checklist: lint typehint test

.PHONY: black
black:
	black -l 79 *.py
```

```
.PHONY: clean
clean:
        find . -type f -name "*.pyc" | xargs rm -fr
        find . -type d -name __pycache__ | xargs rm -fr
```

Here, the command we run (both on our development machines and on the CI environment builds) is the following:

```
make checklist
```

This will run everything in the following steps:

1. It will first check the compliance with the coding guideline (PEP-8, or `black` with the `'--check'` parameter, for instance).
2. Then it will check for the use of types on the code.
3. Finally, it will run the tests.

If any of these steps fail, consider the entire process a failure.

These tools (`black`, `pylint`, `mypy`, and many more) can be integrated with the editor or IDE of your choice to make things even easier. It's a good investment to configure your editor to make these kinds of modifications either when saving the file or through a shortcut.

It's worth mentioning that the use of a `Makefile` comes in handy for a couple of reasons: first, there is a single and easy way to perform the most repetitive tasks automatically. New members of the team can quickly get onboarded by learning that something like `'make format'` automatically formats the code regardless of the underlying tool (and its parameters) being used. In addition, if it's later decided to change the tool (let's say you're switching over from `yapf` to `black`), then the same command (`'make format'`) would still be valid.

Second, it's good to leverage the `Makefile` as much as possible, and that means configuring your CI tool to also call the commands in the `Makefile`. This way there is a standardized way of running the main tasks in your project, and we place as little configuration as possible in the CI tool (which again, might change in the future, and that doesn't have to be a major burden).

Summary

We now have a first idea of what clean code is, and a workable interpretation of it, which will serve us as a reference point for the rest of this book.

More importantly, we now understand that clean code is something much more important than the structure and layout of the code. We have to focus on how ideas are represented in the code to see if they are correct. Clean code is about readability, maintainability of the code, keeping technical debt to a minimum, and effectively communicating our ideas in the code so that others can understand what we intended to write in the first place.

However, we discussed that adherence to coding styles or guidelines is important for multiple reasons. We agreed that this is a condition that is necessary, but not sufficient, and since it is a minimal requirement every solid project should comply with, it is clear that it is something we better leave to the tools. Therefore, automating all of these checks becomes critical, and in this regard, we have to keep in mind how to configure tools such as `mypy`, `pylint`, `black`, and others.

The next chapter is going to be more focused on Python-specific code, and how to express our ideas in idiomatic Python. We will explore the idioms in Python that make for more compact and efficient code. In this analysis, we will see that, in general, Python has different ideas or different ways to accomplish things compared to other languages.

References

- *PEP-8*: https://www.python.org/dev/peps/pep-0008/
- mypy: http://mypy-lang.org/
- pytype: https://google.github.io/pytype/
- *PEP-3107*: https://www.python.org/dev/peps/pep-3107/
- *PEP-484*: https://www.python.org/dev/peps/pep-0484/
- *PEP-526*: https://www.python.org/dev/peps/pep-0526/
- *PEP-557*: https://www.python.org/dev/peps/pep-0557/
- *PEP-585*: https://www.python.org/dev/peps/pep-0585/

2
Pythonic Code

In this chapter, we will explore the way ideas are expressed in Python, with its own peculiarities. If you are familiar with the standard ways of accomplishing some tasks in programming (such as getting the last element of a list, iterating, and searching), or if you come from other programming languages (such as C, C++, and Java), then you will find that, in general, Python provides its own mechanism for most common tasks.

In programming, an idiom is a particular way of writing code in order to perform a specific task. It is something common that repeats and follows the same structure every time. Some could even argue and call them a pattern, but be careful because they are not designed patterns (which we will explore later on). The main difference is that design patterns are high-level ideas, independent from the language (sort of), but they do not translate into code immediately. On the other hand, idioms are actually coded. It is the way things should be written when we want to perform a particular task.

As idioms are code, they are language dependent. Every language will have its idioms, which means the way things are done in that particular language (for example, how you would open and write a file in C, or C++). When the code follows these idioms, it is known as being idiomatic, which in Python is often referred to as Pythonic.

There are multiple reasons to follow these recommendations and write Pythonic code first (as we will see and analyze), since writing code in an idiomatic way usually performs better. It is also more compact and easier to understand. These are traits that we always want in our code so that it works effectively.

Secondly, as introduced in the previous chapter, it is important that the entire development team can get used to the same patterns and structure of the code because this will help them focus on the true essence of the problem, and will help them avoid making mistakes.

The goals of this chapter are as follows:

- To understand indices and slices, and correctly implement objects that can be indexed
- To implement sequences and other iterables
- To learn about good use cases for context managers, and how to write effective ones.
- To implement more idiomatic code through magic methods
- To avoid common mistakes in Python that lead to undesired side effects

We start by exploring the first item on the list (indexes and slices) in the next section.

Indexes and slices

In Python, as in other languages, some data structures or types support accessing its elements by index. Another thing it has in common with most programming languages is that the first element is placed in the index number 0. However, unlike those languages, when we want to access the elements in a different order than usual, Python provides extra features.

For example, how would you access the last element of an array in C? This is something I did the first time I tried Python. Thinking the same way as in C, I would get the element in the position of the length of the array minus one. In Python, this would work too, but we could also use a negative index number, which will start counting from the last element, as shown in the following commands:

```
>>> my_numbers = (4, 5, 3, 9)
>>> my_numbers[-1]
9
>>> my_numbers[-3]
5
```

This is an example of the preferred (Pythonic) way of doing things.

In addition to getting just one element, we can obtain many by using slice, as shown in the following commands:

```
>>> my_numbers = (1, 1, 2, 3, 5, 8, 13, 21)

>>> my_numbers[2:5]
(2, 3, 5)
```

In this case, the syntax on the square brackets means that we get all of the elements on the tuple, starting from the index of the first number (inclusive), up to the index on the second one (not including it). Slices work this way in Python by excluding the end of the selected interval.

You can exclude either one of the intervals, start or stop, and in that case, it will act from the beginning or end of the sequence, respectively, as shown in the following commands:

```
>>> my_numbers[:3]
(1, 1, 2)
>>> my_numbers[3:]
(3, 5, 8, 13, 21)
>>> my_numbers[::]   # also my_numbers[:], returns a copy
(1, 1, 2, 3, 5, 8, 13, 21)
>>> my_numbers[1:7:2]
(1, 3, 8)
```

In the first example, it will get everything up to the index in the position number 3. In the second example, it will get all the numbers from the position 3 (inclusive), up to the end. In the second to last example, where both ends are excluded, it is actually creating a copy of the original tuple.

The last example includes a third parameter, which is the step. This indicates how many elements to jump when iterating over the interval. In this case, it would mean getting the elements between the positions one and seven, jumping by two.

In all of these cases, when we pass intervals to a sequence, what is actually happening is that we are passing slice. Note that slice is a built-in object in Python that you can build yourself and pass directly:

```
>>> interval = slice(1, 7, 2)
>>> my_numbers[interval]
(1, 3, 8)

>>> interval = slice(None, 3)
>>> my_numbers[interval] == my_numbers[:3]
True
```

Notice that when one of the elements is missing (start, stop, or step), it is considered to be None.

 You should always prefer to use this built-in syntax for slices, as opposed to manually trying to iterate the tuple, string, or list inside a for loop, excluding the elements by hand.

Creating your own sequences

The functionality we just discussed works, thanks to a magic method (magic methods are those surrounded by double underscores that Python uses to reserve special behavior) called __getitem__. This is the method that is called when something like myobject[key] is called, passing the key (value inside the square brackets) as a parameter. A sequence, in particular, is an object that implements both __getitem__ and __len__, and for this reason, it can be iterated over. Lists, tuples, and strings are examples of sequence objects in the standard library.

In this section, we care more about getting particular elements from an object by a key than building sequences or iterable objects, which is a topic explored in *Chapter 7, Generators, Iterators, and Asynchronous Programming*.

If you are going to implement __getitem__ in a custom class in your domain, you will have to take into account some considerations in order to follow a Pythonic approach.

In the case that your class is a wrapper around a standard library object, you might as well delegate the behavior as much as possible to the underlying object. This means that if your class is actually a wrapper on the list, call all of the same methods on that list to make sure that it remains compatible. In the following listing, we can see an example of how an object wraps a list, and for the methods we are interested in, we just delegate to its corresponding version on the list object:

```python
from collections.abc import Sequence

class Items(Sequence):
    def __init__(self, *values):
        self._values = list(values)

    def __len__(self):
        return len(self._values)
```

```
    def __getitem__(self, item):
        return self._values.__getitem__(item)
```

To declare that our class is a sequence, it implements the `Sequence` interface from the `collections.abc` module (`https://docs.python.org/3/library/collections.abc.html`). For the classes you write that are intended to behave as standard types of objects (containers, mappings, and so on), it's a good idea to implement the interfaces from this module, because that reveals the intention of what that class is meant to be, and also because using the interfaces will force you to implement the required methods.

This example uses composition (because it contains an internal collaborator that is a list, rather than inheriting from the list class). Another way of doing it is through class inheritance, in which case we will have to extend the `collections.UserList` base class, with the considerations and caveats mentioned in the last part of this chapter.

If, however, you are implementing your own sequence that is not a wrapper or does not rely on any built-in object underneath, then keep in mind the following points:

- When indexing by a range, the result should be an instance of the same type of the class
- In the range provided by `slice`, respect the semantics that Python uses, excluding the element at the end

The first point is a subtle error. Think about it — when you get a slice of a list, the result is a list; when you ask for a range in a tuple, the result is a tuple; and when you ask for a substring, the result is a string. It makes sense in each case that the result is of the same type as the original object. If you are creating, let's say, an object that represents an interval of dates, and you ask for a range on that interval, it would be a mistake to return a list or tuple, or something else. Instead, it should return a new instance of the same class with the new interval set. The best example of this is in the standard library, with the `range` function. If you call `range` with an interval, it will construct an iterable object that knows how to produce the values in the selected range. When you specify an interval for `range`, you get a new range (which makes sense), not a list:

```
>>> range(1, 100)[25:50]
range(26, 51)
```

The second rule is also about consistency—users of your code will find it more familiar and easier to use if it is consistent with Python itself. As Python developers, we are already used to the idea of how the slices work, how the range function works, and so on. Making an exception on a custom class will create confusion, which means that it will be harder to remember, and it might lead to bugs.

Now that we know about indices and slices, and how to create our own, in the next section, we'll take the same approach but for context managers. First, we'll see how context managers from the standard library work, and then we'll go to the next level and create our own.

Context managers

Context managers are a distinctively useful feature that Python provides. The reason why they are so useful is that they correctly respond to a pattern. There are recurrent situations in which we want to run some code that has preconditions and postconditions, meaning that we want to run things before and after a certain main action, respectively. Context managers are great tools to use in those situations.

Most of the time, we see context managers around resource management. For example, in situations when we open files, we want to make sure that they are closed after processing (so we do not leak file descriptors). Or, if we open a connection to a service (or even a socket), we also want to be sure to close it accordingly, or when dealing with temporary files, and so on.

In all of these cases, you would normally have to remember to free all of the resources that were allocated and that is just thinking about the best case—but what about exceptions and error handling? Given the fact that handling all possible combinations and execution paths of our program makes it harder to debug, the most common way of addressing this issue is to put the cleanup code on a `finally` block so that we are sure we do not miss it. For example, a very simple case would look like the following:

```
fd = open(filename)
try:
    process_file(fd)
finally:
    fd.close()
```

Nonetheless, there is a much more elegant and Pythonic way of achieving the same thing:

```
with open(filename) as fd:
    process_file(fd)
```

The `with` statement (PEP-343) enters the context manager. In this case, the `open` function implements the context manager protocol, which means that the file will be automatically closed when the block is finished, even if an exception occurred.

Context managers consist of two magic methods: __enter__ and __exit__. On the first line of the context manager, the `with` statement will call the first method, __enter__, and whatever this method returns will be assigned to the variable labeled after as. This is optional—we don't really need to return anything specific on the __enter__ method, and even if we do, there is still no strict reason to assign it to a variable if it is not required.

After this line is executed, the code enters a new context, where any other Python code can be run. After the last statement on that block is finished, the context will be exited, meaning that Python will call the __exit__ method of the original context manager object we first invoked.

If there is an exception or error inside the context manager block, the __exit__ method will still be called, which makes it convenient for safely managing the cleaning up of conditions. In fact, this method receives the exception that was triggered on the block in case we want to handle it in a custom fashion.

Despite the fact that context managers are very often found when dealing with resources (like the example we mentioned with files, connections, and so on), this is not the sole application they have. We can implement our own context managers in order to handle the particular logic we need.

Context managers are a good way of separating concerns and isolating parts of the code that should be kept independent, because if we mix them, then the logic will become harder to maintain.

As an example, consider a situation where we want to run a backup of our database with a script. The caveat is that the backup is offline, which means that we can only do it while the database is not running, and for this we have to stop it. After running the backup, we want to make sure that we start the process again, regardless of how the process of the backup itself went.

Now, the first approach would be to create a huge monolithic function that tries to do everything in the same place, stop the service, perform the backup task, handle exceptions and all possible edge cases, and then try to restart the service again. You can imagine such a function, and for that reason, I will spare you the details, and instead come up directly with a possible way of tackling this issue with context managers:

```python
def stop_database():
    run("systemctl stop postgresql.service")


def start_database():
    run("systemctl start postgresql.service")


class DBHandler:
    def __enter__(self):
        stop_database()
        return self

    def __exit__(self, exc_type, ex_value, ex_traceback):
        start_database()


def db_backup():
    run("pg_dump database")


def main():
    with DBHandler():
        db_backup()
```

In this example, we don't need the result of the context manager inside the block, and that's why we can consider that, at least for this particular case, the return value of __enter__ is irrelevant. This is something to take into consideration when designing context managers—what do we need once the block is started? As a general rule, it should be good practice (although not mandatory) to always return something on __enter__.

In this block, we only run the task for the backup, independently from the maintenance tasks, as we saw previously. We also mentioned that even if the backup task has an error, __exit__ will still be called.

Notice the signature of the __exit__ method. It receives the values for the exception that was raised on the block. If there was no exception on the block, they are all none.

The return value of __exit__ is something to consider. Normally, we would want to leave the method as it is, without returning anything in particular. If this method returns True, it means that the exception that was potentially raised will not propagate to the caller and will stop there. Sometimes, this is the desired effect, maybe even depending on the type of exception that was raised, but in general, it is not a good idea to swallow the exception. Remember: errors should never pass silently.

> Keep in mind not to accidentally return True on __exit__. If you do, make sure that this is exactly what you want, and that there is a good reason for it.

Implementing context managers

In general, we can implement context managers like the one in the previous example. All we need is just a class that implements the __enter__ and __exit__ magic methods, and then that object will be able to support the context manager protocol. While this is the most common way for context managers to be implemented, it is not the only one.

In this section, we will see not only different (sometimes more compact) ways of implementing context managers, but also how to take full advantage of them by using the standard library, in particular with the contextlib module.

The contextlib module contains a lot of helper functions and objects to either implement context managers or use ones already provided that can help us write more compact code.

Let's start by looking at the contextmanager decorator.

When the contextlib.contextmanager decorator is applied to a function, it converts the code on that function into a context manager. The function in question has to be a particular kind of function called a generator function, which will separate the statements into what is going to be on the __enter__ and __exit__ magic methods, respectively.

If, at this point, you are not familiar with decorators and generators, this is not a problem because the examples we will be looking at will be self-contained, and the recipe or idiom can be applied and understood regardless. These topics are discussed in detail in *Chapter 7, Generators, Iterators, and Asynchronous Programming.*

The equivalent code of the previous example can be rewritten with the `contextmanager` decorator like this:

```
import contextlib


@contextlib.contextmanager
def db_handler():
    try:
        stop_database()
        yield
    finally:
        start_database()


with db_handler():
    db_backup()
```

Here, we define the generator function and apply the `@contextlib.contextmanager` decorator to it. The function contains a `yield` statement, which makes it a generator function. Again, details on generators are not relevant in this case. All we need to know is that when this decorator is applied, everything before the `yield` statement will be run as if it were part of the __enter__ method. Then, the yielded value is going to be the result of the context manager evaluation (what __enter__ would return), and what would be assigned to the variable if we chose to assign it like as x:—in this case, nothing is yielded (which means the yielded value will be none, implicitly), but if we wanted to, we could yield a statement that will become something we might want to use inside the context manager block.

At that point, the generator function is suspended, and the context manager is entered, where, again, we run the backup code for our database. After this completes, the execution resumes, so we can consider that every line that comes after the `yield` statement will be part of the __exit__ logic.

Writing context managers like this has the advantage that it is easier to refactor existing functions, reuse code, and in general is a good idea when we need a context manager that doesn't belong to any particular object (otherwise, you'd be creating a "fake" class for no real purpose, in the object-oriented sense).

Adding the extra magic methods would make another object of our domain more coupled, with more responsibilities, and supporting something that it probably shouldn't. When we just need a context manager function, without preserving many states, and completely isolated and independent from the rest of our classes, this is probably a good way to go.

There are, however, more ways in which we can implement context manager, and once again, the answer is in the contextlib package from the standard library.

Another helper we could use is contextlib.ContextDecorator. This is a base class that provides the logic for applying a decorator to a function that will make it run inside the context manager. The logic for the context manager itself has to be provided by implementing the aforementioned magic methods. The result is a class that works as a decorator for functions, or that can be mixed into the class hierarchy of other classes to make them behave as context managers.

In order to use it, we have to extend this class and implement the logic on the required methods:

```
class dbhandler_decorator(contextlib.ContextDecorator):
    def __enter__(self):
        stop_database()
        return self

    def __exit__(self, ext_type, ex_value, ex_traceback):
        start_database()


@dbhandler_decorator()
def offline_backup():
    run("pg_dump database")
```

Do you notice something different from the previous examples? There is no with statement. We just have to call the function, and offline_backup() will automatically run inside a context manager. This is the logic that the base class provides to use it as a decorator that wraps the original function so that it runs inside a context manager.

The only downside of this approach is that by the way the objects work, they are completely independent (which is a good trait)—the decorator doesn't know anything about the function that is decorating, and vice versa. This, however good, means that the offline_backup function cannot access the decorator object, should this be needed. However, nothing is stopping us from still calling this decorator inside the function to access the object.

This can be done in the following form:

```
def offline_backup():
    with dbhandler_decorator() as handler: ...
```

Being a decorator, this also has the advantage that the logic is defined only once, and we can reuse it as many times as we want by simply applying the decorators to other functions that require the same invariant logic.

Let's explore one last feature of `contextlib`, to see what we can expect from context managers and get an idea of the sort of thing we could use them for.

In this library, we can find `contextlib.suppress`, which is a utility to avoid certain exceptions in situations where we know it is safe to ignore them. It's similar to running that same code on a `try/except` block and passing an exception or just logging it, but the difference is that calling the `suppress` method makes it more explicit that those exceptions are controlled as part of our logic.

For example, consider the following code:

```
import contextlib

with contextlib.suppress(DataConversionException):
    parse_data(input_json_or_dict)
```

Here, the presence of the exception means that the input data is already in the expected format, so there is no need for conversion, hence making it safe to ignore it.

Context managers are quite a peculiar feature that differentiates Python. Therefore, using context managers can be considered idiomatic. In the next section, we explore another interesting trait of Python that will help us write more concise code; comprehensions and assignment expressions.

Comprehensions and assignment expressions

We will see comprehension expressions many times throughout the book. This is because they're usually a more concise way of writing code, and in general, code written this way tends to be easier to read. I say in general, because sometimes if we need to do some transformations on the data we're collecting, using a comprehension might lead to some more complicated code. In these cases, writing a simple `for` loop should be preferred instead.

There is, however, one last resort we could apply to try to salvage the situation: assignment expressions. In this section, we discuss these alternatives.

The use of comprehensions is recommended to create data structures in a single instruction, instead of multiple operations. For example, if we wanted to create a list with calculations over some numbers in it, instead of writing it like this:

```
numbers = []
for i in range(10):
    numbers.append(run_calculation(i))
```

We would create the list directly:

```
numbers = [run_calculation(i) for i in range(10)]
```

Code written in this form usually performs better because it uses a single Python operation, instead of calling `list.append` repeatedly. If you are curious about the internals or differences between different versions of the code, you can check out the `dis` module, and call it with these examples.

Let's see the example of a function that will take some strings that represent resources on a cloud computing environment (for example ARNs), and returns the set with the account IDs found on them. Something like this would be the most naïve way of writing such a function:

```
from typing import Iterable, Set

def collect_account_ids_from_arns(arns: Iterable[str]) -> Set[str]:
    """Given several ARNs in the form

        arn:partition:service:region:account-id:resource-id

    Collect the unique account IDs found on those strings, and return them.
    """
    collected_account_ids = set()
    for arn in arns:
        matched = re.match(ARN_REGEX, arn)
        if matched is not None:
            account_id = matched.groupdict()["account_id"]
            collected_account_ids.add(account_id)
    return collected_account_ids
```

Clearly the code has many lines, and it's doing something relatively simple. A reader of this code might get confused by these multiple statements, and perhaps inadvertently make a mistake when working with that code. If we could simplify it, that would be better. We can achieve the same functionality in fewer lines by using a few comprehension expressions in a way that resembles functional programming:

```python
def collect_account_ids_from_arns(arns):
    matched_arns = filter(None, (re.match(ARN_REGEX, arn) for arn in arns))
    return {m.groupdict()["account_id"] for m in matched_arns}
```

The first line of the function seems similar to applying `map` and `filter`: first, we apply the result of trying to match the regular expression to all the strings provided, and then we filter those that aren't `None`. The result is an iterator that we will later use to extract the account ID in a set comprehension expression.

The previous function should be more maintainable than our first example, but still requires two statements. Before Python 3.8, it wasn't possible to achieve a more compact version. But with the introduction of assignment expressions in PEP-572 (`https://www.python.org/dev/peps/pep-0572/`), we can rewrite this in a single statement:

```python
def collect_account_ids_from_arns(arns: Iterable[str]) -> Set[str]:
    return {
        matched.groupdict()["account_id"]
        for arn in arns
        if (matched := re.match(ARN_REGEX, arn)) is not None
    }
```

Note the syntax on the third line inside the comprehension. This sets a temporary identifier inside the scope, which is the result of applying the regular expression to the string, and it can be reused in more parts within the same scope.

In this particular example, it's arguable if the third example is better than the second one (but there should be no doubts that both of them are better than the first one!). I believe this last example to be more expressive because it has fewer indirections in the code, and everything that the reader needs to know on how the values are being collected belongs to the same scope.

Keep in mind that a more compact code does not always mean better code. If to write a one-liner, we have to create a convoluted expression, then it's not worth it, and we would be better off with the naïve approach. This is related to the *keep it simple* principle that we'll discuss in the next chapter.

Take into consideration the readability of the comprehension expressions, and don't force your code to be a one-liner, if this one won't be actually easier to understand.

Another good reason for using assignment expressions in general (not just in comprehensions) is the performance considerations. If we have to use a function as part of our transformation logic, we don't want to call that more than is necessary. Assigning the result of the function to a temporary identifier (as it's done by assignment expressions in new scopes) would be a good optimization technique that, at the same time, keeps the code more readable.

Evaluate the performance improvements that can be made by using assignment expressions.

In the next section, we'll review another idiomatic feature of Python: properties. Moreover, we'll discuss the different ways of exposing or hiding data in Python objects.

Properties, attributes, and different types of methods for objects

All of the properties and functions of an object are public in Python, which is different from other languages where properties can be public, private, or protected. That is, there is no point in preventing caller objects from invoking any attributes an object has. This is another difference compared to other programming languages in which you can mark some attributes as private or protected.

There is no strict enforcement, but there are some conventions. An attribute that starts with an underscore is meant to be private to that object, and we expect that no external agent calls it (but again, nothing is preventing this).

Before jumping into the details of properties, it's worth mentioning some traits of underscores in Python, understanding the convention, and the scope of attributes.

Underscores in Python

There are some conventions and implementation details that make use of underscores in Python, which is an interesting topic that's worthy of analysis.

Like we mentioned previously, by default, all attributes of an object are `public`. Consider the following example to illustrate this:

```
>>> class Connector:
...     def __init__(self, source):
...         self.source = source
...         self._timeout = 60
...
>>> conn = Connector("postgresql://localhost")
>>> conn.source
'postgresql://localhost'
>>> conn._timeout
60
>>> conn.__dict__
{'source': 'postgresql://localhost', '_timeout': 60}
```

Here, a `Connector` object is created with `source`, and it starts with two attributes—the aforementioned `source` and `timeout`. The former is `public` and the latter `private`. However, as we can see from the following lines when we create an object like this, we can actually access both of them.

The interpretation of this code is that `_timeout` should be accessed only within connector itself and never from a caller. This means that you should organize the code in a way so that you can safely refactor the timeout at all of the times it's needed, relying on the fact that it's not being called from outside the object (only internally), hence preserving the same interface as before. Complying with these rules makes the code easier to maintain and more robust because we don't have to worry about ripple effects when refactoring the code if we maintain the interface of the object. The same principle applies to methods as well.

 Classes should only expose those attributes and methods that are relevant to an external caller object, namely, entailing its interface. Everything that is not strictly part of an object's interface should be kept prefixed with a single underscore.

Attributes that start with an underscore must be respected as private and not be
called externally. On the other hand, as an exception to this rule, we could say that
in unit tests, it might be allowed to access internal attributes if this makes things
easier to test (but note that adhering to this pragmatic approach still suffers from the
maintainability cost when you decide to refactor the main class). However, keep in
mind the following recommendation:

> Using too many internal methods and attributes could be a sign
> that the class has too many tasks and doesn't comply with the
> single responsibility principle. This could indicate that you need to
> extract some of its responsibilities into more collaborating classes.

Using a single underscore as prefix is the Pythonic way of clearly delimiting
the interface of an object. There is, however, a common misconception that
some attributes and methods can be actually made private. This is, again, a
misconception. Let's imagine that now the timeout attribute is defined with a leading
double underscore instead:

```
>>> class Connector:
...     def __init__(self, source):
...         self.source = source
...         self.__timeout = 60
...
...     def connect(self):
...         print("connecting with {0}s".format(self.__timeout))
...         # ...
...
>>> conn = Connector("postgresql://localhost")
>>> conn.connect()
connecting with 60s
>>> conn.__timeout
Traceback (most recent call last):
  File "<stdin>", line 1, in <module>
AttributeError: 'Connector' object has no attribute '__timeout'
```

Some developers use this method to hide some attributes, thinking, like in this
example, that timeout is now private and that no other object can modify it. Now,
take a look at the exception that is raised when trying to access __timeout. It's
AttributeError, saying that it doesn't exist. It doesn't say something like "this is
private" or "this can't be accessed", and so on. It says it does not exist. This should
give us a clue that, in fact, something different is happening and that this behavior
is instead just a side effect, but not the real effect we want.

What's actually happening is that with the double underscores, Python creates a different name for the attribute (this is called name mangling). What it does is create the attribute with the following name instead: "_<class-name>__<attribute-name>". In this case, an attribute named '_Connector__timeout' will be created, and this attribute can be accessed (and modified) as follows:

```
>>> vars(conn)
{'source': 'postgresql://localhost', '_Connector__timeout': 60}
>>> conn._Connector__timeout
60
>>> conn._Connector__timeout = 30
>>> conn.connect()
connecting with 30s
```

Notice the side effect that we mentioned earlier—the attribute still exists, only with a different name, and for that reason, the AttributeError was raised on our first attempt to access it.

The idea of the double underscore in Python is completely different. It was created as a means to override different methods of a class that is going to be extended several times, without the risk of having collisions with the method names. Even that is a too far-fetched use case as to justify the use of this mechanism.

Double underscores are a non-Pythonic approach. If you need to define attributes as private, use a single underscore, and respect the Pythonic convention that it is a private attribute.

Do not define attributes with leading double underscores.

By the same token, do not define your own "dunder" methods (methods whose names are surrounded by double underscores)

Let's now explore the opposite case, that is, when we do want to access some attributes of an object that are intended to be public. Typically, we'd use properties for this, which we will explore in the next section.

Properties

Typically, in object-oriented design, we create objects to represent an abstraction over an entity of the domain problem. In this sense, objects can encapsulate behavior or data. And more often than not, the accuracy of the data determines if an object can be created or not. That is to say, some entities can only exist for certain values of the data, whereas incorrect values shouldn't be allowed.

This is why we create validation methods, typically to be used in the setter operations. However, in Python, sometimes we can encapsulate these setter and getter methods more compactly by using properties.

Consider the example of a geographical system that needs to deal with coordinates. There is only a certain range of values for which latitude and longitude make sense. Outside of those values, a coordinate cannot exist. We can create an object to represent a coordinate, but in doing so we must ensure that the values for latitude are at all times within the acceptable ranges. And for this we can use properties:

```python
class Coordinate:
    def __init__(self, lat: float, long: float) -> None:
        self._latitude = self._longitude = None
        self.latitude = lat
        self.longitude = long

    @property
    def latitude(self) -> float:
        return self._latitude

    @latitude.setter
    def latitude(self, lat_value: float) -> None:
        if lat_value not in range(-90, 90 + 1):
            raise ValueError(f"{lat_value} is an invalid value for
latitude")
        self._latitude = lat_value

    @property
    def longitude(self) -> float:
        return self._longitude

    @longitude.setter
    def longitude(self, long_value: float) -> None:
        if long_value not in range(-180, 180 + 1):
            raise ValueError(f"{long_value} is an invalid value for
longitude")
        self._longitude = long_value
```

Here, we're using a property to define the latitude and longitude. In doing so, we establish that retrieving any of these attributes will return the internal value held in the private variables. More importantly, when any user wants to modify values for any of these properties in the following form:

```python
coordinate.latitude = <new-latitude-value>  # similar for longitude
```

The validation method that's declared with the `@latitude.setter` decorator will be automatically (and transparently) invoked, and it will pass the value on the right-hand-side of the statement (`<new-latitude-value>`) as the parameter (named `lat_value` in the preceding code).

> Don't write custom `get_*` and `set_*` methods for all attributes on your objects. Most of the time, leaving them as regular attributes is just enough. If you need to modify the logic for when an attribute is retrieved or modified, then use `properties`.

We have seen the case for when an object needs to hold values, and how `properties` help us to manage their internal data in a consistent and transparent way, but sometimes, we might also need to do some computations based on the state of the object and its internal data. Most of the time, properties are a good choice for this.

For example, if you have an object that needs to return a value in a particular format, or data type, a property can be used to do this computation. In the previous example, if we decided that we wanted to return the coordinates with a precision of up to four decimal places (regardless of how many decimal places the original number was provided with), we can make the computation for rounding this in the `@property` method that reads the value.

You might find that properties are a good way to achieve command and query separation (CC08). The command and query separation principle states that a method of an object should either answer to something or do something, but not both. If a method is doing something, and at the same time it returns a status answering a question of how that operation went, then it's doing more than one thing, clearly violating the principle that says that functions should do one thing, and one thing only.

Depending on the name of the method, this can create even more confusion, making it harder for readers to understand what the actual intention of the code is. For example, if a method is called `set_email`, and we use it as if `self.set_email("a@j.com"): ...`, what is that code doing? Is it setting the email to a@j.com? Is it checking if the email is already set to that value? Both (setting and then checking if the status is correct)?

With `properties`, we can avoid this kind of confusion. The `@property` decorator is the query that will answer to something, and `@<property_name>.setter` is the command that will do something.

Another piece of good advice derived from this example is as follows—don't do more than one thing in a method. If you want to assign something and then check the value, break that down into two or more statements.

To illustrate what this means, using the previous example, we would have one setter or getter method, to set the email of the user, and then another property to simply ask for the email. This is because, in general, any time we ask an object about its current state, it should return it without side effects (without changing its internal representation). Perhaps the only exception I can think of to this rule would be in the case of a lazy property: something we want to precompute only once, and then use the computed value. For the rest of the cases, try to make properties idempotent, and then methods that are allowed to change the internal representation of the object, but don't mix both.

 Methods should do one thing only. If you have to run an action and then check for the status, do that in separate methods that are called by different statements.

Creating classes with a more compact syntax

Continuing with the idea that sometimes, we need objects to hold values, there's a common boilerplate in Python when it comes to the initialization of objects, which is to declare in the __init__ method all attributes that the object will have, and then set that to internal variables, typically in the following form:

```
def __init__(self, x, y, … ):
    self.x = x
    self.y = y
```

Since Python 3.7, we can simplify this by using the dataclasses module. This has been introduced by PEP-557. We have seen this module in the previous chapter, in the context of using annotations on the code, and here we'll review it briefly in terms of how it helps us write more compact code.

This module provides a @dataclass decorator, which, when applied to a class, it'll take all the class attributes with annotations, and treat them as instance attributes, as if they were declared in the initialization method. When using this decorator, it will automatically generate the __init__ method on the class, so we don't have to.

Additionally, this module provides a field object that will help us define particular traits for some of the attributes. For example, if one of the attributes we need needs to be mutable (such as a list), we'll see later in the chapter (in the section for avoiding caveats in Python) that we cannot pass this default empty list in the __init__ method, and that instead we should pass None, and set it to a default list inside __init__, if None was provided.

When using the `field` object, what we would do instead is to use the `default_factory` argument, and provide the `list` class to it. This argument is meant to be used with a callable that takes no arguments, and will be called to construct the object, when nothing is provided for the value of that attribute.

Because there's no `__init__` method to be implemented, what happens if we need to run validations? Or if we want to have some attributes computed or derived from previous ones? To answer the latter, we can rely on `properties`, as we have just explored in the previous section. As per the former, the data classes allow us to have a `__post_init__` method that will be called automatically by `__init__`, so this would be a good place to write our logic for post-initialization.

To put all of this into practice, let's consider the example of modeling a node for an R-Trie data structure (where R stands for *radix*, which means it is an indexed tree over some base R). The details of this data structure, and the algorithms associated with it, are beyond the scope of this book, but for the purposes of the example, I'll mention that is a data structure designed to answer queries over text or strings (such as prefixes, and finding similar or related words). In a very basic form, this data structure contains a value (that holds a character, and it can be its integer representation, for instance), and then an array or length R with references to the next nodes (it's a recursive data structure, in the same sense as a `linked list` or a `tree` for example). The idea is that each position of the array defines implicitly a reference to the next node. For example, imagine the value 0 is mapped to the character `'a'`, then if the next node contains a value different than `None` in its 0 position, then this means there's a reference for `'a'`, and that points to another R-Trie node.

Graphically, the data structure might look something like this:

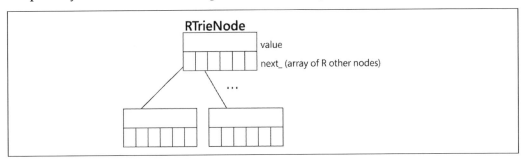

Figure 2.1: Generic structure for an R-Trie node

And we could write a code block like the following one to represent it. In the following code, the attribute named next_ contains a trailing underscore, just as a way to differentiate it from the built-in next function. We can argue that in this case, there's no collision, but if we needed to use the next() function within the `RTrieNode` class, that could be problematic (and those are usually hard-to-catch subtle errors):

```python
from typing import List
from dataclasses import dataclass, field

R = 26


@dataclass
class RTrieNode:
    size = R
    value: int
    next_: List["RTrieNode"] = field(
        default_factory=lambda: [None] * R)

    def __post_init__(self):
        if len(self.next_) != self.size:
            raise ValueError(f"Invalid length provided for next list")
```

The preceding example contains several different combinations. First, we define an R-Trie with R=26 to represent the characters in the English alphabet (this is not important to understand the code itself, but it gives more context). The idea is that if we want to store a word, we create a node for each letter, starting with the first one. When there's a link to the next character, we store it in the position of the next_ array corresponding to that character, another node for that one, and so on.

Note the first attribute in the class: size. This one doesn't have an annotation, so it's a regular class attribute (shared for all node objects), and not something that belongs exclusively to the object. Alternatively, we could have defined this by setting field(init=False), but this form is more compact. However, if we wanted to annotate the variable, but not consider it as part of __init__, then this syntax is the only viable alternative.

Then follow two other attributes, both of which have annotations, but with different considerations. The first one, value, is an integer, but it doesn't have a default argument, so when we create a new node, we must always provide a value as a first parameter. The second one is a mutable argument (a list of itself), and it does have a default factory: in this case a lambda function that will create a new list of size R, initialized with None on all slots. Note that if we had used field(default_factory=list) for this, we would still have constructed a new list for each object on creation, but this loses control over the length of that list. And finally, we wanted to validate that we don't create nodes that have a list of next nodes with the wrong length, so this is validated in the __post_init__ method. Any attempt to create such a list will be prevented with a ValueError at initialization time.

Data classes provide a more compact way of writing classes, without the boilerplate of having to set all variables with the same name in the __init__ method.

When you have objects that don't do many complex validations or transformations on the data, consider this alternative. Keep in mind this last point. Annotations are great, but they don't enforce data conversion. This means that for example, if you declare an attribute that needs to be a float, or an integer, then you must do this conversion in the __init__ method. Writing this as a data class won't do it, and it might hide subtle errors. This is for cases when validations aren't strictly required and type casts are possible. For example, it's perfectly fine to define an object that can be created from multiple other types, like converting a float from a numeric string (after all, this leverages Python's dynamic typing nature), provided this is correctly converted to the required data type within the __init__ method.

Probably a good use case for data classes would be all those places when we need to use objects as data containers or wrappers, namely situations on which we used named tuples or simple namespaces. Consider data classes as another alternative to named tuples or namespaces when you're evaluating options in your code.

Iterable objects

In Python, we have objects that can be iterated by default. For example, lists, tuples, sets, and dictionaries can not only hold data in the structure we want, but also be iterated over a for loop to get those values repeatedly.

However, the built-in iterable objects are not the only kind that we can have in a for loop. We could also create our own iterable, with the logic we define for iteration.

In order to achieve this, we rely, once again, on magic methods.

Iteration works in Python by its own protocol (namely the iterator protocol). When you try to iterate an object in the form for e in myobject:..., what Python checks at a very high level are the following two things, in order:

- If the object contains one of the iterator methods— __next__ or __iter__
- If the object is a sequence and has __len__ and __getitem__

Therefore, as a fallback mechanism, sequences can be iterated, and so there are two ways of customizing our objects to be able to work on for loops.

Creating iterable objects

When we try to iterate an object, Python will call the iter() function over it. One of the first things this function checks for is the presence of the __iter__ method on that object, which, if present, will be executed.

The following code creates an object that allows iterating over a range of dates, producing one day at a time on every round of the loop:

```python
from datetime import timedelta


class DateRangeIterable:
    """An iterable that contains its own iterator object."""

    def __init__(self, start_date, end_date):
        self.start_date = start_date
        self.end_date = end_date
        self._present_day = start_date

    def __iter__(self):
        return self

    def __next__(self):
        if self._present_day >= self.end_date:
            raise StopIteration()
        today = self._present_day
        self._present_day += timedelta(days=1)
        return today
```

This object is designed to be created with a pair of dates, and when iterated, it will produce each day in the interval of specified dates, which is shown in the following code:

```python
>>> from datetime import date
>>> for day in DateRangeIterable(date(2018, 1, 1), date(2018, 1, 5)):
...     print(day)
...
2018-01-01
2018-01-02
2018-01-03
2018-01-04
>>>
```

Here, the for loop is starting a new iteration over our object. At this point, Python will call the iter() function on it, which, in turn, will call the __iter__ magic method. On this method, it is defined to return self, indicating that the object is an iterable itself, so at that point every step of the loop will call the next() function on that object, which delegates to the __next__ method. In this method, we decide how to produce the elements and return one at a time. When there is nothing else to produce, we have to signal this to Python by raising the StopIteration exception.

This means that what is actually happening is similar to Python calling next() every time on our object until there is a StopIteration exception, on which it knows it has to stop the for loop:

```
>>> r = DateRangeIterable(date(2018, 1, 1), date(2018, 1, 5))
>>> next(r)
datetime.date(2018, 1, 1)
>>> next(r)
datetime.date(2018, 1, 2)
>>> next(r)
datetime.date(2018, 1, 3)
>>> next(r)
datetime.date(2018, 1, 4)
>>> next(r)
Traceback (most recent call last):
  File "<stdin>", line 1, in <module>
  File ... __next__
    raise StopIteration
StopIteration
>>>
```

This example works, but it has a small problem—once exhausted, the iterable will continue to be empty, hence raising StopIteration. This means that if we use this on two or more consecutive for loops, only the first one will work, while the second one will be empty:

```
>>> r1 = DateRangeIterable(date(2018, 1, 1), date(2018, 1, 5))
>>> ", ".join(map(str, r1))

'2018-01-01, 2018-01-02, 2018-01-03, 2018-01-04'
>>> max(r1)
Traceback (most recent call last):
  File "<stdin>", line 1, in <module>
ValueError: max() arg is an empty sequence
>>>
```

This is because of the way the iteration protocol works—an iterable constructs an iterator, and this one is the one being iterated over. In our example, __iter__ just returned self, but we can make it create a new iterator every time it is called. One way of fixing this would be to create new instances of DateRangeIterable, which is not a terrible issue, but we can make __iter__ use a generator (which are iterator objects), which is being created every time:

```
class DateRangeContainerIterable:
    def __init__(self, start_date, end_date):
        self.start_date = start_date
        self.end_date = end_date

    def __iter__(self):
        current_day = self.start_date
        while current_day < self.end_date:
            yield current_day
            current_day += timedelta(days=1)
```

And this time it works:

```
>>> r1 = DateRangeContainerIterable(date(2018, 1, 1), date(2018, 1, 5))
>>> ", ".join(map(str, r1))
'2018-01-01, 2018-01-02, 2018-01-03, 2018-01-04'
>>> max(r1)
datetime.date(2018, 1, 4)
>>>
```

The difference is that each for loop is calling __iter__ again, and each one of those is creating the generator again.

This is called a container iterable.

 In general, it is a good idea to work with container iterables when dealing with generators.

Details on generators will be explained in more detail in *Chapter 7, Generators, Iterators, and Asynchronous Programming*.

Creating sequences

Maybe our object does not define the __iter__() method, but we still want to be able to iterate over it. If __iter__ is not defined on the object, the iter() function will look for the presence of __getitem__, and if this is not found, it will raise TypeError.

A sequence is an object that implements __len__ and __getitem__ and expects to be able to get the elements it contains, one at a time, in order, starting at zero as the first index. This means that you should be careful in the logic so that you correctly implement __getitem__ to expect this type of index, or the iteration will not work.

The example from the previous section had the advantage that it uses less memory. This means that it is only holding one date at a time and knows how to produce the days one by one. However, it has the drawback that if we want to get the nth element, we have no way to do so but iterate n-times until we reach it. This is a typical trade-off in computer science between memory and CPU usage.

The implementation with an iterable will use less memory, but it takes up to $O(n)$ to get an element, whereas implementing a sequence will use more memory (because we have to hold everything at once), but supports indexing in constant time, $O(1)$.

The preceding notation (for example, $O(n)$) is called asymptotic notation (or "big-O" notation) and it describes the order of complexity of the algorithm. At a very high level, this means how many operations the algorithm needs to perform as a function of the size of the input (n). For more information on this, you can check out (ALGO01) listed at the end of the chapter, which contains a detailed study of asymptotic notation.

This is what the new implementation might look like:

```
class DateRangeSequence:
    def __init__(self, start_date, end_date):
        self.start_date = start_date
        self.end_date = end_date
        self._range = self._create_range()

    def _create_range(self):
        days = []
        current_day = self.start_date
        while current_day < self.end_date:
            days.append(current_day)
            current_day += timedelta(days=1)
        return days
```

```
    def __getitem__(self, day_no):
        return self._range[day_no]

    def __len__(self):
        return len(self._range)
```

Here is how the object behaves:

```
>>> s1 = DateRangeSequence(date(2018, 1, 1), date(2018, 1, 5))
>>> for day in s1:
...     print(day)
...
2018-01-01
2018-01-02
2018-01-03
2018-01-04
>>> s1[0]
datetime.date(2018, 1, 1)
>>> s1[3]
datetime.date(2018, 1, 4)
>>> s1[-1]
datetime.date(2018, 1, 4)
```

In the preceding code, we can see that negative indices also work. This is because the DateRangeSequence object delegates all of the operations to its wrapped object (a list), which is the best way to maintain compatibility and a consistent behavior.

 Evaluate the trade-off between memory and CPU usage when deciding which one of the two possible implementations to use. In general, the iteration is preferable (and generators even more), but keep in mind the requirements of every case.

Container objects

Containers are objects that implement a __contains__ method (that usually returns a Boolean value). This method is called in the presence of the in keyword of Python.

Something like the following:

```
element in container
```

When used in Python, becomes this:

```
container.__contains__(element)
```

You can imagine how much more readable (and Pythonic!) the code can be when this method is properly implemented.

Let's say we have to mark some points on a map of a game that has two-dimensional coordinates. We might expect to find a function like the following:

```
def mark_coordinate(grid, coord):
    if 0 <= coord.x < grid.width and 0 <= coord.y < grid.height:
        grid[coord] = MARKED
```

Now, the part that checks the condition of the first if statement seems convoluted; it doesn't reveal the intention of the code, it's not expressive, and worst of all it calls for code duplication (every part of the code where we need to check the boundaries before proceeding will have to repeat that if statement).

What if the map itself (called grid on the code) could answer this question? Even better, what if the map could delegate this action to an even smaller (and hence more cohesive) object?

We could solve this problem in a more elegant way with object-oriented design and with the help of a magic method. In this case, we can create a new abstraction to represent the limits of the grid, which can be made an object in itself. *Figure 2.2* helps illustrate the point:

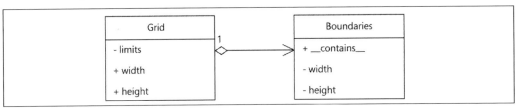

Figure 2.2: An example using composition, distributing responsibilities in different classes, and using the container magic method

Parenthetically, I'll mention that it's true that in general, class names refer to nouns, and they're usually singular. So, it might sound strange to have a class named Boundaries, but if we think about it, perhaps for this particular case, it makes sense to say that we have an object representing all the boundaries of a grid, especially because of the way it's being used (in this case, we're using it to validate if a particular coordinate is within those boundaries).

With this design, we can ask the `map` if it contains a coordinate, and the `map` itself can have information about its limit and pass the query down to its internal collaborator:

```
class Boundaries:
    def __init__(self, width, height):
        self.width = width
        self.height = height

    def __contains__(self, coord):
        x, y = coord
        return 0 <= x < self.width and 0 <= y < self.height


class Grid:
    def __init__(self, width, height):
        self.width = width
        self.height = height
        self.limits = Boundaries(width, height)

    def __contains__(self, coord):
        return coord in self.limits
```

This code alone is a much better implementation. First, it is doing a simple composition and it's using delegation to solve the problem. Both objects are really cohesive, having the minimal possible logic; the methods are short, and the logic speaks for itself—`coord in self.limits` is pretty much a declaration of the problem to solve, expressing the intention of the code.

From the outside, we can also see the benefits. It's almost as if Python is solving the problem for us:

```
def mark_coordinate(grid, coord):
    if coord in grid:
        grid[coord] = MARKED
```

Dynamic attributes for objects

It is possible to control the way attributes are obtained from objects by means of the __getattr__ magic method. When we call something like <myobject>.<myattribute>, Python will look for <myattribute> in the dictionary of the object, calling __getattribute__ on it. If this is not found (namely, the object does not have the attribute we are looking for), then the extra method, __getattr__, is called, passing the name of the attribute (myattribute) as a parameter.

By receiving this value, we can control the way things should be returned to our objects. We can even create new attributes, and so on.

In the following listing, the __getattr__ method is demonstrated:

```
class DynamicAttributes:

    def __init__(self, attribute):
        self.attribute = attribute

    def __getattr__(self, attr):
        if attr.startswith("fallback_"):
            name = attr.replace("fallback_", "")
            return f"[fallback resolved] {name}"
        raise AttributeError(
            f"{self.__class__.__name__} has no attribute {attr}"
        )
```

Here are some calls to an object of this class:

```
>>> dyn = DynamicAttributes("value")
>>> dyn.attribute
'value'

>>> dyn.fallback_test
'[fallback resolved] test'

>>> dyn.__dict__["fallback_new"] = "new value"
>>> dyn.fallback_new
'new value'

>>> getattr(dyn, "something", "default")
'default'
```

The first call is straightforward—we just request an attribute that the object has and get its value as a result. The second is where this method takes action because the object does not have anything called fallback_test, so __getattr__ will run with that value. Inside that method, we placed the code that returns a string, and what we get is the result of that transformation.

The third example is interesting because a new attribute named fallback_new is created (actually, this call would be the same as running dyn. fallback_new = "new value"), so when we request that attribute, notice that the logic we put in __getattr__ does not apply, simply because that code is never called.

Now, the last example is the most interesting one. There is a subtle detail here that makes a huge difference. Take another look at the code in the __getattr__ method. Notice the exception it raises when the value is not retrievable, AttributeError. This is not only for consistency (as well as the message in the exception), but also required by the built-in getattr() function. Had this exception been any other, it would raise, and the default value would not be returned.

 Be careful when implementing a method so dynamic as __getattr__, and use it with caution. When implementing __getattr__, raise AttributeError.

The __getattr__ magic method is useful in many situations. It can be used to create a proxy to another object. For example, if you're creating a wrapper object on top of another one by means of composition, and you want to delegate most of the methods to the wrapped object, instead of copying and defining all of those methods, you can implement __getattr__ that will internally call the same method on the wrapped object.

Another example is when you know you need attributes that are dynamically computed. I've used it on a past project working with GraphQL (https://graphql.org/) with Graphene (https://graphene-python.org/). The way the library worked was by using resolver methods. Basically, every method named resolve_X was used when property X was requested. Since there were already domain objects that could resolve each property X in the class of the Graphene object, __getattr__ was implemented to know where to get each property from, without having to write a massive boilerplate code.

Use the __getattr__ magic method when you see an opportunity to avoid lots of duplicated code and boilerplate, but don't abuse this method, as it'll render the code harder to understand and reason about. Keep in mind that having attributes that aren't explicitly declared and just appear dynamically will make the code harder to understand. When using this method, you're always weighing code compactness versus maintainability.

Callable objects

It is possible (and often convenient) to define objects that can act as functions. One of the most common applications for this is to create better decorators, but it's not limited to that.

The magic method __call__ will be called when we try to execute our object as if it were a regular function. Every argument passed to it will be passed along to the __call__ method.

The main advantage of implementing functions this way, through objects, is that objects have states, so we can save and maintain information across calls. This means that using a callable object might be a more convenient way of implementing functions if we need to maintain an internal state across different calls. Examples of this can be functions we would like to implement with memoization, or internal caches.

When we have an object, a statement like this, object(*args, **kwargs), is translated in Python to object.__call__(*args, **kwargs).

This method is useful when we want to create callable objects that will work as parametrized functions, or in some cases, functions with memory.

The following listing uses this method to construct an object that, when called with a parameter, returns the number of times it has been called with the very same value:

```python
from collections import defaultdict


class CallCount:

    def __init__(self):
        self._counts = defaultdict(int)

    def __call__(self, argument):
        self._counts[argument] += 1
        return self._counts[argument]
```

Some examples of this class in action are as follows:

```python
>>> cc = CallCount()
>>> cc(1)
1
>>> cc(2)
1
>>> cc(1)
2
>>> cc(1)
3
>>> cc("something")
```

```
1
>>> callable(cc)
    True
```

Later in this book, we will find out that this method comes in handy when creating decorators.

Summary of magic methods

We can summarize the concepts we described in the previous sections in the form of a cheat sheet like the one presented as follows. For each action in Python, the magic method involved is presented, along with the concept that it represents:

Statement	Magic method	Behavior
obj[key] obj[i:j] obj[i:j:k]	__getitem__(key)	Subscriptable object
with obj: ...	__enter__ / __exit__	Context manager
for i in obj: ...	__iter__ / __next__	Iterable object
	__len__ / __getitem__	Sequence
obj.<attribute>	__getattr__	Dynamic attribute retrieval
obj(*args, **kwargs)	__call__(*args, **kwargs)	Callable object

Table 2.1: Magic methods and their behavior in Python

The best way to implement these methods correctly (and to know the set of methods that need to be implemented together) is to declare our class to implement the corresponding class following the abstract base classes defined in the collections.abc module (https://docs.python.org/3/library/collections.abc.html#collections-abstract-base-classes). These interfaces provide the methods that need to be implemented, so it'll make it easier for you to define the class correctly, and it'll also take care of creating the type correctly (something that works well when the isinstance() function is called on your object).

We have seen the main features of Python with respect to its peculiar syntax. With the features we have learned (context managers, callable objects, creating our own sequences, and suchlike), we are now able to write code that will blend well with Python's reserved words (for example, we can use the with statements with our own context managers, or the in operator with a container of our own.)

With practice and experience, you'll become more fluent with these features of Python, until it becomes second nature for you to wrap the logic you're writing behind abstractions with nice and small interfaces. Give it enough time, and the reverse effect will take place: Python will start programming you. That is, you'll naturally think of having small, clean interfaces in your programs, so even when you're creating software in a different language, you'll try to use these concepts. For example, if you find yourself programming in, let's say, Java or C (or even Bash), you might identify a scenario where a context manager might be useful. Now the language itself might not support this out of the box, but that might not stop you from writing your own abstraction that provides similar guarantees. And that's a good thing. It means you have internalized good concepts beyond a specific language, and you can apply them in different situations.

All programming languages have their caveats, and Python is no exception, so in order to have a more complete understanding of Python, we'll review some of them in the next section.

Caveats in Python

Besides understanding the main features of the language, being able to write idiomatic code is also about being aware of the potential problems of some idioms, and how to avoid them. In this section, we will explore common issues that might cause you long debugging sessions if they catch you off guard.

Most of the points discussed in this section are things to avoid entirely, and I will dare to say that there is almost no possible scenario that justifies the presence of the anti-pattern (or idiom, in this case). Therefore, if you find this on the code base you are working on, feel free to refactor it in the way that is suggested. If you find these traits while doing a code review, this is a clear indication that something needs to change.

Mutable default arguments

Simply put, don't use mutable objects as the default arguments of functions. If you use mutable objects as default arguments, you will get results that are not the expected ones.

Consider the following erroneous function definition:

```
def wrong_user_display(user_metadata: dict = {"name": "John", "age":
30}):
    name = user_metadata.pop("name")
```

```
    age = user_metadata.pop("age")

    return f"{name} ({age})"
```

This has two problems, actually. Besides the default mutable argument, the body of the function is mutating a mutable object, and hence creating a side effect. But the main problem is the default argument for user_metadata.

This will actually only work the first time it is called without arguments. For the second time, we call it without explicitly passing something to user_metadata. It will fail with a KeyError, like so:

```
>>> wrong_user_display()
'John (30)'
>>> wrong_user_display({"name": "Jane", "age": 25})
'Jane (25)'
>>> wrong_user_display()
Traceback (most recent call last):
  File "<stdin>", line 1, in <module>
  File ... in wrong_user_display
    name = user_metadata.pop("name")
KeyError: 'name'
```

The explanation is simple — by assigning the dictionary with the default data to user_metadata on the definition of the function, this dictionary is actually created once and the user_metadata variable points to it. When the Python interpreter parses the file, it'll read the function, and find a statement in the signature that creates the dictionary and assigns it to the parameter. From that point on, the dictionary is created only once, and it's the same for the entire life of the program.

Then, the body of the function modifies this object, which remains alive in memory so long as the program is running. When we pass a value to it, this will take the place of the default argument we just created. When we don't want this object, it is called again, and it has been modified since the previous run; the next time we run it, will not contain the keys since they were removed on the previous call.

The fix is also simple — we need to use None as a default sentinel value and assign the default on the body of the function. Because each function has its own scope and life cycle, user_metadata will be assigned to the dictionary every time None appears:

```
def user_display(user_metadata: dict = None):
    user_metadata = user_metadata or {"name": "John", "age": 30}

    name = user_metadata.pop("name")
```

```
    age = user_metadata.pop("age")

    return f"{name} ({age})"
```

Let's conclude the section by understanding the quirks of extending built-in types.

Extending built-in types

The correct way of extending built-in types such as lists, strings, and dictionaries is by means of the `collections` module.

If you create a class that directly extends `dict`, for example, you will obtain results that are probably not what you are expecting. The reason for this is that in CPython (a C optimization), the methods of the class don't call each other (as they should), so if you override one of them, this will not be reflected by the rest, resulting in unexpected outcomes. For example, you might want to override __getitem__, and then when you iterate the object with a `for` loop, you will notice that the logic you have put on that method is not applied.

This is all solved by using `collections.UserDict`, for example, which provides a transparent interface to actual dictionaries, and is more robust.

Let's say we want a list that was originally created from numbers to convert the values to strings, adding a prefix. The first approach might look like it solves the problem, but it is erroneous:

```
class BadList(list):
    def __getitem__(self, index):
        value = super().__getitem__(index)
        if index % 2 == 0:
            prefix = "even"
        else:
            prefix = "odd"
        return f"[{prefix}] {value}"
```

At first sight, it looks like the object behaves as we want it to. But then, if we try to iterate it (after all, it is a `list`), we find that we don't get what we wanted:

```
>>> bl = BadList((0, 1, 2, 3, 4, 5))
>>> bl[0]
'[even] 0'
>>> bl[1]
'[odd] 1'
>>> "".join(bl)
```

```
Traceback (most recent call last):
...
TypeError: sequence item 0: expected str instance, int found
```

The join function will try to iterate (run a for loop over) the list but expects values of the string type. We would expect this to work because we modified the __getitem__ method so that it always returns a string. However, based on the result, we can conclude that our modified version of __getitem__ is not being called.

This issue is actually an implementation detail of CPython, while in other platforms such as PyPy this doesn't happen (see the differences between PyPy and CPython in the references at the end of this chapter).

Regardless of this, we should write code that is portable and compatible with all implementations, so we will fix it by extending not from list, but UserList:

```python
from collections import UserList


class GoodList(UserList):
    def __getitem__(self, index):
        value = super().__getitem__(index)
        if index % 2 == 0:
            prefix = "even"
        else:
            prefix = "odd"
        return f"[{prefix}] {value}"
```

And now things look much better:

```python
>>> gl = GoodList((0, 1, 2))
>>> gl[0]
'[even] 0'
>>> gl[1]
'[odd] 1'
>>> "; ".join(gl)
'[even] 0; [odd] 1; [even] 2'
```

 Don't extend directly from dict; use collections.UserDict instead. For lists, use collections.UserList, and for strings, use collections.UserString.

At this point, we know all the main concepts of Python. Not only how to write idiomatic code that blends well with Python itself, but also to avoid certain pitfalls. The next section is complementary.

Before finishing the chapter, I wanted to give a quick introduction to asynchronous programming, because while it is not strictly related to clean code *per se*, asynchronous code has become more and more popular, following up with the idea that, in order to work effectively with code, we must be able to read it and understand it, because being able to read asynchronous code is important.

A brief introduction to asynchronous code

Asynchronous programming is not related to clean code. Therefore, the features of Python described in this section won't make the code base easier to maintain. This section introduces the syntax in Python to work with coroutines, because it might be of use for the reader, and examples with coroutines might appear later in the book.

The idea behind asynchronous programming is to have parts in our code that are able to suspend so that other parts of our code can run. Typically, when we are running I/O operations, we would very much like to keep that code running, and use the CPU on something else during that time.

This changes the programming model. Instead of us making calls synchronously, we would write our code in a way that is being called by an event loop, which is in charge of scheduling the coroutines for running all of them in the same process and thread.

The idea is that we create a series of coroutines, and they're added to the event loop. When the event loop starts, it'll pick among the coroutines it has, and schedule them to run. At some point, when one of our coroutines needs to do an I/O operation, we can trigger it and signal the event loop back to take control again, and then schedule another coroutine whilst this operation was kept running. At some point, the event loop will resume our coroutine from the last point it got stopped at, and will continue from there. Keep in mind that the advantage of asynchronous programming is to not block on I/O operations. This means the code can jump to something else while an I/O operation is in place and then come back at it, but it doesn't mean that there are multiple processes running simultaneously. The execution model is still single-threaded.

In order to achieve this in Python, there were (and still are) lots of frameworks available. But in older versions of Python, there wasn't a specific syntax that allowed this, so the way the frameworks worked was a bit complicated, or non-obvious at first glance. Starting with Python 3.5, specific syntax for declaring coroutines was added to the language, and that changed the way we write asynchronous code in Python. Slightly prior to that, a default event loop module, `asyncio`, was introduced in the standard library. With these two milestones of Python, making asynchronous programming is much better.

While this section uses `asyncio` as the module for asynchronous processing, this is not the only one. You can write asynchronous code using any library (there are plenty of them available outside the standard library, such as `trio` (`https://github.com/python-trio/trio`) and `curio` (`https://github.com/dabeaz/curio`) to name just a couple). The syntax that Python provides for writing coroutines can be considered an API. As long as the library you choose complies with that API, you should be able to use it, without having to change how your coroutines were declared.

The syntactic differences compared with asynchronous programming are that coroutines are like functions, but they're defined with `async def` before their name. When inside a coroutine and we want to call another one (which can be ours, or defined in a third-party library), we would typically use the `await` keyword before its invocation. When `await` is called, this signals the event loop to take back control. At this point, the event loop will resume its execution, and the coroutine will be left there waiting for its non-blocking operation to continue, and in the meantime, another part of the code will run (another coroutine will be called by the event loop). At some point, the event loop will call our original coroutine again, and this one will resume from the point where it left off (right after the line with the `await` statement).

A typical coroutine we might define in our code has the following structure:

```
async def mycoro(*args, **kwargs):
    # … logic
    await third_party.coroutine(…)
    # … more of our logic
```

As mentioned before, there's new syntax for defining coroutines. One difference that this syntax introduces is that as opposed to regular functions, when we call this definition, it will not run the code within it. Instead, it will create a coroutine object. This object will be included in the event loop, and at some point, must be awaited (otherwise the code inside the definition will never run):

```
result = await mycoro(…)   #  doing result = mycoro() would be erroneous
```

Don't forget to await your coroutines, or their code will never be run. Pay attention to the warnings given by `asyncio`.

As mentioned, there are several libraries for asynchronous programming in Python, with event loops that can run coroutines like the preceding one defined. In particular, for `asyncio`, there's a built-in function to run a coroutine until its completion:

```
import asyncio
asyncio.run(mycoro(…))
```

The details of how coroutines work in Python are beyond the scope of this book, but this introduction should get the reader more familiar with the syntax. That said, coroutines are technically implemented on top of generators, which we will explore in detail in *Chapter 7, Generators, Iterators, and Asynchronous Programming*.

Summary

In this chapter, we have explored the main features of Python, with the goal of understanding its most distinctive features, those that make Python a peculiar language compared to the rest. Along this path, we have explored different methods of Python, protocols, and their internal mechanics.

As opposed to the previous chapter, this one is more Python-focused. A key takeaway of the topics of this book is that clean code goes beyond following the formatting rules (which, of course, are essential to a good code base). They are a necessary condition, but not sufficient. Over the next few chapters, we will see ideas and principles that relate more to the code, with the goal of achieving a better design and implementation of our software solution.

With the concepts and the ideas of this chapter, we explored the core of Python: its protocols and magic methods. It should be clear by now that the best way of having Pythonic, idiomatic code is not only by following the formatting conventions, but also by taking full advantage of all the features Python has to offer. This means that you can write more maintainable code by using a particular magic method, a context manager, or writing more concise statements by using comprehensions and assignment expressions.

We also got acquainted with asynchronous programming, and now we should feel comfortable reading asynchronous code in Python. This is important because asynchronous programming is becoming increasingly popular, and it'll be useful for future topics, explored later in the book.

In the next chapter, we will put these concepts into action, relating general concepts of software engineering with the way they can be written in Python.

References

The reader will find more information about some of the topics that we have covered in this chapter in the following references. The decision of how indices work in Python is based on (EWD831), which analyzes several alternatives for ranges in math and programming languages:

- *EWD831: Why numbering should start at zero* (`https://www.cs.utexas.edu/users/EWD/transcriptions/EWD08xx/EWD831.html`)

- *PEP-343: The "with" statement* (`https://www.python.org/dev/peps/pep-0343/`)

- *CC08*: The book written by *Robert C. Martin* entitled *Clean Code: A Handbook of Agile Software Craftsmanship*

- *The iter() function*: `https://docs.python.org/3/library/functions.html#iter`

- *Differences between PyPy and CPython*: `https://pypy.readthedocs.io/en/latest/cpython_differences.html#subclasses-of-built-in-types`

- *The Art of Enbugging*: `http://media.pragprog.com/articles/jan_03_enbug.pdf`

- *ALGO01*: The book written by *Thomas H. Cormen, Charles E. Leiserson, Ronald L. Rivest,* and *Clifford Stein* entitled *Introduction to Algorithms, 3rd Edition (The MIT Press)*

3
General Traits of Good Code

This is a book about software construction with Python. Good software is built from a good design. By saying things such as clean code, you may be thinking that we will explore good practices that relate only to the implementation details of the software, instead of its design. However, this assumption would be wrong since the code is not something different from the design—the code *is* the design.

The code is probably the most detailed representation of the design. In the first two chapters, we discussed why structuring the code in a consistent way was important, and we have seen idioms for writing more compact and idiomatic code. Now it's time to understand that clean code is that, and much more—the ultimate goal is to make the code as robust as possible, and to write it in a way that minimizes defects or makes them utterly evident, should they occur.

This chapter, and the one following, is focused on design principles at a higher level of abstraction. I will present the general principles of software engineering that are applied in Python.

In particular, for this chapter, we will review different principles that make for good software design. Good quality software should be built around these ideas, and they will serve as design tools. That does not mean that all of them should always be applied; in fact, some of them represent different points of view (such is the case with the **Design by Contract (DbC)** approach, as opposed to defensive programming). Some of them depend on the context and are not always applicable.

High-quality code is a concept that has multiple dimensions. We can think of this similarly to how we think about the quality attributes of a software architecture. For example, we want our software to be secure and to have good performance, reliability, and maintainability, to name just a few attributes.

The goals of this chapter are as follows:

- To understand the concepts behind robust software
- To learn how to deal with erroneous data during the workflow of the application
- To design maintainable software that can easily be extended and adapted to new requirements
- To design reusable software
- To write effective code that will keep the productivity of the development team high

Design by contract

Some parts of the software we are working on are not meant to be called directly by users, but instead by other parts of the code. Such is the case when we divide the responsibilities of the application into different components or layers, and we have to think about the interaction between them.

We have to encapsulate some functionality behind each component and expose an interface to clients who are going to use that functionality, namely, an **Application Programming Interface (API)**. The functions, classes, or methods we write for that component have a particular way of working under certain considerations that, if they are not met, will make our code crash. Conversely, clients calling that code expect a particular response, and any failure of our function to provide this would represent a defect.

That is to say that if, for example, we have a function that is expected to work with a series of parameters of type integers, and some other function invokes ours by passing strings, it is clear that it should not work as expected, but in reality, the function should not run at all because it was called incorrectly (the client made a mistake). This error should not pass silently.

Of course, when designing an API, the expected input, output, and side effects should be documented. But documentation cannot enforce the behavior of the software at runtime. These rules, what every part of the code expects in order to work properly and what the caller is expecting from them, should be part of the design, and here is where the concept of a **contract** comes into place.

The idea behind the DbC approach is that, instead of implicitly placing in the code what every party is expecting, both parties agree on a contract that, if violated, will raise an exception, clearly stating why it cannot continue.

In our context, a contract is a construction that enforces some rules that must be honored during the communication of software components. A contract entails mainly preconditions and postconditions, but in some cases, invariants, and side effects are also described:

- **Preconditions**: We can say that these are all the checks the code will perform before running. It will check for all the conditions that have to be made before the function can proceed. In general, it's implemented by validating the dataset provided in the parameters passed, but nothing should stop us from running all sorts of validations (for example, validating a set in a database, a file, or another method that was called before) if we consider that their side effects are overshadowed by the importance of such validations. Note that this imposes a constraint on the caller.

- **Postconditions**: The opposite of preconditions, here, the validations are done after the function call is returned. Postcondition validations are run to validate what the caller is expecting from this component.

- **Invariants**: Optionally, it would be a good idea to document, in the docstring of a function, the invariants, the things that are kept constant while the code of the function is running, as an expression of the logic of the function to be correct.

- **Side effects**: Optionally, we can mention any side effects of our code in the docstring.

While conceptually, all of these items form part of the contract for a software component, and this is what should go to the documentation of such a piece, only the first two (preconditions and postconditions) are to be enforced at a low level (code).

The reason why we would design by contract is that if errors occur, they must be easy to spot (and by noticing whether it was either the precondition or postcondition that failed, we will find the culprit much more easily) so that they can be quickly corrected. More importantly, we want critical parts of the code to avoid being executed under the wrong assumptions. This should help to clearly mark the limits for the responsibilities and errors if they occur, as opposed to something saying that this part of the application is failing. But the caller code provided the wrong arguments, so where should we apply the fix?

The idea is that preconditions bind the client (they have an obligation to meet them if they want to run some part of the code), whereas postconditions bind the component in relation to some guarantees that the client can verify and enforce.

This way, we can quickly identify responsibilities. If the precondition fails, we know it is due to a defect on the client. On the other hand, if the postcondition check fails, we know the problem is in the routine or class (supplier) itself.

Specifically, regarding preconditions, it is important to highlight that they can be checked at runtime, and if they occur, the code that is being called should not be run at all (it does not make sense to run it because its conditions do not hold, and doing so might end up making things worse).

Preconditions

Preconditions are all of the guarantees a function or method expects to receive in order to work correctly. In general programming terms, this usually means providing data that is properly formed, for example, objects that are initialized, non-null values, and many more. For Python, in particular, being dynamically typed, this also means that sometimes we need to check for the exact type of data that is provided. This is not exactly the same as type checking, the mypy kind would do this, but rather verify the exact values that are needed.

Part of these checks can be detected early on by using static analysis tools, such as mypy, which we already introduced in *Chapter 1, Introduction, Code Formatting, and Tools*, but these checks are not enough. A function should have proper validation for the information that it is going to handle.

Now, this poses the question of where to place the validation logic, depending on whether we let the clients validate all the data before calling the function, or allow this one to validate everything that it received prior to running its own logic. The former equates to a tolerant approach (because the function itself is still allowing any data, potentially malformed data as well), whereas the latter equates to a demanding approach.

For the purposes of this analysis, we prefer a demanding approach when it comes to DbC because it is usually the safest choice in terms of robustness, and usually the most common practice in the industry.

Regardless of the approach we decide to take, we should always keep in mind the non-redundancy principle, which states that the enforcement of each precondition for a function should be done by only one of the two parts of the contract, but not both. This means that we put the validation logic on the client, or we leave it to the function itself, but in no case should we duplicate it (which also relates to the DRY principle, which we will discuss later on in this chapter).

Postconditions

Postconditions are the part of the contract that is responsible for enforcing the state after the method or function has returned.

Assuming that the function or method has been called with the correct properties (that is, with its preconditions met), then the postconditions will guarantee that certain properties are preserved.

The idea is to use postconditions to check and validate everything that a client might need. If the method executed properly, and the postcondition validations pass, then any client calling that code should be able to work with the returned object without problems, as the contract has been fulfilled.

Pythonic contracts

At the time of writing this book, a PEP-316, named *Programming by Contract for Python*, is deferred. That doesn't mean that we cannot implement it in Python because, as introduced at the beginning of the chapter, this is a general design principle.

Probably the best way to enforce this is by adding control mechanisms to our methods, functions, and classes, and if they fail, raise a RuntimeError exception or ValueError. It's hard to devise a general rule for the correct type of exception, as that would pretty much depend on the application in particular. These previously mentioned exceptions are the most common types of exception, but if they don't fit accurately with the problem, creating a custom exception would be the best choice.

We would also like to keep the code as isolated as possible. That is, the code for the preconditions in one part, the one for the postconditions in another, and the core of the function separated. We could achieve this separation by creating smaller functions, but in some cases implementing a decorator would be an interesting alternative.

Design by contract – conclusions

The main value of this design principle is to effectively identify where the problem is. By defining a contract, when something fails at runtime, it will be clear what part of the code is broken, and what broke the contract.

As a result of following this principle, the code will be more robust. Each component is enforcing its own constraints and maintaining some invariants, and the program can be proven correct as long as these invariants are preserved.

It also serves the purpose of clarifying the structure of the program better. Instead of trying to run ad hoc validations, or trying to surmount all possible failure scenarios, the contracts explicitly specify what each function or method expects to work properly, and what is expected from them.

Of course, following these principles also adds extra work, because we are not just programming the core logic of our main application, but also the contracts. In addition, we might want to consider adding unit tests for these contracts as well. However, the quality gained by this approach pays off in the long run; hence, it is a good idea to implement this principle for critical components of the application.

Nonetheless, for this method to be effective, we should carefully think about what we are willing to validate, and this has to be a meaningful value. For example, it would not make much sense to define contracts that only check for the correct data types of the parameters provided to a function. Many programmers would argue that this would be like trying to make Python a statically typed language. Regardless of this, tools such as mypy, in combination with the use of annotations, would serve this purpose much better and with less effort. With that in mind, design contracts so that there is actually value in them, checking, for example, the properties of the objects being passed and returned, the conditions they have to abide by, and so on.

Defensive programming

Defensive programming follows a somewhat different approach to DbC. Instead of stating all conditions that must be held in a contract, which, if unmet, will raise an exception and make the program fail, this is more about making all parts of the code (objects, functions, or methods) able to protect themselves against invalid inputs.

Defensive programming is a technique that has several aspects, and it is particularly useful if it is combined with other design principles (this means that the fact that it follows a different philosophy to DbC does not mean that it is a case of either one or the other—it could mean that they might complement one another).

The main ideas on the subject of defensive programming are how to handle errors for scenarios that we might expect to occur, and how to deal with errors that should never occur (when impossible conditions happen). The former will fall into error handling procedures, while the latter will be the case for assertions. Both topics are explored in the following sections.

Error handling

In our programs, we resort to error handling procedures for situations that we anticipate as prone to cause errors. This is usually the case for data input.

The idea behind error handling is to gracefully respond to these expected errors in an attempt to either continue our program execution or decide to fail if the error turns out to be insurmountable.

There are different approaches by which we can handle errors on our programs, but not all of them are always applicable. Some of these approaches are as follows:

- Value substitution
- Error logging
- Exception handling

In the next two sections, we'll focus on value substitution and exception handling, because these forms of error handling provide more interesting analysis. Error logging is a complementary practice (and a good one; we should always log errors), but most of the time we only log when there's nothing else to be done, so the other methods provide more interesting alternatives.

Value substitution

In some scenarios, when there is an error and there is a risk of the software producing an incorrect value or failing entirely, we might be able to replace the result with another, safer value. We call this value substitution, since we are, in fact, replacing the actual erroneous result for a value that is to be considered non-disruptive (it could be a default, a well-known constant, a sentinel value, or simply something that does not affect the result at all, such as returning zero in a case where the result is intended to be applied to a sum).

Value substitution is not always possible, however. This strategy has to be carefully chosen for cases where the substituted value is a safe option. Making this decision is a trade-off between robustness and correctness. A software program is robust when it does not fail, even in the presence of an erroneous scenario. But this is not correct either.

This might not be acceptable for some kinds of software. If the application is critical, or the data being handled is too sensitive, this is not an option, since we cannot afford to provide users (or other parts of the application) with erroneous results. In these cases, we opt for correctness, rather than let the program explode when yielding the wrong results.

A slightly different, and safer, version of this decision is to use default values for data that is not provided. This can be the case for parts of the code that can work with a default behavior, for example, default values for environment variables that are not set, for missing entries in configuration files, or for parameters of functions.

We can find examples of Python supporting this throughout different methods of its API, for example, dictionaries have a get method, whose (optional) second parameter allows you to indicate a default value:

```
>>> configuration = {"dbport": 5432}
>>> configuration.get("dbhost", "localhost")

'localhost'
>>> configuration.get("dbport")
5432
```

Environment variables have a similar API:

```
>>> import os
>>> os.getenv("DBHOST")
'localhost'
>>> os.getenv("DPORT", 5432)
5432
```

In both previous examples, if the second parameter is not provided, None will be returned because it's the default value those functions are defined with. We can also define default values for the parameters of our own functions:

```
>>> def connect_database(host="localhost", port=5432):
...     logger.info("connecting to database server at %s:%i", host,
port)
```

In general, replacing missing parameters with default values is acceptable, but substituting erroneous data with legal close values is more dangerous and can mask some errors. Take this criterion into consideration when deciding on this approach.

Exception handling

In the presence of incorrect or missing input data, sometimes it is possible to correct the situation with some examples, such as the ones mentioned in the previous section. In other cases, however, it is better to stop the program from continuing to run with the wrong data than to leave it computing under erroneous assumptions. In those cases, failing and notifying the caller that something is wrong is a good approach, and this is the case for a precondition that was violated, as we saw in DbC.

Nonetheless, erroneous input data is not the only possible way in which a function can go wrong. After all, functions are not just about passing data around; they also have side effects and connect to external components.

It could be possible that a fault in a function call is due to a problem on one of these external components, and not in our function itself. If that is the case, our function should communicate this properly. This will make it easier to debug. The function should clearly, and unambiguously, notify the rest of the application regarding errors that cannot be ignored so that they can be addressed accordingly.

The mechanism for accomplishing this is an exception. It is important to emphasize that this is what exceptions should be used for—clearly announcing an exceptional situation, and not altering the flow of the program according to business logic.

If the code tries to use exceptions to handle expected scenarios or business logic, the flow of the program will become harder to read. This will lead to a situation where exceptions are used as a sort of go-to statement, which (to make things worse) could span multiple levels on the call stack (up to caller functions), violating the encapsulation of the logic into its correct level of abstraction. The case could get even worse if these except blocks are mixing business logic with truly exceptional cases that the code is trying to defend against; in that case, it will be harder to distinguish between the core logic we have to maintain and the errors to be handled.

> Do not use exceptions as a go-to mechanism for business logic. Raise exceptions when there is something wrong with the code that callers need to be aware of.

This last concept is an important one; exceptions are usually about notifying the caller about something amiss. This means that exceptions should be used carefully because they weaken encapsulation. The more exceptions a function has, the more the caller function will have to anticipate, therefore knowing about the function it is calling. And if a function raises too many exceptions, this means that it is not so context-free, because every time we want to invoke it, we will have to keep all of its possible side effects in mind.

This can be used as a heuristic to tell when a function is not sufficiently cohesive and has too many responsibilities. If it raises too many exceptions, it could be a sign that it has to be broken down into multiple, smaller ones.

Here are some recommendations that relate to exceptions in Python.

Handling exceptions at the right level of abstraction

Exceptions are also part of the principal functions that do one thing, and one thing only. The exception the function is handling (or raising) has to be consistent with the logic encapsulated on it.

In the following example, we can see what we mean by mixing different levels of abstractions. Imagine an object that acts as a transport for some data in our application. It connects to an external component where the data is going to be sent upon decoding. In the following listing, we will focus on the deliver_event method:

```python
class DataTransport:
    """An example of an object handling exceptions of different
levels."""
    _RETRY_BACKOFF: int = 5
    _RETRY_TIMES: int = 3

    def __init__(self, connector: Connector) -> None:
        self._connector = connector
        self.connection = None

    def deliver_event(self, event: Event):
        try:
            self.connect()
            data = event.decode()
            self.send(data)
        except ConnectionError as e:
            logger.info("connection error detected: %s", e)
            raise
        except ValueError as e:
            logger.error("%r contains incorrect data: %s", event, e)
            raise

    def connect(self):
        for _ in range(self._RETRY_TIMES):
            try:
                self.connection = self._connector.connect()
            except ConnectionError as e:
                logger.info(
                    "%s: attempting new connection in %is", e, self._
RETRY_BACKOFF,
                )
                time.sleep(self._RETRY_BACKOFF)
            else:
                return self.connection
        raise ConnectionError(f"Couldn't connect after {self._RETRY_
TIMES} times")

    def send(self, data: bytes):
        return self.connection.send(data)
```

For our analysis, let's zoom in and focus on how the `deliver_event()` method handles exceptions.

What does `ValueError` have to do with `ConnectionError`? Not much. By looking at these two highly different types of error, we can get an idea of how responsibilities should be divided.

`ConnectionError` should be handled inside the `connect` method. This allows a clear separation of behavior. For example, if this method needs to support retries, then handling said exception would be a way of doing it.

Conversely, `ValueError` belongs to the `decode` method of the event. With this new implementation (shown in the next example), this method does not need to catch any exception—the exceptions we were worrying about before are either handled by internal methods or deliberately left to be raised.

We should separate these fragments into different methods or functions. For the connection management, a small function should be enough. This function will be in charge of trying to establish the connection, catching exceptions (should they occur), and logging them accordingly:

```
def connect_with_retry(connector: Connector, retry_n_times: int, retry_
backoff: int = 5):
    """Tries to establish the connection of <connector> retrying
    <retry_n_times>, and waiting <retry_backoff> seconds between
attempts.

    If it can connect, returns the connection object.
    If it's not possible to connect after the retries have been
exhausted, raises ``ConnectionError``.

    :param connector:        An object with a ``.connect()`` method.
    :param retry_n_times int: The number of times to try to call
                             ``connector.connect()``.

    :param retry_backoff int: The time lapse between retry calls.

    """
    for _ in range(retry_n_times):
        try:
            return connector.connect()
        except ConnectionError as e:
            logger.info("%s: attempting new connection in %is", e,
retry_backoff)
```

```
            time.sleep(retry_backoff)
    exc = ConnectionError(f"Couldn't connect after {retry_n_times}
times")
    logger.exception(exc)
    raise exc
```

Then, we will call this function in our method. As for the `ValueError` exception on the event, we could separate it with a new object and do composition, but for this limited case it would be overkill, so just moving the logic to a separate method would be enough. With these two considerations in place, the new version of the method looks much more compact and easier to read:

```
class DataTransport:
    """An example of an object that separates the exception handling by
    abstraction levels.
    """

    _RETRY_BACKOFF: int = 5
    _RETRY_TIMES: int = 3

    def __init__(self, connector: Connector) -> None:
        self._connector = connector
        self.connection = None

    def deliver_event(self, event: Event):
        self.connection = connect_with_retry(self._connector, self._
RETRY_TIMES, self._RETRY_BACKOFF)
        self.send(event)

    def send(self, event: Event):
        try:
            return self.connection.send(event.decode())
        except ValueError as e:
            logger.error("%r contains incorrect data: %s", event, e)
            raise
```

See now how the separation of the exception classes also delimits a separation in responsibilities. In the first example shown, everything was mixed, and there wasn't a clear separation of concerns. Then we decided the connection as a concern on itself, so in the next example, the `connect_with_retry` function was created, and `ConnectionError` was being handled as part of this function, if we needed to modify that function (as we had). On the other hand, the `ValueError` wasn't part of that same logic, so it was left in the send method where it belongs.

Exceptions carry a meaning. For that reason, it's important to handle each type of exception at its right level of abstraction (that means, depending on the layer of our application they belong to). But they can also carry important information sometimes. And since this information might be sensitive, we don't want it to fall into the wrong hands, so in the next section we'll discuss the security implications of exceptions.

Do not expose tracebacks to end users

This is a security consideration. When dealing with exceptions, it might be acceptable to let them propagate if the error is too important, and maybe even let the program fail if this is the decision for that particular scenario and correctness was favored over robustness.

When there is an exception that denotes a problem, it's important to log in with as much detail as possible (including the traceback information, message, and all we can gather) so that the issue can be corrected efficiently. At the same time, we want to include as much detail as possible for ourselves—we don't want any of this becoming visible to users.

In Python, tracebacks of exceptions contain very rich and useful debugging information. Unfortunately, this information is also very useful for attackers or malicious users who want to try and harm the application, not to mention that the leak would represent an important information disclosure, jeopardizing the intellectual property of your organization (as parts of the code will be exposed).

If you choose to let exceptions propagate, make sure not to disclose any sensitive information. Also, if you have to notify users about a problem, choose generic messages (such as `Something went wrong`, or `Page not found`). This is a common technique used in web applications that display generic informative messages when an HTTP error occurs.

Avoid empty except blocks

This was even referred to as the most diabolical Python anti-pattern (REAL 01). While it is good to anticipate and defend our programs against some errors, being too defensive might lead to even worse problems. In particular, the only problem with being too defensive is that there is an empty except block that silently passes without doing anything.

Python is so flexible that it allows us to write code that can be faulty and yet, will not raise an error, like this:

```
try:
    process_data()
except:
    pass
```

The problem with this is that it will not fail, ever, even when it should. It is also non-Pythonic if you remember from the Zen of Python that errors should never pass silently.

 Configure your continuous integration environment (by using tools such as those explored in *Chapter 1, Introduction, Code Formatting, and Tools*) to automatically report on empty exception blocks.

In the event of an exception, this block of code will not fail, which might be what we wanted in the first place. But what if there is a defect? There might occur an actual failure when the process_data() function runs, and we would like to know if there is an error in our logic in order to be able to correct it. Writing blocks such as this one will mask problems, making things harder to maintain.

There are two alternatives:

- Catch a more specific exception (not too broad, such as an Exception). In fact, some linting tools and IDEs will warn you in some cases when the code is handling too broad an exception.
- Perform some actual error handling on the except block.

The best thing to do would be to apply both recommendations. Handling a more specific exception (for example, AttributeError or KeyError) will make the program more maintainable because the reader will know what to expect and can get an idea of the *why* of it. It will also leave other exceptions free to be raised, and if that happens, this probably means a bug, only this time it can be discovered.

Handling the exception itself can mean multiple things. In its simplest form, it could be just about logging the exception (make sure to use logger.exception or logger. error to provide the full context of what happened). Other alternatives could be to return a default value (substitution, only that in this case after detecting an error, not prior to causing it), or raising a different exception.

If you choose to raise a different exception, include the original exception that caused the problem (see the next section).

Another reason to avoid having an empty except block (using `pass`) is the implicitness of it: it doesn't tell readers of the code that we actually expect that exception to be ignored. A more explicit way of doing so would be to use the `contextlib.suppress` function, which can accept all exceptions as arguments that are to be ignored, and it can be used as a context manager.

In our example, it might look like this:

```
import contextlib

with contextlib.suppress(KeyError):
    process_data()
```

Again, as with the previous case, try to avoid passing the general `Exception` to this context manager, because the effect will be the same.

Include the original exception

As part of our error handling logic, we might decide to raise a different one, and maybe even change its message. If that is the case, it is recommended to include the original exception that led to that.

We can use the `raise <e> from <original_exception>` syntax (PEP-3134). When using this construction, the original traceback will be embedded into the new exception, and the original exception will be set in the `__cause__` attribute of the resulting one.

For example, if we desire to wrap default exceptions with custom ones internally to our project, we could still do that while including information about the root exception:

```
class InternalDataError(Exception):
    """An exception with the data of our domain problem."""


def process(data_dictionary, record_id):
    try:
        return data_dictionary[record_id]
    except KeyError as e:
        raise InternalDataError("Record not present") from e
```

Always use the `raise <e> from <o>` syntax when changing the
type of the exception.

Using this syntax will make the tracebacks contain more information about the
exception or the error that has just occurred, which will help significantly when
debugging.

Using assertions in Python

Assertions are to be used for situations that should never happen, so the expression
on the `assert` statement has to mean an impossible condition. Should this condition
happen, it means there is a defect in the software.

In contrast to the error handling approach, there are situations in which we don't
want our program to continue its execution if a particular error occurred. This is
because, in some cases, the error cannot be surmounted, and our program cannot
correct its course of execution (or self-heal), so it's better to fail fast, and let the
error be noticed, so it can be corrected with the next version upgrade.

The idea of using assertions is to prevent the program from causing further damage
if such an invalid scenario is presented. Sometimes, it is better to stop and let the
program crash rather than let it continue processing under the wrong assumptions.

By definition, an assertion is a Boolean condition in the code that must hold true
for the program to be correct. If the program fails because of an `AssertionError`, it
means a defect has just been uncovered.

For this reason, assertions should not be mixed with the business logic, or used as
control flow mechanisms for the software. The following example is a bad idea:

```
try:
    assert condition.holds(), "Condition is not satisfied"
except AssertionError:
    alternative_procedure()
```

Do not catch the `AssertionError` exception because it might be
confusing for readers of the code. If you're expecting some part of
your code to raise an exception, try to use a more specific one.

The previous advice of catching the `AssertionError` goes along the lines of not letting your program fail silently. But it could fail gracefully. So, instead of letting the application have a hard crash, you can catch the `AssertionError` and show a generic error message, while still logging all the internal error details to the logging platform of your company. The point is not exactly about whether or not to catch this exception, but that assertion errors are a valuable source of information that will help you improve the quality of your software.

Make sure that the program terminates when an assertion fails. This means that assertions are usually put in the code to identify erroneous parts of the program. There's a tendency in many programming languages to think that assertions can be suppressed when the program is running in production, but that defeats its purpose, because the point of them is to precisely let us know about those parts of the program that need to be fixed.

In Python, in particular, running with the –O flag will suppress the `assert` statements, but this is discouraged for the aforementioned reasons.

 Do not run your production programs with `python -O ...` as you'd like to take advantage of the assertions in the code to correct defects.

Include a descriptive error message in the assertion statement and log the errors to make sure that you can properly debug and correct the problem later on.

Another important reason why the previous code is a bad idea is that besides catching `AssertionError`, the statement in the assertion is a function call. Function calls can have side effects, and they aren't always repeatable (we don't know if calling `condition.holds()` again will yield the same result). Moreover, if we stop the debugger at that line, we might not be able to conveniently see the result that causes the error, and, again, even if we call that function again, we don't know if that was the offending value.

A better alternative requires a few more lines of code, but provides more useful information:

```
result = condition.holds()
assert result > 0, f"Error with {result}"
```

When using assertions, try to avoid using function calls directly, and write the expression in terms of local variables.

What's the relationship between assertions and exception handling? Some might ask if assertions are moot, in the light of exception handling. Why would you want to assert for a condition if we can check that with an `if` statement and raise an exception? There's a subtle difference, though. In general, exceptions are for handling unexpected situations in relation to the business logic that our program will want to consider, whereas assertions are like self-checking mechanisms put in the code, to validate (assert) its correctness.

For this reason, exception raising will be much more common than having `assert` statements. Typical uses of `assert` are situations where an algorithm maintains an invariant logic that must be kept at all times: in that case, you might want to assert for the invariant. If this is broken at some point, it means either the algorithm is wrong or poorly implemented.

We have explored defensive programming in Python, and some related topics regarding exception handling. Now, we move on to the next big topic, as the next section discusses the separation of concerns.

Separation of concerns

This is a design principle that is applied at multiple levels. It is not just about the low-level design (code), but it is also relevant at a higher level of abstraction, so it will come up later when we talk about architecture.

Different responsibilities should go into different components, layers, or modules of the application. Each part of the program should only be responsible for a part of the functionality (what we call its concerns) and should know nothing about the rest.

The goal of separating concerns in software is to enhance maintainability by minimizing ripple effects. A **ripple** effect means the propagation of a change in the software from a starting point. This could be the case of an error or exception triggering a chain of other exceptions, causing failures that will result in a defect on a remote part of the application. It can also be that we have to change a lot of code scattered through multiple parts of the code base, as a result of a simple change in a function definition.

Clearly, we do not want these scenarios to happen. The software has to be easy to change. If we have to modify or refactor some part of the code, this has to have a minimal impact on the rest of the application, and the way to achieve this is through proper encapsulation.

In a similar way, we want any potential errors to be contained so that they don't cause major damage.

This concept is related to the DbC principle in the sense that each concern can be enforced by a contract. When a contract is violated, and an exception is raised as a result of such a violation, we know what part of the program has the failure, and what responsibilities failed to be met.

Despite this similarity, separation of concerns goes further. We normally think of contracts between functions, methods, or classes, and while this also applies to responsibilities that have to be separated, the idea of the separation of concerns also applies to Python modules, packages, and basically any software component.

Cohesion and coupling

These are important concepts for good software design.

On the one hand, `cohesion` means that objects should have a small and well-defined purpose, and they should do as little as possible. It follows a similar philosophy as Unix commands that do only one thing and do it well. The more cohesive our objects are, the more useful and reusable they become, making our design better.

On the other hand, `coupling` refers to the idea of how two or more objects depend on each other. This dependency poses a limitation. If two parts of the code (objects or methods) are too dependent on each other, they bring with them some undesired consequences:

- **No code reuse**: If one function depends too much on a particular object, or takes too many parameters, it's coupled with this object, which means that it will be really difficult to use that function in a different context (to do so, we will have to find a suitable parameter that complies with a very restrictive interface).

- **Ripple effects**: Changes in one of the two parts will certainly impact the other, as they are too close.

- **Low level of abstraction**: When two functions are so closely related, it is hard to see them as different concerns resolving problems at different levels of abstraction.

Rule of thumb: Well-defined software will achieve high cohesion and low coupling.

Acronyms to live by

In this section, we will review some principles that yield some good design ideas. The point is to quickly relate to good software practices by acronyms that are easy to remember, working as a sort of mnemonic rule. If you keep these words in mind, you will be able to associate them with good practices more easily and finding the right idea behind a particular line of code that you are looking at will be faster.

These are by no means formal or academic definitions, but more like empirical ideas that emerged from years of working in the software industry. Some of them do appear in books, as they were coined by important authors (see the references to investigate them in more detail), and others have their roots probably in blog posts, papers, or conference talks.

DRY/OAOO

The ideas of **Don't Repeat Yourself (DRY)** and **Once and Only Once (OAOO)** are closely related, so they were included together here. They are self-explanatory, and you should avoid duplication at all costs.

Things in the code, knowledge, have to be defined only once and in a single place. When you have to make a change to the code, there should be only one rightful location to modify. Failure to do so is a sign of a poorly designed system.

Code duplication is a problem that directly impacts maintainability. It is very undesirable to have code duplication because of its many negative consequences:

- **It's error prone**: When some logic is repeated multiple times throughout the code, and this needs to change, it means we depend on efficiently correcting all the instances with this logic, without forgetting any of them, because in that case there will be a bug.

- **It's expensive**: Linked to the previous point, making a change in multiple places takes much more time (development and testing effort) than if it was defined only once. This will slow the team down.

- **It's unreliable**: Also linked to the first point, when multiple places need to be changed for a single change in the context, you rely on the person who wrote the code to remember all the instances where the modification has to be made. There is no single source of truth.

Duplication is often caused by ignoring (or forgetting) that code represents knowledge. By giving meaning to certain parts of the code, we are identifying and labeling that knowledge.

Let's see what this means with an example. Imagine that, in a study center, students are ranked by the following criteria: 11 points per exam passed, minus five points per exam failed, and minus two per year in the institution. The following is not actual code, but just a representation of how this might be scattered in a real code base:

```
def process_students_list(students):
    # do some processing...

    students_ranking = sorted(
        students, key=lambda s: s.passed * 11 - s.failed * 5 - s.years
* 2
    )
    # more processing
    for student in students_ranking:
        print(
            "Name: {0}, Score: {1}".format(
                student.name,
                (student.passed * 11 - student.failed * 5 - student.
years * 2),
            )
        )
```

Notice how the lambda, which is in the key of the sorted function, represents some valid knowledge from the domain problem, yet it doesn't reflect it (it doesn't have a name, a proper and rightful location, there is no meaning assigned to that code, nothing). This lack of meaning in the code leads to the duplication we find when the score is printed out while listing the raking.

We should reflect our knowledge of our domain problem in our code, and our code will then be less likely to suffer from duplication and will be easier to understand:

```
def score_for_student(student):
    return student.passed * 11 - student.failed * 5 - student.years * 2
```

```
def process_students_list(students):
    # do some processing...

    students_ranking = sorted(students, key=score_for_student)
    # more processing
    for student in students_ranking:
        print(
            "Name: {0}, Score: {1}".format(
                student.name, score_for_student(student)
            )
        )
```

A fair disclaimer: This is just an analysis of one of the traits of code duplication. In reality, there are more cases, types, and taxonomies of code duplication. Entire chapters could be dedicated to this topic, but here we focus on one particular aspect to make the idea behind the acronym clear.

In this example, we have taken what is probably the simplest approach to eliminating duplication: creating a function. Depending on the case, the best solution would be different. In some cases, there might be an entirely new object that has to be created (maybe an entire abstraction was missing). In other cases, we can eliminate duplication with a context manager. Iterators or generators (described in *Chapter 7, Generators, Iterators, and Asynchronous Programming*) could also help to avoid repetition in the code, and decorators (explained in *Chapter 5, Using Decorators to Improve Our Code*) will also help.

Unfortunately, there is no general rule or pattern to tell you which of the features of Python are the most suitable when it comes to addressing code duplication, but hopefully, after seeing the examples in this book, and how the elements of Python are used, the reader will be able to develop their own intuition.

YAGNI

YAGNI (short for **You Ain't Gonna Need It**) is an idea you might want to keep in mind very often when writing a solution if you do not want to over-engineer it.

We want to be able to easily modify our programs, so we want to make them future-proof. In line with that, many developers think that they have to anticipate all future requirements and create solutions that are very complex, and so create abstractions that are hard to read, maintain, and understand. Sometime later, it turns out that those anticipated requirements do not show up, or they do but in a different way (surprise!), and the original code that was supposed to handle precisely that does not work.

The problem is that now it is even harder to refactor and extend our programs. What happened was that the original solution did not handle the original requirements correctly, and neither do the current ones, simply because it is the wrong abstraction.

Having maintainable software is not about anticipating future requirements (do not do futurology!). It is about writing software that only addresses current requirements in such a way that it will be possible (and easy) to change later on. In other words, when designing, make sure that your decisions don't tie you down, and that you will be able to keep on building, but do not build more than what's necessary.

It's usually tempting to not follow this idea in some cases in which we're aware of principles that we think might apply or save time for us. For example, later in the book, we'll review design patterns, which are common solutions for typical situations of object-oriented design. While it's important to study design patterns, we must refuse the temptation to apply them prematurely as it might fall into a violation of the YAGNI principle.

For example, imagine you're creating a class to encapsulate the behavior of a component. You know it's needed, but then you think that more (and similar) requirements will come in the future, so it might be tempting to create a base class (as to define an interface with the methods that must be implemented), and then make the class you were just creating a subclass that implement that interface. This would be wrong for several reasons. First, all you need now is the class that was being created in the first place (investing more time in over-generalizing a solution that we don't know we'll need is not a good way of managing our resources). And then, that base class is being biased by the current requirements, so it'll likely not be the correct abstraction.

The best approach would be to write only what's needed now in a way that doesn't hinder further improvements. If, later on, more requirements come in, we can think about creating a base class, abstract some methods, and perhaps we will discover a design pattern that emerged for our solution. This is also the way object-oriented design is supposed to work: bottom-up.

Finally, I wanted to emphasize that YAGNI is an idea that also applies to software architecture (not just detailed code).

KIS

KIS (stands for **Keep It Simple**) relates very much to the previous point. When you are designing a software component, avoid over-engineering it. Ask yourself if your solution is the minimal one that fits the problem.

Implement minimal functionality that correctly solves the problem and does not complicate your solution more than is necessary. Remember, the simpler the design, the more maintainable it will be.

This design principle is an idea we will want to keep in mind at all levels of abstraction, whether we are thinking of a high-level design, or addressing a particular line of code.

At a high level, think about the components we are creating. Do we really need all of them? Does this module actually require being utterly extensible right now? Emphasize the last part—maybe we want to make that component extensible, but now is not the right time, or it is not appropriate to do so because we still do not have enough information to create the proper abstractions, and trying to come up with generic interfaces at this point will only lead to even worse problems.

In terms of code, keeping it simple usually means using the smallest data structure that fits the problem. You will most likely find it in the standard library.

Sometimes, we might over-complicate code, creating more functions or methods than are necessary. The following class creates a namespace from a set of keyword arguments that have been provided, but it has a rather complicated code interface:

```python
class ComplicatedNamespace:
    """A convoluted example of initializing an object with some
    properties."""


    ACCEPTED_VALUES = ("id_", "user", "location")

    @classmethod
    def init_with_data(cls, **data):
        instance = cls()
        for key, value in data.items():
            if key in cls.ACCEPTED_VALUES:
                setattr(instance, key, value)
        return instance
```

Having an extra class method for initializing the object doesn't seem necessary. Then, the iteration and the call to setattr inside it make things even more strange, and the interface that is presented to the user is not very clear:

```python
>>> cn = ComplicatedNamespace.init_with_data(
...     id_=42, user="root", location="127.0.0.1", extra="excluded"
... )
```

```
>>> cn.id_, cn.user, cn.location
(42, 'root', '127.0.0.1')

>>> hasattr(cn, "extra")
False
```

The user has to know of the existence of this other method, which is not convenient. It would be better to keep it simple, and just initialize the object as we initialize any other object in Python (after all, there is a method for that) with the __init__ method:

```
class Namespace:
    """Create an object from keyword arguments."""

    ACCEPTED_VALUES = ("id_", "user", "location")

    def __init__(self, **data):
        for attr_name, attr_value in data.items():
            if attr_name in self.ACCEPTED_VALUES:
                setattr(self, attr_name, attr_value)
```

Remember the Zen of Python: Simple is better than complex.

There are many scenarios in Python in which we would like to keep our code simple. One of them relates to something we've explored before: code duplication. A common way to abstract code in Python is by using decorators (which we'll see later on, in *Chapter 5*, *Using Decorators to Improve Our Code*). But what if we're trying to avoid duplication of a small section, let's say three lines of code? In that case, writing the decorator would probably take more lines and be more trouble for the simple duplicated lines we're trying to solve. In this case, apply common sense and be pragmatic. Accept that a small amount of duplication might be better than a complicated function (that is, of course, unless you find an even simpler way of removing the duplication and keeping the code simple!).

As part of keeping the code simple, I would recommend avoiding advanced features of Python, like meta-classes (or anything related to meta-programming in general), because not only are these features hardly required (there are very special justifications for their use!), but also, they make the code much more complicated to read, and harder to maintain.

EAFP/LBYL

EAFP stands for **Easier to Ask Forgiveness than Permission**, while LBYL stands for **Look Before You Leap**.

The idea of EAFP is that we write our code so that it performs an action directly, and then we take care of the consequences later in case it doesn't work. Typically, this means try running some code, expecting it to work, but catching an exception if it doesn't, and then handling the corrective code on the except block.

This is the opposite of LBYL. As its name says, in the *look before you leap* approach, we first check what we are about to use. For example, we might want to check whether a file is available before trying to operate with it:

```python
if os.path.exists(filename):
    with open(filename) as f:
        ...
```

The EAFP version of the previous code would look like this:

```python
try:
    with open(filename) as f:
        ...
except FileNotFoundError as e:
    logger.error(e)
```

If you are coming from other languages, such as C, which doesn't have exceptions, then it's logical that will find the LBYL approach of more use. And in other languages such as C++, there is some discouragement towards the use of exceptions due to performance considerations, but this doesn't generally hold true in Python.

Particular cases might of course apply, but most of the time, you'll find the EAFP version to be more intention-revealing. The code written this way would be easier to read, because it goes directly to the task needed instead of preventively checking conditions. Put another way, in the last example, you'll see a part of the code that tries to open a file and then process it. If the file doesn't exist, then we handle that case. In the first example, we'll see a function checking whether a file exists, and then trying to do something. You might argue that this is also clear, but we don't know for sure. Maybe the file being asked about is a different one or is a function that belongs to a different layer of the program, or a leftover, and such like. The second approach is less error-prone when you look at the code at first glance.

You can apply both ideas as they make sense in your particular code, but in general, code written in an EAFP fashion would be easier to pick at first glance, so in case of doubt, I'd recommend you choose this variant.

Inheritance in Python

In object-oriented software design, there are often discussions as to how to address some problems by using the main ideas of the paradigm (polymorphism, inheritance, and encapsulation).

Probably the most commonly used of these ideas is inheritance—developers often start by creating a class hierarchy with the classes they are going to need and decide the methods each one should implement.

While inheritance is a powerful concept, it does come with its perils. The main one is that every time we extend a base class, we are creating a new one that is tightly coupled with the parent. As we have already discussed, coupling is one of the things we want to reduce to a minimum when designing software.

One of the main scenarios developers relate inheritance with is code reuse. While we should always embrace code reuse, it is not a good idea to force our design to use inheritance to reuse code just because we get the methods from the parent class for free. The proper way to reuse code is to have highly cohesive objects that can be easily composed and that could work on multiple contexts.

When inheritance is a good decision

We have to be careful when creating a derived class because this is a double-edged sword—on the one hand, it has the advantage that we get all the code of the methods from the parent class for free, but on the other hand, we are carrying all of them to a new class, meaning that we might be placing too much functionality in a new definition.

When creating a new subclass, we have to think if it is actually going to use all of the methods it has just inherited, as a heuristic to see whether the class is correctly defined. If instead, we find out that we do not need most of the methods, and have to override or replace them, this is a design mistake that could be caused by a number of reasons:

- The superclass is vaguely defined and contains too much responsibility, instead of a well-defined interface

- The subclass is not a proper specialization of the superclass it is trying to extend

A good case for using inheritance is the type of situation when you have a class that defines certain components with its behavior that are defined by the interface of this class (its `public` methods and attributes), and then you need to specialize this class in order to create objects that do the same but with something else added, or with some particular parts of its behavior changed.

You can find examples of good uses of inheritance in the Python standard library itself. For example, in the `http.server` package (`https://docs.python.org/3/library/http.server.html#http.server.BaseHTTPRequestHandler`), we can find a base class such as `BaseHTTPRequestHandler`, and subclasses such as `SimpleHTTPRequestHandler`, that extend this one by adding or changing part of its base interface.

Speaking of interface definition, this is another good use of inheritance. When we want to enforce the interface of some objects, we can create an abstract base class that does not implement the behavior itself, but instead just defines the interface—every class that extends this one will have to implement these to be a proper subtype.

Finally, another good case for inheritance is exceptions. We can see that the standard exception in Python derives from `Exception`. This is what allows you to have a generic clause such as `except Exception`, which will catch every possible error. The important point is the conceptual one; they are classes derived from `Exception` because they are more specific exceptions. This also works in well-known libraries such as `requests`, for instance, in which an `HTTPError` is a `RequestException`, which, in turn, is an `IOError`.

Anti-patterns for inheritance

If the previous section had to be summarized in a single word, it would be *specialization*. The correct use of inheritance is to specialize objects and create more detailed abstractions starting from base ones.

The parent (or base) class is part of the `public` definition of the new derived class. This is because the methods that are inherited will be part of the interface of this new class. For this reason, when we read the `public` methods of a class, they have to be consistent with what the parent class defines.

For example, if we see that a class derived from `BaseHTTPRequestHandler` implements a method named `handle()`, it would make sense because it is overriding one of the parents. If it had any other method whose name relates to an action that has to do with an HTTP request, then we could also think that is correctly placed (but we would not think that if we found something called `process_purchase()` on that class).

The previous illustration might seem obvious, but it is something that happens very often, especially when developers try to use inheritance with the sole goal of reusing code. In the next example, we will see a typical situation that represents a common anti-pattern in Python—there is a domain problem that has to be represented, and a suitable data structure is devised for that problem, but instead of creating an object that uses such a data structure, the object becomes the data structure itself.

Let's see these problems more concretely through an example. Imagine we have a system for managing insurance, with a module in charge of applying policies to different clients. We need to keep in memory a set of customers that are being processed at the time in order to apply those changes before further processing or persistence. The basic operations we need are to store a new customer with its records as satellite data, apply a change to a policy, or edit some of the data, to name but a few. We also need to support a batch operation. That is, when something on the policy itself changes (the one this module is currently processing), we have to apply these changes overall to customers on the current transaction.

Thinking in terms of the data structure we need, we realize that accessing the record for a particular customer in constant time is a nice trait. Therefore, something like `policy_transaction[customer_id]` looks like a nice interface. From this, we might think that a `subscriptable` object is a good idea, and further on, we might get carried away into thinking that the object we need is a dictionary:

```python
class TransactionalPolicy(collections.UserDict):
    """Example of an incorrect use of inheritance."""

    def change_in_policy(self, customer_id, **new_policy_data):
        self[customer_id].update(**new_policy_data)
```

With this code, we can get information about a policy for a customer by its identifier:

```python
>>> policy = TransactionalPolicy({
...     "client001": {
...         "fee": 1000.0,
...         "expiration_date": datetime(2020, 1, 3),
...     }
... })
>>> policy["client001"]
{'fee': 1000.0, 'expiration_date': datetime.datetime(2020, 1, 3, 0, 0)}
>>> policy.change_in_policy("client001", expiration_date=datetime(2020, 1, 4))
>>> policy["client001"]
{'fee': 1000.0, 'expiration_date': datetime.datetime(2020, 1, 4, 0, 0)}
```

Sure, we achieved the interface we wanted in the first place, but at what cost? Now, this class has a lot of extra behavior from carrying out methods that weren't necessary:

```
>>> dir(policy)
[ # all magic and special method have been omitted for brevity...
 'change_in_policy', 'clear', 'copy', 'data', 'fromkeys', 'get',
 'items', 'keys', 'pop', 'popitem', 'setdefault', 'update', 'values']
```

There are (at least) two major problems with this design. On the one hand, the hierarchy is wrong. Creating a new class from a base one conceptually means that it's a more specific version of the class it's extending (hence the name). How is it that a TransactionalPolicy is a dictionary? Does this make sense? Remember, this is part of the public interface of the object, so users will see this class and its hierarchy and will notice such an odd specialization as well as its public methods.

This leads us to the second problem—coupling. The interface of the transactional policy now includes all methods from a dictionary. Does a transactional policy really need methods such as pop() or items()? However, there they are. They are also public, so any user of this interface is entitled to call them, with whatever undesired side effect they may carry. More on this point—we don't really gain much by extending a dictionary. The only method it actually needs to update for all customers affected by a change in the current policy (change_in_policy()) is not on the base class, so we will have to define it ourselves either way.

This is a problem of mixing implementation objects with domain objects. A dictionary is an implementation object, a data structure, suitable for certain kinds of operation, and with a trade-off like all data structures. A transactional policy should represent something in the domain problem, an entity that is part of the problem we are trying to solve.

 Don't mix implementation data structures with business domain classes in the same hierarchy.

Hierarchies like this one are incorrect, and just because we get a few magic methods from a base class (to make the object subscriptable by extending a dictionary) is not reason enough to create such an extension. Implementation classes should be extended solely when creating other, more specific, implementation classes. In other words, extend a dictionary if you want to create another (more specific, or slightly modified) dictionary. The same rule applies to classes of the domain problem.

The correct solution here is to use composition. `TransactionalPolicy` is not a dictionary—it uses a dictionary. It should store a dictionary in a `private` attribute, and implement __getitem__() by proxying from that dictionary and then only implementing the rest of the `public` method it requires:

```python
class TransactionalPolicy:
    """Example refactored to use composition."""

    def __init__(self, policy_data, **extra_data):
        self._data = {**policy_data, **extra_data}

    def change_in_policy(self, customer_id, **new_policy_data):
        self._data[customer_id].update(**new_policy_data)

    def __getitem__(self, customer_id):
        return self._data[customer_id]

    def __len__(self):
        return len(self._data)
```

This way is not only conceptually correct, but also more extensible. If the underlying data structure (which, for now, is a dictionary) is changed in the future, callers of this object will not be affected, so long as the interface is maintained. This reduces coupling, minimizes ripple effects, allows for better refactoring (unit tests ought not to be changed), and makes the code more maintainable.

Multiple inheritance in Python

Python supports multiple inheritance. As inheritance, when improperly used, leads to design problems, you could also expect that multiple inheritance will also yield even bigger problems when it's not correctly implemented.

Multiple inheritance is, therefore, a double-edged sword. It can also be very beneficial in some cases. Just to be clear, there is nothing wrong with multiple inheritance—the only problem it has is that when it's not implemented correctly, it will multiply the problems.

Multiple inheritance is a perfectly valid solution when used correctly, and this opens up new patterns (such as the adapter pattern we discussed in *Chapter 9, Common Design Patterns*) and mixins.

One of the most powerful applications of multiple inheritance is perhaps that which enables the creation of mixins. Before exploring mixins, we need to understand how multiple inheritance works, and how methods are resolved in a complex hierarchy.

Method Resolution Order (MRO)

Some people don't like multiple inheritance because of the constraints it has in other programming languages, for instance, the so-called diamond problem. When a class extends from two or more classes, and all of those classes also extend from other base classes, the bottom ones will have multiple ways to resolve the methods coming from the top-level classes. The question is: Which of these implementations is used?

Consider the following diagram, which has a structure with multiple inheritance. The top-level class has a class attribute and implements the __str__ method. Think of any of the concrete classes, for example, ConcreteModuleA12—it extends from BaseModule1 and BaseModule2, and each one of them will take the implementation of __str__ from BaseModule. Which of these two methods is going to be the one for ConcreteModuleA12?

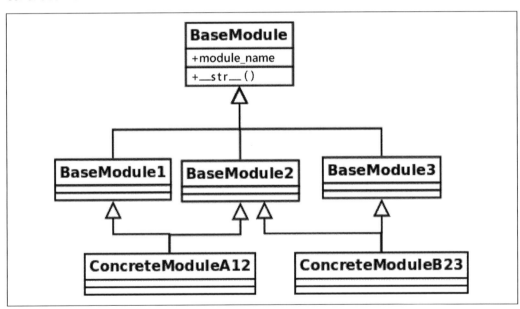

Figure 3.1: Method Resolution Order

With the value of the class attribute, this will become evident:

```
class BaseModule:
    module_name = "top"
```

```
    def __init__(self, module_name):
        self.name = module_name

    def __str__(self):
        return f"{self.module_name}:{self.name}"


class BaseModule1(BaseModule):
    module_name = "module-1"


class BaseModule2(BaseModule):
    module_name = "module-2"


class BaseModule3(BaseModule):
    module_name = "module-3"


class ConcreteModuleA12(BaseModule1, BaseModule2):
    """Extend 1 & 2"""

class ConcreteModuleB23(BaseModule2, BaseModule3):
    """Extend 2 & 3"""
```

Now, let's test this to see what method is being called:

```
>>> str(ConcreteModuleA12("test"))
'module-1:test'
```

There is no collision. Python resolves this by using an algorithm called C3 linearization or MRO, which defines a deterministic way in which methods are going to be called.

In fact, we can specifically ask the class for its resolution order:

```
>>> [cls.__name__ for cls in ConcreteModuleA12.mro()]
['ConcreteModuleA', 'BaseModule1', 'BaseModule2', 'BaseModule',
'object']
```

Knowing about how the method is going to be resolved in a hierarchy can be used to our advantage when designing classes because we can make use of mixins.

Mixins

A mixin is a base class that encapsulates some common behavior with the goal of reusing code. Typically, a mixin class is not useful on its own, and extending this class alone will certainly not work, because most of the time it depends on methods and properties that are defined in other classes. The idea is to use mixin classes along with other ones, through multiple inheritance, so that the methods or properties used on the mixin will be available.

Imagine we have a simple parser that takes a string and provides iteration over it by its values separated by hyphens (-):

```python
class BaseTokenizer:

    def __init__(self, str_token):
        self.str_token = str_token

    def __iter__(self):
        yield from self.str_token.split("-")
```

This is quite straightforward:

```python
>>> tk = BaseTokenizer("28a2320b-fd3f-4627-9792-a2b38e3c46b0")
>>> list(tk)
['28a2320b', 'fd3f', '4627', '9792', 'a2b38e3c46b0']
```

But now we want the values to be sent in uppercase, without altering the base class. For this simple example, we could just create a new class, but imagine that a lot of classes are already extending from `BaseTokenizer`, and we don't want to replace all of them. We can mix a new class into the hierarchy that handles this transformation:

```python
class UpperIterableMixin:
    def __iter__(self):
        return map(str.upper, super().__iter__())


class Tokenizer(UpperIterableMixin, BaseTokenizer):
    pass
```

The new `Tokenizer` class is really simple. It doesn't need any code because it takes advantage of the mixin. This type of mixin acts as a sort of decorator. Based on what we just saw, `Tokenizer` will take `__iter__` from the mixin, and this one, in turn, delegates to the next class on the line (by calling `super()`), which is `BaseTokenizer`, but it converts its values to uppercase, thereby creating the desired effect.

As we have discussed inheritance in Python, we've seen topics such as cohesion and coupling that are important to the design of our software. These concepts appear repeatedly in software design, and they can also be analyzed from the lens of functions and their arguments, which we explore in the next section.

Arguments in functions and methods

In Python, functions can be defined to receive arguments in several different ways, and these arguments can also be provided by callers in multiple ways.

There is also an industry-wide set of practices for defining interfaces in software engineering that closely relate to the definition of arguments in functions.

In this section, we will first explore the mechanics of arguments in Python functions and then review the general principles of software engineering that relate to good practices regarding this subject to finally relate both concepts.

How function arguments work in Python

First, let's review the particularities of how arguments are passed to functions in Python.

By first understanding the possibilities that Python offers for handling parameters, we will be able to assimilate general rules more easily, and the idea is that after having done so, we can easily draw conclusions on what good patterns or idioms are when handling arguments. Then, we can identify in which scenarios the Pythonic approach is the correct one, and in which cases we might be abusing the features of the language.

How arguments are copied to functions

The first rule in Python is that all arguments are passed by a value. Always. This means that when passing values to functions, they are assigned to the variables on the signature definition of the function to be later used on it.

You will notice that a function may or may not mutate the parameters it receives, depending on their type. If we are passing `mutable` objects, and the body of the function modifies this, then of course, we have the side effect that they will have been changed by the time the function returns.

In the following, we can see the difference:

```
>>> def function(argument):
...         argument += " in function"
...         print(argument)
...
>>> immutable = "hello"
>>> function(immutable)
hello in function
>>> mutable = list("hello")
>>> immutable
'hello'
>>> function(mutable)
['h', 'e', 'l', 'l', 'o', ' ', 'i', 'n', ' ', 'f', 'u', 'n', 'c', 't',
'i', 'o', 'n']
>>> mutable
['h', 'e', 'l', 'l', 'o', ' ', 'i', 'n', ' ', 'f', 'u', 'n', 'c', 't',
'i', 'o', 'n']
>>>
```

This might look like an inconsistency, but it's not. When we pass the first argument, a string, this is assigned to the argument on the function. Since string objects are immutable, a statement such as argument += <expression> will, in fact, create the new object, argument + <expression>, and assign that back to the argument. At that point, an argument is just a local variable inside the scope of the function and has nothing to do with the original one in the caller.

On the other hand, when we pass list, which is a mutable object, then that statement has a different meaning (it is equivalent to calling .extend() on that list). This operator acts by modifying the list in place over a variable that holds a reference to the original list object, hence modifying it. What happened in this second case is that the list's reference was passed by a value to the function. But since it's a reference, it is mutating the original list object, so we see the mutation after the function has finished. It's roughly equivalent to this:

```
>>> a = list(range(5))
>>> b = a  # the function call is doing something like this
>>> b.append(99)
>>> b
[0, 1, 2, 3, 4, 99]
>>> a
[0, 1, 2, 3, 4, 99]
```

We have to be careful when dealing with mutable objects because it can lead to unexpected side effects. Unless you are absolutely sure that it is correct to manipulate mutable arguments in this way, I would recommend avoiding it and going for alternatives without these problems.

 Don't mutate function arguments. In general, try to avoid unnecessary side effects in functions as much as possible.

Arguments in Python can be passed by position, as in many other programming languages, but also by keyword. This means that we can explicitly tell the function which values we want for which of its parameters. The only caveat is that after a parameter is passed by a keyword, the rest that follow must also be passed this way, otherwise, SyntaxError will be raised.

Variable number of arguments

Python, as well as other languages, has built-in functions and constructions that can take a variable number of arguments. Consider, for example, string interpolation functions (whether it be by using the % operator or the format method for strings), which follow a similar structure to the printf function in C, a first positional parameter with the string format, followed by any number of arguments that will be placed on the markers of that formatting string.

Besides taking advantage of these functions that are available in Python, we can also create our own, which will work in a similar fashion. In this section, we will cover the basic principles of functions with a variable number of arguments, along with some recommendations, so that in the next section, we can explore how to use these features to our advantage when dealing with common problems, issues, and constraints that functions might have if they have too many arguments.

For a variable number of positional arguments, the star symbol (*) is used, preceding the name of the variable that is packing those arguments. This works through the packing mechanism of Python.

Let's say there is a function that takes three positional arguments. In one part of the code, we conveniently happen to have the arguments we want to pass to the function inside a list, in the same order as they are expected by the function.

Instead of passing them one by one by the position (that is, list[0] to the first element, list[1] to the second, and so on), which would be really un-Pythonic, we can use the packing mechanism and pass them all together in a single instruction:

```
>>> def f(first, second, third):
...     print(first)
...     print(second)
...     print(third)
...
>>> l = [1, 2, 3]
>>> f(*l)
1
2
3
```

The nice thing about the packing mechanism is that it also works the other way around. If we want to extract the values of a list to variables, by their respective position, we can assign them like this:

```
>>> a, b, c = [1, 2, 3]
>>> a
1
>>> b
2
>>> c
3
```

Partial unpacking is also possible. Let's say we are just interested in the first values of a sequence (this can be a list, tuple, or something else), and after some point we just want the rest to be kept together. We can assign the variables we need and leave the rest under a packaged list. The order in which we unpack is not limited. If there is nothing to place in one of the unpacked subsections, the result will be an empty list. Try the following examples on a Python terminal and also explore how unpacking works with generators as well:

```
>>> def show(e, rest):
...     print("Element: {0} - Rest: {1}".format(e, rest))
...
>>> first, *rest = [1, 2, 3, 4, 5]
>>> show(first, rest)
Element: 1 - Rest: [2, 3, 4, 5]
>>> *rest, last = range(6)
>>> show(last, rest)
```

```
Element: 5 - Rest: [0, 1, 2, 3, 4]
>>> first, *middle, last = range(6)
>>> first
0
>>> middle
[1, 2, 3, 4]
>>> last
5
>>> first, last, *empty = 1, 2
>>> first
1
>>> last
2
>>> empty
[]
```

One of the best uses for unpacking variables can be found in iteration. When we have to iterate over a sequence of elements, and each element is, in turn, a sequence, it is a good idea to unpack at the same time each element is being iterated over. To see an example of this in action, we are going to pretend that we have a function that receives a list of database rows, and that it is in charge of creating users out of that data. The first implementation takes the values to construct the user with from the position of each column in the row, which is not idiomatic at all. The second implementation uses unpacking while iterating:

```python
from dataclasses import dataclass


USERS = [
    (i, f"first_name_{i}", f"last_name_{i}")
    for i in range(1_000)
]


@dataclass
class User:
    user_id: int
    first_name: str
    last_name: str

def bad_users_from_rows(dbrows) -> list:
    """A bad case (non-pythonic) of creating ``User``s from DB rows."""
    return [User(row[0], row[1], row[2]) for row in dbrows]
```

```
def users_from_rows(dbrows) -> list:
    """Create ``User``s from DB rows."""
    return [
        User(user_id, first_name, last_name)
        for (user_id, first_name, last_name) in dbrows
    ]
```

Notice that the second version is much easier to read. In the first version of the function (bad_users_from_rows), we have data expressed in the form row[0], row[1], and row[2], which doesn't tell us anything about what they are. On the other hand, variables such as user_id, first_name, and last_name speak for themselves.

We could also use the star operator to pass all the positional parameters from the tuple when constructing the User object:

```
[User(*row) for row in dbrows]
```

We can leverage this kind of functionality to our advantage when designing our own functions.

An example of this that we can find in the standard library lies in the max function, which is defined as follows:

```
max(...)
    max(iterable, *[, default=obj, key=func]) -> value
    max(arg1, arg2, *args, *[, key=func]) -> value

    With a single iterable argument, return its biggest item. The
    default keyword-only argument specifies an object to return if
    the provided iterable is empty.
    With two or more arguments, return the largest argument.
```

There is a similar notation, with two stars (**) for keyword arguments. If we have a dictionary and we pass it with a double star to a function, what it will do is pick the keys as the name for the parameter, and pass the value for that key as the value for that parameter in that function.

For instance, check this out:

```
function(**{"key": "value"})
```

It is the same as the following:

```
function(key="value")
```

Conversely, if we define a function with a parameter starting with two star symbols, the opposite will happen — keyword-provided parameters will be packed into a dictionary:

```
>>> def function(**kwargs):
...     print(kwargs)
...
>>> function(key="value")
{'key': 'value'}
```

This feature of Python is really powerful as it lets us choose dynamically the values we want to pass to a function. However, abusing this functionality, and making excessive use of it, will render the code harder to understand.

When we define a function as in the previous example, on which one of its parameters has a double star, meaning that arbitrary keyword arguments are allowed, Python will place them in a dictionary that we can access at our discretion. From the previously defined function, the kwargs argument is a dictionary. A good recommendation is to not use this dictionary to extract particular values from it.

Namely, don't look for particular keys of the dictionary. Instead, extract these arguments directly on the function definition.

For example, instead of doing something like this:

```
def function(**kwargs):  # wrong
    timeout = kwargs.get("timeout", DEFAULT_TIMEOUT)
    ...
```

Let Python do the unpacking and set the default argument at the signature:

```
def function(timeout=DEFAULT_TIMEOUT, **kwargs):  # better
    ...
```

In this example, timeout is not strictly keyword-only. We'll see how to make keyword-only arguments in a few sections, but the idea that should prevail is to not manipulate the kwargs dictionary, and instead execute proper unpacking at the signature level.

Before diving into keyword-only arguments, let's start with those that are positional-only first.

Positional-only parameters

As we have seen already, positional arguments (variable or not) are those that are first provided to functions in Python. The values for these arguments are interpreted based on the position they're provided to the function, meaning they're assigned respectively to the parameters in the function's definition.

If we don't make use any special syntax when defining the function arguments, by default, they can be passed by position or keyword. For example, in the following function, all calls to the function are equivalent:

```
>>> def my_function(x, y):
...     print(f"{x=}, {y=}")
...
>>> my_function(1, 2)
x=1, y=2
>>> my_function(x=1, y=2)
x=1, y=2
>>> my_function(y=2, x=1)
x=1, y=2
>>> my_function(1, y=2)
x=1, y=2
```

This means, in the first case, we pass the values 1 and 2, and by their position, they're assigned to the parameters x and y, respectively. With this syntax, nothing stops us from passing the same arguments with their keyword (even in reverse order), should that be needed (for example, to be more explicit). The only constraint here is that if we pass one argument as a keyword, all the following ones must be provided as a keyword as well (the last example wouldn't work with the parameters reversed).

However, starting from Python 3.8 (PEP-570), new syntax was introduced that allows parameters to be defined that are strictly positional (meaning we can't provide their name when passing values by). To use this, a / must be added to the end of the last positional-only argument). For example:

```
>>> def my_function(x, y, /):
...     print(f"{x=}, {y=}")
...
>>> my_function(1, 2)
x=1, y=2
>>> my_function(x=1, y=2)
Traceback (most recent call last):
  File "<stdin>", line 1, in <module>
TypeError: my_function() got some positional-only arguments passed as
```

```
keyword arguments: 'x, y'
```

Note how the first invocation of the function worked (just as before), but from now on, any attempt to pass a keyword argument will fail. The exception that is raised will tell us in its message the positional-only parameters that attempted to be passed as keyword-only. In general, using keyword arguments makes the code more readable because you'll know at all times which values are provided for which arguments, but there could be situations in which this syntax is useful, for example, in cases where the names of the arguments aren't meaningful (because they can't be, not because we did a poor job on naming them!), and attempting to use their name would be counterproductive.

To give a really simple example, imagine a function to check whether two words are anagrams. That function takes two strings and does some processing. It doesn't really matter how we name those two strings (and frankly their order doesn't matter, it would just be a first word and a second word). Trying to come up with good names for those arguments wouldn't make much sense, nor would assigning their keyword values when calling the function.

For the rest of the cases, this should be avoided.

 Don't force meaningful arguments to be positional-only.

In very particular cases, positional-only parameters might be a good idea, but most of the time this shouldn't be required. But in general, this isn't a feature you'd want to use many times because we can take advantage of passing arguments as keywords, because that will make it easier to understand which values are being passed to which parameters. For that reason, the opposite case is something you'd want to do more often, making the arguments keyword-only, as we'll discuss in the next section.

Keyword-only arguments

Analogous to the previous feature is the possibility of making some arguments keyword-only. This probably makes more sense, because we can find meaning when assigning the keyword argument on a function call, and now we can enforce this explicitness.

In this case (and contrary to the previous one), we use the * symbol to signal when the keyword-only arguments start. In the function signature, everything that comes after the variable number of positional arguments (*args) will be keyword-only.

For example, the following definition takes two positional arguments, then any number of positional parameters, and then two final arguments, which are to be passed as keyword-only. The last one has a default value (although this is not mandatory, as in the third case):

```
>>> def my_function(x, y, *args, kw1, kw2=0):
...     print(f"{x=}, {y=}, {kw1=}, {kw2=}")
...
>>> my_function(1, 2, kw1=3, kw2=4)
x=1, y=2, kw1=3, kw2=4
>>> my_function(1, 2, kw1=3)
x=1, y=2, kw1=3, kw2=0
```

The function calls make it clear how this behaves. If we didn't want any number of positional arguments after the first two, we can simply put * instead of *args.

This functionality is useful for extending functions or classes that are already defined (and being used) in a backward-compatible fashion. If, for example, you have a function that takes two arguments, and it's being called several times throughout the code (sometimes with the parameters by position, sometimes by keyword), and you'd want to add a third parameter, you'd have to set a default for it, if you want the current calls to keep working. But even better would be to make this last parameter keyword-only, so new calls have to make it explicit that they intend to use the new definition.

Along the same lines, this functionality is also useful when refactoring and keeping compatibility. Imagine you have a function that you're replacing with a new implementation, but you keep the original function as a wrapper, in order to preserve compatibility. Let's analyze the difference between a function call such as the following:

```
result = my_function(1, 2, True)
```

And another call as follows:

```
result = my_function(1, 2, use_new_implementation=True)
```

It's clear that the second example is much more explicit, and you get a clear idea of what's going on as soon as you glance at the function call. For that reason, it makes sense to make the new parameter (which determines which implementation to use) keyword-only.

In cases like this, where there's an argument that really needs context in order to be understood, making that parameter keyword-only is a good idea.

These are the basics in terms of how arguments and parameters work in Python functions. Now we can use that knowledge to discuss this in terms of good design ideas.

The number of arguments in functions

In this section, we agree on the idea that having functions or methods that take too many arguments is a sign of bad design (a code smell). Then, we propose ways of dealing with this issue.

The first alternative is a more general principle of software design—reification (creating a new object for all of those arguments that we are passing, which is probably the abstraction we are missing). Compacting multiple arguments into a new object is not a solution specific to Python, but rather something that we can apply in any programming language.

Another option would be to use the Python-specific features we saw in the previous section, making use of variable positional and keyword arguments to create functions that have a dynamic signature. While this might be a Pythonic way of proceeding, we have to be careful not to abuse the feature, because we might be creating something that is so dynamic that it is hard to maintain. In this case, we should take a look at the body of the function. Regardless of the signature, and whether the parameters seem to be correct, if the function is doing too many different things responding to the values of the parameters, then it is a sign that it has to be broken down into multiple smaller functions (remember, functions should do one thing, and one thing only!).

Function arguments and coupling

The more arguments a function signature has, the more likely this one is going to be tightly coupled with the caller function.

Let's say we have two functions, f1, and f2, and the latter takes five parameters. The more parameters f2 takes, the more difficult it would be for anyone trying to call that function to gather all that information and pass it along so that it can work properly.

Now, f1 seems to have all of this information because it can call it correctly. From this, we can derive two conclusions. First, f2 is probably a leaky abstraction, which means that since f1 knows everything that f2 requires, it can pretty much figure out what it is doing internally and will be able to do it by itself.

So, all in all, f2 is not abstracting that much. Second, it looks like f2 is only useful to f1, and it is hard to imagine using this function in a different context, making it harder to reuse.

When functions have a more general interface and are able to work with higher-level abstractions, they become more reusable.

This applies to all sorts of functions and object methods, including the __init__ method for classes. The presence of a method like this could generally (but not always) mean that a new higher-level abstraction should be passed instead, or that there is a missing object.

 If a function needs too many parameters to work properly, consider it a code smell.

In fact, this is such a design problem that static analysis tools such as pylint (discussed in *Chapter 1, Introduction, Code Formatting, and Tools*) will, by default, raise a warning when they encounter such a case. When this happens, don't suppress the warning—refactor it instead.

Compact function signatures that take too many arguments

Suppose we find a function that requires too many parameters. We know that we cannot leave the code base like that, and a refactor process is imperative. But what are the options?

Depending on the case, some of the following rules might apply. This is by no means extensive, but it does provide an idea of how to solve some scenarios that occur quite often.

Sometimes, there is an easy way to change parameters if we can see that most of them belong to a common object. For example, consider a function call like this one:

```
track_request(request.headers, request.ip_addr, request.request_id)
```

Now, the function might or might not take additional arguments, but something is really obvious here: All of the parameters depend upon request, so why not pass the request object instead? This is a simple change, but it significantly improves the code. The correct function call should be track_request(request)—not to mention that, semantically, it also makes much more sense.

While passing around parameters like this is encouraged, in all cases where we pass `mutable` objects to functions, we must be really careful about side effects. The function we are calling should not make any modifications to the object we are passing because that will mutate the object, creating an undesired side effect. Unless this is actually the desired effect (in which case, it must be made explicit), this kind of behavior is discouraged. Even when we actually want to change something on the object we are dealing with, a better alternative would be to copy it and return a (new) modified version of it.

> Work with immutable objects and avoid side effects as much as possible.

This brings us to a similar topic—grouping parameters. In the previous example, the parameters were already grouped, but the group (in this case, the request object) was not being used. But other cases are not as obvious as that one, and we might want to group all the data in the parameters in a single object that acts as a container. Needless to say, this grouping has to make sense. The idea here is to *reify*: Create the abstraction that was missing from our design.

If the previous strategies don't work, as a last resort we can change the signature of the function to accept a variable number of arguments. If the number of arguments is too big, using *args or **kwargs will make things harder to follow, so we have to make sure that the interface is properly documented and correctly used, but in some cases, this is worth doing.

It's true that a function defined with *args and **kwargs is really flexible and adaptable, but the disadvantage is that it loses its signature, and with that, part of its meaning, and almost all of its legibility. We have seen examples of how names for variables (including function arguments) make the code much easier to read. If a function will take any number of arguments (positional or keyword), we might find out that when we want to take a look at that function in the future, we probably won't know exactly what it was supposed to do with its parameters, unless it has a very good docstring.

> Try to only define functions with the most generic arguments (*args, **kwargs) when you want a perfect wrapper over another function (for example, a method that will call super(), or a decorator).

Final remarks on good practices for software design

Good software design involves a combination of following good practices of software engineering and taking advantage of most of the features of the language. There is great value in using everything that Python has to offer, but there is also a great risk of abusing this and trying to fit complex features into simple designs.

In addition to this general principle, it would be good to add some final recommendations.

Orthogonality in software

This word is very general and can have multiple meanings or interpretations. In math, orthogonal means that two elements are independent. If two vectors are orthogonal, their scalar product is zero. It also means they are not related at all. A change in one of them doesn't affect the other one at all. That's the way we should think about our software.

Changing a module, class, or function should have no impact on the outside world to that component that is being modified. This is, of course, highly desirable, but not always possible. But even for cases where it's not possible, a good design will try to minimize the impact as much as possible. We have seen ideas such as separation of concerns, cohesion, and isolation of components.

In terms of the runtime structure of software, orthogonality can be interpreted as the process of making changes (or side effects) local. This means, for instance, that calling a method on an object should not alter the internal state of other (unrelated) objects. We have already (and will continue to do so) emphasized in this book the importance of minimizing side effects in our code.

In the example with the mixin class, we created a tokenizer object that returned an `iterable`. The fact that the `__iter__` method returned a new generator increases the chances that all three classes (the base, the mixing, and the concrete class) are orthogonal. If this had returned something in concrete (a `list`, let's say), this would have created a dependency on the rest of the classes, because when we changed the `list` to something else, we might have needed to update other parts of the code, revealing that the classes were not as independent as they should be.

Let's show you a quick example. Python allows passing functions by parameter because they are just regular objects. We can use this feature to achieve some orthogonality. We have a function that calculates a price, including taxes and discounts, but afterward we want to format the final price that's obtained:

```python
def calculate_price(base_price: float, tax: float, discount: float) ->
float:
    return (base_price * (1 + tax)) * (1 - discount)


def show_price(price: float) -> str:
    return "$ {0:,.2f}".format(price)


def str_final_price(
    base_price: float, tax: float, discount: float, fmt_function=str
) -> str:
    return fmt_function(calculate_price(base_price, tax, discount))
```

Notice that the top-level function is composing two orthogonal functions. One thing to notice is how we calculate price, which is how the other one is going to be represented. Changing one does not change the other. If we don't pass anything in particular, it will use string conversion as the default representation function, and if we choose to pass a custom function, the resulting string will change. However, changes in show_price do not affect calculate_price. We can make changes to either function, knowing that the other one will remain as it was:

```python
>>> str_final_price(10, 0.2, 0.5)
'6.0'

>>> str_final_price(1000, 0.2, 0)
'1200.0'

>>> str_final_price(1000, 0.2, 0.1, fmt_function=show_price)
'$ 1,080.00'
```

There is an interesting quality aspect that relates to orthogonality. If two parts of the code are orthogonal, it means one can change without affecting the other. This implies that the part that changed has unit tests that are also orthogonal to the unit tests of the rest of the application. Under this assumption, if those tests pass, we can assume (up to a certain degree) that the application is correct without needing full regression testing.

More broadly, orthogonality can be thought of in terms of features. Two functionalities of the application can be totally independent so that they can be tested and released without having to worry that one might break the other (or the rest of the code, for that matter). Imagine that the project requires a new authentication mechanism (oauth2, let's say, but just for the sake of the example), and at the same time another team is also working on a new report.

Unless there is something fundamentally wrong in that system, neither of those features should impact the other. Regardless of which one of those gets merged first, the other one should not be affected at all.

Structuring the code

The way code is organized also impacts the performance of the team and its maintainability.

In particular, having large files with lots of definitions (classes, functions, constants, and so on) is a bad practice and should be discouraged. This doesn't mean going to the extreme of placing one definition per file, but a good code base will structure and arrange components by similarity.

Luckily, most of the time, changing a large file into smaller ones is not a hard task in Python. Even if other multiple parts of the code depend on definitions made on that file, this can be broken down into a package, and will maintain total compatibility. The idea would be to create a new directory with a __init__.py file on it (this will make it a Python package). Alongside this file, we will have multiple files with all the particular definitions each one requires (fewer functions and classes grouped by a certain criterion). Then, the __init__.py file will import from all the other files the definitions it previously had (which is what guarantees its compatibility). Additionally, these definitions can be mentioned in the __all__ variable of the module to make them exportable.

There are many advantages to this. Other than the fact that each file will be easier to navigate, and things will be easier to find, we could argue that it will be more efficient for the following reasons:

- It contains fewer objects to parse and load into memory when the module is imported.
- The module itself will probably be importing fewer modules because it needs fewer dependencies, like before.

It also helps to have a convention for the project. For example, instead of placing constants in all of the files, we can create a file specific to the constant values to be used in the project, and import it from there:

```
from myproject.constants import CONNECTION_TIMEOUT
```

Centralizing information in this way makes it easier to reuse code and helps to avoid inadvertent duplication.

More details about separating modules and creating Python packages will be discussed in *Chapter 10*, *Clean Architecture*, when we explore this in the context of software architecture.

Summary

In this chapter, we have explored several principles to achieve a clean design. Understanding that the code is part of the design is key to achieving high-quality software. This and the following chapter are focused precisely on that.

With these ideas, we can now construct more robust code. For example, by applying DbC, we can create components that are guaranteed to work within their constraints. More importantly, if errors occur, this will not happen out of the blue, but instead, we will have a clear idea of who the offender is and which part of the code broke the contract. This compartmentalization is key to effective debugging.

Along similar lines, each component can be made more robust if it defends itself from malicious intent or incorrect input. Although this idea goes in a different direction from DbC, it might complement it very well. Defensive programming is a good idea, especially for critical parts of the application.

For both approaches (DbC and defensive programming), it's important to correctly handle assertions. Keep in mind how they should be used in Python, and don't use assertions as part of the control flow logic of the program. Don't catch this exception, either.

Speaking of exceptions, it's important to know how and when to use them, and the most important concept here is to avoid using exception as a control flow (go-to) kind of construction.

We have explored a recurrent topic in object-oriented design—deciding between using inheritance or composition. The main lesson here is not to use one over the other, but to use whichever option is better; we should also avoid some common anti-patterns, which we might often see in Python (especially given its highly dynamic nature).

Finally, we discussed the number of arguments in functions, along with heuristics for a clean design, always with the particularities of Python in mind.

These concepts are fundamental design ideas that lay the foundations for what's coming in the next chapter. We need to first understand these ideas so that we can move on to more advanced topics, such as SOLID principles.

References

Here is a list of information you can refer to:

- *PEP-570: Python Positional-Only Parameters* (`https://www.python.org/dev/peps/pep-0570/`)

- *PEP-3102: Keyword-Only Arguments* (`https://www.python.org/dev/peps/pep-3102/`)

- *Object-Oriented Software Construction, Second Edition*, written by *Bertrand Meyer*

- *The Pragmatic Programmer: From Journeyman to Master*, by *Andrew Hunt* and *David Thomas*, published by *Addison-Wesley*, 2000.

- *PEP-316: Programming by Contract for Python* (`https://www.python.org/dev/peps/pep-0316/`)

- *REAL 01: The Most Diabolical Python Antipattern* (`https://realpython.com/blog/python/the-most-diabolical-python-antipattern/`)

- *PEP-3134: Exception Chaining and Embedded Tracebacks*: (`https://www.python.org/dev/peps/pep-3134/`)

- *Idiomatic Python: EAFP versus LBYL*: `https://blogs.msdn.microsoft.com/pythonengineering/2016/06/29/idiomatic-python-eafp-versus-lbyl/`

- *Composition vs. Inheritance: How to Choose?* `https://www.thoughtworks.com/insights/blog/composition-vs-inheritance-how-choose`

- *Python HTTP*: `https://docs.python.org/3/library/http.server.html#http.server.BaseHTTPRequestHandler`

- Source reference for exceptions in the requests library: `http://docs.python-requests.org/en/master/_modules/requests/exceptions/`

- *Code Complete: A Practical Handbook of Software Construction, Second Edition*, written by *Steve McConnell*

4
The SOLID Principles

In this chapter, we will continue to explore concepts of clean design applied to Python. In particular, we will review the **SOLID** principles and how to implement them in a Pythonic way. These principles entail a series of good practices to achieve better-quality software. In case some of you aren't aware of what SOLID stands for, here it is:

- **S**: Single responsibility principle
- **O**: Open/closed principle
- **L**: Liskov's substitution principle
- **I**: Interface segregation principle
- **D**: Dependency inversion principle

The goals of this chapter are as follows:

- To become acquainted with SOLID principles for software design
- To design software components that follow the single responsibility principle
- To achieve more maintainable code through the open/closed principle
- To implement proper class hierarchies in object-oriented design, by complying with Liskov's substitution principle
- To design with interface segregation and dependency inversion

The single responsibility principle

The **single responsibility principle (SRP)** states that a software component (in general, a class) must have only one responsibility. The fact that the class has a sole responsibility means that it is in charge of doing just one concrete thing, and as a consequence of that, we can conclude that it must have only one reason to change.

Only if one thing on the domain problem changes will the class have to be updated. If we have to make modifications to a class for different reasons, it means the abstraction is incorrect, and that the class has too many responsibilities. This is probably an indication that there is at least one abstraction missing: more objects need to be created to address the extra responsibility that's overloading the current class in question.

As introduced in *Chapter 2, Pythonic Code*, this design principle helps us build more cohesive abstractions—objects that do one thing, and just one thing, well, following the Unix philosophy. What we want to avoid in all cases is having objects with multiple responsibilities (often called **God objects**, because they know too much, or more than they should). These objects group different (mostly unrelated) behaviors, thus making them harder to maintain.

Again, the smaller the class, the better.

The SRP is closely related to the idea of cohesion in software design, which we already explored in *Chapter 3, General Traits of Good Code*, when we discussed the separation of concerns in software. What we strive to achieve here is that classes are designed in such a way that most of their properties and their attributes are used by their methods, most of the time. When this happens, we know they are related concepts, and therefore it makes sense to group them under the same abstraction.

In a way, this idea is somewhat analogous to the concept of normalization in relational database design. When we detect that there are partitions on the attributes or methods of the interface of an object, they might as well be moved somewhere else—it is a sign that they are two or more different abstractions mixed into one.

There is another way of looking at this principle. If, when looking at a class, we find methods that are mutually exclusive and do not relate to each other, they are the different responsibilities that have to be broken down into smaller classes.

A class with too many responsibilities

In this example, we are going to create a case for an application that is in charge of reading information about events from a source (this could be log files, a database, or many more sources), and identify the actions corresponding to each particular log.

A design that fails to conform to the SRP would look like this:

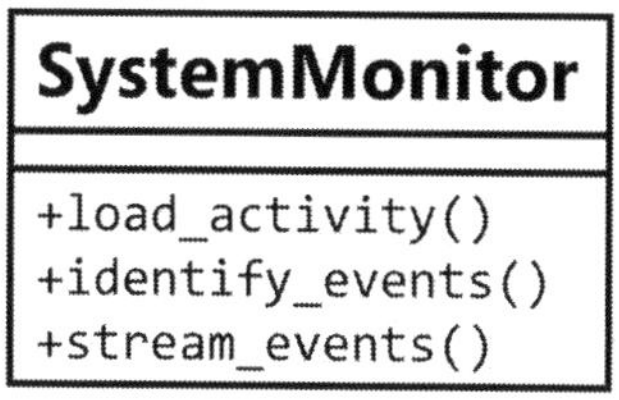

SystemMonitor
+load_activity() +identify_events() +stream_events()

Figure 4.1: A class with too many responsibilities

Without considering the implementation, the code for the class might look as in the following listing:

```
# srp_1.py
class SystemMonitor:
    def load_activity(self):
        """Get the events from a source, to be processed."""

    def identify_events(self):
        """Parse the source raw data into events (domain objects)."""

    def stream_events(self):
        """Send the parsed events to an external agent."""
```

The problem with this class is that it defines an interface with a set of methods that correspond to actions that are orthogonal: each one can be done independently of the rest.

This design flaw makes the class rigid, inflexible, and error-prone because it is hard to maintain. In this example, each method represents a responsibility of the class. Each responsibility entails a reason why the class might need to be modified. In this case, each method represents one of the various reasons why the class will have to be modified.

Consider the loader method, which retrieves the information from a particular source. Regardless of how this is done (we can abstract the implementation details here), it will have its own sequence of steps, for instance, connecting to the data source, loading the data, parsing it into the expected format, and so on. If we need to change something (for example, we want to change the data structure used for holding the data), the SystemMonitor class will need to change. Ask yourself whether this makes sense. Does a system monitor object have to change because we changed the representation of the data? No.

The same reasoning applies to the other two methods. If we change how we fingerprint events, or how we deliver them to another data source, we end up making changes to the same class.

It should be clear by now that this class is rather fragile and not very maintainable. There are lots of different reasons that will impact changes in this class. Instead, we want external factors to impact our code as little as possible. The solution, again, is to create smaller and more cohesive abstractions.

Distributing responsibilities

To make the solution more maintainable, we separate every method into a different class. This way, each class will have a single responsibility:

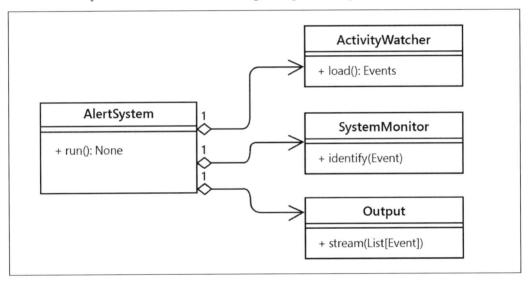

Figure 4.2: Distributing responsibilities throughout classes

The same behavior is achieved by using an object that interacts with instances of these new classes, using those objects as collaborators, but the idea remains that each class encapsulates a specific set of methods that are independent of the rest. The idea now is that changes to any of these classes do not impact the rest, and all of them have a clear and specific meaning. If we need to change something in how we load events from the data sources, the alert system is not even aware of these changes, so we do not have to modify anything on the system monitor (as long as the contract is still preserved), and the data target is also unmodified.

Changes are now local, the impact is minimal, and each class is easier to maintain.

The new classes define interfaces that are not only more maintainable but also reusable. Imagine that now, in another part of the application, we also need to read the activity from the logs, but for different purposes. With this design, we can simply use objects of the `ActivityWatcher` type (which would actually be an interface, but for the purposes of this section, that detail is not relevant and will be explained later for the next principles). This would make sense, whereas it would not have made sense in the previous design, because attempts to reuse the only class we had defined would have also carried extra methods (such as `identify_events()` or `stream_events()`) that were not needed at all.

One important clarification is that the principle does not mean at all that each class must have a single method. Any of the new classes might have extra methods, as long as they correspond to the same logic that that class is in charge of handling.

An interesting observation of most (if not all) of the principles we're exploring in this chapter is that we shouldn't try to get them right from the very first design. The idea is to design software that can be easily extended and changed, and that can evolve toward a more stable version.

In particular, you can use the SRP as a thought process. For example, if you're designing a component (let's say a class), and there are a lot of different things that need to be done (as in the previous example), right from the beginning you can anticipate that this will not end well, and that you need to separate responsibilities. That's a good start, but then the question is: what are the right boundaries to separate responsibilities? So, to understand this, you can start writing a monolithic class, in order to understand what the internal collaborations are and how responsibilities are distributed. This will help you get a clearer picture of the new abstractions that need to be created.

The open/closed principle

The **open/closed principle** (**OCP**) states that a module should be both open and closed (but with respect to different aspects).

When designing a class, for instance, we should carefully encapsulate the implementation details, so that it has good maintenance, meaning that we want it to be open to extension but closed to modification.

What this means in simple terms is that, of course, we want our code to be extensible, to adapt to new requirements or changes in the domain problem. That means when something new appears on the domain problem, we only want to add new things to our model, not change anything existing that is closed to modification.

If for some reason, when something new has to be added we find ourselves modifying the code, then that logic is probably poorly designed. Ideally, when requirements change, we want to just have to extend the module with the new behavior, but without having to alter the current logic significantly.

This principle applies to several software abstractions. It could be a class or even a module we're talking about, but the idea remains the same. We will see examples of each one in the following two subsections.

Example of maintainability perils for not following the OCP

Let's begin with an example of a system that is designed in such a way that does not follow the OCP, in order to see the maintainability problems this carries, and the inflexibility of such a design.

The idea is that we have a part of the system that is in charge of identifying events as they occur in another system, which is being monitored. At each point, we want this component to identify the type of event, correctly, according to the values of the data that was previously gathered (for simplicity, we will assume it is packaged into a dictionary, and was previously retrieved through another means such as logs, queries, and many more). We have a class that, based on this data, will retrieve the event, which is another type with its own hierarchy.

From the class diagram in *Figure 4.3*, we see an object that works with an interface (a base class, with several subclasses that can be used polymorphically):

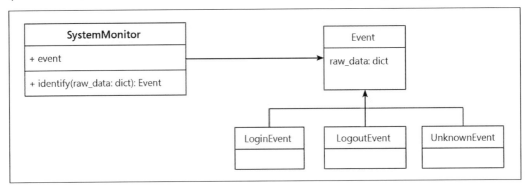

Figure 4.3: A design that's not closed for modification

At first glance this might look like it's an extensible design: adding a new event would be about creating a new subclass of Event, and then the system monitor should be able to work with them. However, this is not quite accurate, as it all depends on the actual implementation within the method used in the system monitor class.

A first attempt to solve this problem might look like this:

```python
# openclosed_1.py
@dataclass
class Event:
    raw_data: dict


class UnknownEvent(Event):
    """A type of event that cannot be identified from its data."""


class LoginEvent(Event):
    """A event representing a user that has just entered the system."""


class LogoutEvent(Event):
    """An event representing a user that has just left the system."""


class SystemMonitor:
    """Identify events that occurred in the system."""

    def __init__(self, event_data):
        self.event_data = event_data

    def identify_event(self):
        if (
            self.event_data["before"]["session"] == 0
            and self.event_data["after"]["session"] == 1
        ):
            return LoginEvent(self.event_data)
        elif (
            self.event_data["before"]["session"] == 1
            and self.event_data["after"]["session"] == 0
        ):
            return LogoutEvent(self.event_data)

        return UnknownEvent(self.event_data)
```

The following is the expected behavior of the preceding code:

```
>>> l1 = SystemMonitor({"before": {"session": 0}, "after": {"session":
1}})
>>> l1.identify_event().__class__.__name__
'LoginEvent'

>>> l2 = SystemMonitor({"before": {"session": 1}, "after": {"session":
0}})
>>> l2.identify_event().__class__.__name__
'LogoutEvent'

>>> l3 = SystemMonitor({"before": {"session": 1}, "after": {"session":
1}})
>>> l3.identify_event().__class__.__name__
'UnknownEvent'
```

Notice the hierarchy of event types, and some business logic to construct them. For instance, when there was no previous flag for a session, but there is now, we identify that record as a login event. Conversely, when the opposite happens, it means that it was a logout event. If it was not possible to identify an event, an event of type unknown is returned. This is to preserve polymorphism by following the null object pattern (instead of returning None, it retrieves an object of the corresponding type with some default logic). The null object pattern is described in *Chapter 9, Common Design Patterns*.

This design has some problems. The first issue is that the logic for determining the types of events is centralized inside a monolithic method. As the number of events we want to support grows, this method will as well, and it could end up being a very long method, which is bad because, as we have already discussed, it will not be doing just one thing and one thing well.

On the same line, we can see that this method is not closed for modification. Every time we want to add a new type of event to the system, we will have to change something in this method (not to mention that the chain of elif statements will be a nightmare to read!).

We want to be able to add new types of events without having to change this method (closed for modification). We also want to be able to support new types of events (open for extension) so that when a new event is added, we only have to add code, not change the code that already exists.

Refactoring the events system for extensibility

The problem with the previous example was that the SystemMonitor class was interacting directly with the concrete classes it was going to retrieve.

In order to achieve a design that honors the open/closed principle, we have to design towards abstractions.

A possible alternative would be to think of this class as it collaborates with the events, and then we delegate the logic for each particular type of event to its corresponding class:

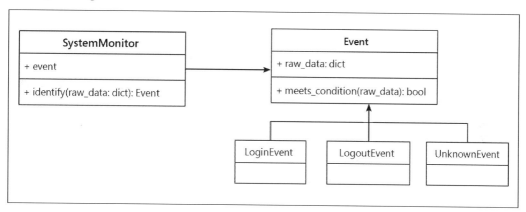

Figure 4.4: A design that follows the OCP

Then we have to add a new (polymorphic) method to each type of event with the single responsibility of determining if it corresponds to the data being passed or not, and we also have to change the logic to go through all events, finding the right one.

The new code should look like this:

```python
# openclosed_2.py
class Event:
    def __init__(self, raw_data):
        self.raw_data = raw_data

    @staticmethod
    def meets_condition(event_data: dict) -> bool:
        return False


class UnknownEvent(Event):
```

```
    """A type of event that cannot be identified from its data"""


class LoginEvent(Event):
    @staticmethod
    def meets_condition(event_data: dict):
        return (
            event_data["before"]["session"] == 0
            and event_data["after"]["session"] == 1
        )


class LogoutEvent(Event):
    @staticmethod
    def meets_condition(event_data: dict):
        return (
            event_data["before"]["session"] == 1
            and event_data["after"]["session"] == 0
        )


class SystemMonitor:
    """Identify events that occurred in the system."""

    def __init__(self, event_data):
        self.event_data = event_data

    def identify_event(self):
        for event_cls in Event.__subclasses__():
            try:
                if event_cls.meets_condition(self.event_data):
                    return event_cls(self.event_data)
            except KeyError:
                continue
        return UnknownEvent(self.event_data)
```

Notice how the interaction is now oriented towards an abstraction (in this case, it would be the generic base class Event, which might even be an abstract base class or an interface, but for the purposes of this example it is enough to have a concrete base class). The method no longer works with specific types of events, but just with generic events that follow a common interface—they are all polymorphic with respect to the meets_condition method.

Notice how events are discovered through the __subclasses__() method. Supporting new types of events is now just about creating a new class for that event that has to extend Event and implement its own meets_condition() method, according to its particular criteria.

This example relies on the __subclasses__() method, because it's enough to illustrate the idea of an extensible design. Other alternatives can be used as well, such as registering classes using the abc module, or creating our own registry, but the main idea is the same, and the relationship between the objects wouldn't change.

With this design, the original identify_event method is closed: it doesn't have to be modified when we add a new type of event to our domain. Conversely, the hierarchy of events is open for extension: when a new event appears in the domain, we only need to create a new entity and define its criteria according to the interface it implements.

Extending the events system

Now, let's prove that this design is actually as extensible as we wanted it to be. Imagine that a new requirement arises, and we have to also support events that correspond to transactions that the user executed on the monitored system.

The class diagram for the design has to include this new event type, as shown in *Figure 4.5*:

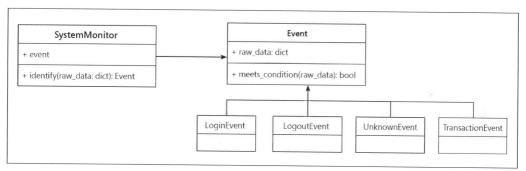

Figure 4.5: The design extended

We create the new class, implement the criteria on its meets_condition method, and the rest of the logic should continue to work as before (with the new behavior included).

Assuming all the rest of the previous definitions don't change, here's the code for the new class:

```
# openclosed_3.py

class TransactionEvent(Event):
    """Represents a transaction that has just occurred on the
system."""

    @staticmethod
    def meets_condition(event_data: dict):
        return event_data["after"].get("transaction") is not None
```

We can verify that the previous cases work as before and that the new event is also correctly identified:

```
>>> l1 = SystemMonitor({"before": {"session": 0}, "after": {"session":
1}})
>>> l1.identify_event().__class__.__name__
'LoginEvent'

>>> l2 = SystemMonitor({"before": {"session": 1}, "after": {"session":
0}})
>>> l2.identify_event().__class__.__name__
'LogoutEvent'

>>> l3 = SystemMonitor({"before": {"session": 1}, "after": {"session":
1}})
>>> l3.identify_event().__class__.__name__
'UnknownEvent'

>>> l4 = SystemMonitor({"after": {"transaction": "Tx001"}})
>>> l4.identify_event().__class__.__name__
'TransactionEvent'
```

Notice that the SystemMonitor.identify_event() method did not change at all when we added the new event type. We therefore say that this method is closed with respect to new types of events.

Conversely, the Event class allowed us to add a new type of event when we were required to do so. We then say that events are open for an extension with respect to new types.

This is the true essence of this principle—when something new appears on the domain problem, we only want to add new code, not modify any existing code.

Final thoughts about the OCP

As you might have noticed, this principle is closely related to the effective use of polymorphism. We want to work towards designing abstractions that respect a polymorphic contract that the client can use, to a structure that is generic enough that extending the model is possible, as long as the polymorphic relationship is preserved.

This principle tackles an important problem in software engineering: maintainability. The perils of not following the OCP are ripple effects and problems in the software where a single change triggers changes all over the code base, or risks breaking other parts of the code.

One important final note is that, in order to achieve this design in which we do not change the code to extend behavior, we need to be able to create proper closure against the abstractions we want to protect (in this example, new types of events). This is not always possible in all programs, as some abstractions might collide (for example, we might have a proper abstraction that provides closure against a requirement but does not work for other types of requirements). In these cases, we need to be selective and apply a strategy that provides the best closure for the types of requirements that require being the most extensible.

Liskov's substitution principle

Liskov's substitution principle (LSP) states that there is a series of properties that an object type must hold to preserve the reliability of its design.

The main idea behind LSP is that, for any class, a client should be able to use any of its subtypes indistinguishably, without even noticing, and therefore without compromising the expected behavior at runtime. That means that clients are completely isolated and unaware of changes in the class hierarchy.

More formally, this is the original definition (LISKOV 01) of LSP: if S is a subtype of T, then objects of type T may be replaced by objects of type S, without breaking the program.

This can be understood with the help of a generic diagram such as the following one. Imagine that there is some client class that requires (includes) objects of another type. Generally speaking, we will want this client to interact with objects of some type, namely, it will work through an interface.

Now, this type might as well be just a generic interface definition, an abstract class or an interface, not a class with the behavior itself. There may be several subclasses extending this type (described in *Figure 4.6* with the name Subtype, up to N). The idea behind this principle is that if the hierarchy is correctly implemented, the client class has to be able to work with instances of any of the subclasses without even noticing. These objects should be interchangeable, as *Figure 4.6* shows:

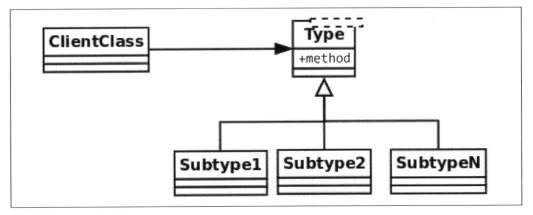

Figure 4.6: A generic subtypes hierarchy

This is related to other design principles we have already visited, like designing for interfaces. A good class must define a clear and concise interface, and as long as subclasses honor that interface, the program will remain correct.

As a consequence of this, the principle also relates to the ideas behind designing by contract. There is a contract between a given type and a client. By following the rules of LSP, the design will make sure that subclasses respect the contracts as they are defined by parent classes.

Detecting LSP issues with tools

There are some scenarios so notoriously wrong with respect to the LSP that they can be easily identified by the tools we have learned to configure in *Chapter 1, Introduction, Code Formatting, and Tools* (mainly mypy and pylint).

Using mypy to detect incorrect method signatures

By using type annotations (as recommended previously in *Chapter 1, Introduction, Code Formatting, and Tools*), throughout our code, and configuring mypy, we can quickly detect some basic errors early, and check basic compliance with LSP for free.

If one of the subclasses of the Event class were to override a method in an incompatible fashion, mypy would notice this by inspecting the annotations:

```
class Event:
    ...
    def meets_condition(self, event_data: dict) -> bool:
        return False


class LoginEvent(Event):
    def meets_condition(self, event_data: list) -> bool:
        return bool(event_data)
```

When we run mypy on this file, we will get an error message saying the following:

```
error: Argument 1 of "meets_condition" incompatible with supertype
"Event"
```

The violation to LSP is clear—since the derived class is using a type for the event_ data parameter that is different from the one defined on the base class, we cannot expect them to work equally. Remember that, according to this principle, any caller of this hierarchy has to be able to work with Event or LoginEvent transparently, without noticing any difference. Interchanging objects of these two types should not make the application fail. Failure to do so would break the polymorphism on the hierarchy.

The same error would have occurred if the return type was changed for something other than a Boolean value. The rationale is that clients of this code are expecting a Boolean value to work with. If one of the derived classes changes this return type, it would be breaking the contract, and again, we cannot expect the program to continue working normally.

A quick note about types that are not the same but share a common interface: even though this is just a simple example to demonstrate the error, it is still true that both dictionaries and lists have something in common; they are both iterables. This means that in some cases, it might be valid to have a method that expects a dictionary and another one expecting to receive a list, as long as both treat the parameters through the iterable interface. In this case, the problem would not lie in the logic itself (LSP might still apply), but in the definition of the types of the signature, which should read neither list nor dict, but a union of both. Regardless of the case, something has to be modified, whether it is the code of the method, the entire design, or just the type annotations, but in no case should we silence the warning and ignore the error given by mypy.

Do not ignore errors such as this by using # type: ignore or something similar. Refactor or change the code to solve the real problem. The tools are reporting an actual design flaw for a valid reason.

This principle also makes sense from an object-oriented design perspective. Remember that subclassing should create more specific types, but each subclass must be what the parent class declares. With the example from the previous section, the system monitor wants to be able to work with any of the event types interchangeably. But each of these event types is an event (a LoginEvent must be an Event, and so must the rest of the subclasses). If any of these objects break the hierarchy by not implementing a message from the base Event class, implementing another public method not declared in this one, or changing the signature of the methods, then the identify_event method might no longer work.

Detecting incompatible signatures with pylint

Another strong violation of LSP is when, instead of varying the types of the parameters on the hierarchy, the signatures of the methods differ completely. This might seem like quite a blunder, but detecting it might not always be so easy to remember; Python is interpreted, so there is no compiler to detect these types of errors early on, and therefore they will not be caught until runtime. Luckily, we have static code analyzers such as mypy and pylint to catch errors such as this one early on.

While mypy will also catch these types of errors, it is a good idea to also run pylint to gain more insight.

In the presence of a class that breaks the compatibility defined by the hierarchy (for example, by changing the signature of the method, adding an extra parameter, and so on) such as the following:

```
# lsp_1.py
class LogoutEvent(Event):
    def meets_condition(self, event_data: dict, override: bool) ->
bool:
        if override:
            return True

    ...
```

`pylint` will detect it, printing an informative error:

```
Parameters differ from overridden 'meets_condition' method (arguments-
differ)
```

Once again, like in the previous case, do not suppress these errors. Pay attention to the warnings and errors the tools give and adapt the code accordingly.

More subtle cases of LSP violations

In other cases, however, the way LSP is broken is not so clear or obvious that a tool can automatically identify it for us, and we have to rely upon careful code inspection when doing a code review.

Cases where contracts are modified are particularly harder to detect automatically. Given that the entire idea of LSP is that subclasses can be used by clients just like their parent class, it must also be true that contracts are correctly preserved on the hierarchy.

Remember from *Chapter 3, General Traits of Good Code*, when designing by contract, the contract between the client and supplier sets some rules—the client must provide the preconditions to the method, which the supplier might validate, and it returns some result to the client that it will check in the form of postconditions.

The parent class defines a contract with its clients. Subclasses of this one must respect such a contract. This means that for example:

- A subclass can never make preconditions stricter than they are defined on the parent class
- A subclass can never make postconditions weaker than they are defined on the parent class

Consider the example of the events hierarchy defined in the previous section, but now with a change to illustrate the relationship between LSP and DbC.

This time, we are going to assume a precondition for the method that checks the criteria based on the data, that the provided parameter must be a dictionary that contains both keys "before" and "after", and that their values are also nested dictionaries. This allows us to encapsulate even further, because now the client does not need to catch the KeyError exception, but instead just calls the precondition method (assuming that it is acceptable to fail if the system is operating under the wrong assumptions).

As a side note, it is good that we can remove this from the client, as now, SystemMonitor does not need to know which types of exceptions the methods of the collaborator class might raise (remember that exceptions weaken encapsulation, as they require the caller to know something extra about the object they are calling).

Such a design might be represented with the following changes in the code:

```
# lsp_2.py
from collections.abc import Mapping


class Event:
    def __init__(self, raw_data):
        self.raw_data = raw_data

    @staticmethod
    def meets_condition(event_data: dict) -> bool:
        return False

    @staticmethod
    def validate_precondition(event_data: dict):
        """Precondition of the contract of this interface.

        Validate that the ``event_data`` parameter is properly formed.
        """
        if not isinstance(event_data, Mapping):
            raise ValueError(f"{event_data!r} is not a dict")
        for moment in ("before", "after"):
            if moment not in event_data:
                raise ValueError(f"{moment} not in {event_data}")
            if not isinstance(event_data[moment], Mapping):
                raise ValueError(f"event_data[{moment!r}] is not a
    dict")
```

And now the code that tries to detect the correct event type just checks the precondition once, and proceeds to find the right type of event:

```
# lsp_2.py
class SystemMonitor:
    """Identify events that occurred in the system."""

    def __init__(self, event_data):
        self.event_data = event_data
```

```
def identify_event(self):
    Event.validate_precondition(self.event_data)
    event_cls = next(
        (
            event_cls
            for event_cls in Event.__subclasses__()
            if event_cls.meets_condition(self.event_data)
        ),
        UnknownEvent,
    )
    return event_cls(self.event_data)
```

The contract only states that the top-level keys "before" and "after" are mandatory and that their values should also be dictionaries. Any attempt in the subclasses to demand a more restrictive parameter will fail.

The class for the transaction event was originally correctly designed. Look at how the code does not impose a restriction on the internal key named "transaction"; it only uses its value if it is there, but this is not mandatory:

```
# lsp_2.py
class TransactionEvent(Event):
    """Represents a transaction that has just occurred on the
system."""

    @staticmethod
    def meets_condition(event_data: dict) -> bool:
        return event_data["after"].get("transaction") is not None
```

However, the original two methods are not correct, because they demand the presence of a key named "session", which is not part of the original contract. This breaks the contract, and now the client cannot use these classes in the same way it uses the rest of them because it will raise KeyError.

After fixing this (changing the square brackets for the .get() method), the order on the LSP has been reestablished, and polymorphism prevails:

```
>>> l1 = SystemMonitor({"before": {"session": 0}, "after": {"session":
1}})
>>> l1.identify_event().__class__.__name__
'LoginEvent'

>>> l2 = SystemMonitor({"before": {"session": 1}, "after": {"session":
```

```
0}})
>>> l2.identify_event().__class__.__name__
'LogoutEvent'

>>> l3 = SystemMonitor({"before": {"session": 1}, "after": {"session":
1}})
>>> l3.identify_event().__class__.__name__
'UnknownEvent'

>>> l4 = SystemMonitor({"before": {}, "after": {"transaction":
"Tx001"}})
>>> l4.identify_event().__class__.__name__
'TransactionEvent'
```

It is unreasonable to expect automated tools (regardless of how good and helpful they are) to detect cases such as this one. We have to be careful when designing classes that we do not accidentally change the input or output of the methods in a way that would be incompatible with what the clients are originally expecting.

Remarks on the LSP

The LSP is fundamental to good object-oriented software design because it emphasizes one of its core traits—polymorphism. It is about creating correct hierarchies so that classes derived from a base one are polymorphic along the parent one, with respect to the methods on their interface.

It is also interesting to notice how this principle relates to the previous one—if we attempt to extend a class with a new one that is incompatible, it will fail, the contract with the client will be broken, and as a result such an extension will not be possible (or, to make it possible, we would have to break the other end of the principle and modify code in the client that should be closed for modification, which is completely undesirable and unacceptable).

Carefully thinking about new classes in the way that LSP suggests helps us to extend the hierarchy correctly. We could then say that LSP contributes to the OCP.

Interface segregation

The **interface segregation principle (ISP)** provides some guidelines for an idea that we have revisited quite repeatedly already: that interfaces should be small.

In object-oriented terms, an **interface** is represented by the set of methods and properties an object exposes. That is to say that all the messages that an object is able to receive or interpret constitute its interface, and this is what other clients can request. The interface separates the definition of the exposed behavior for a class from its implementation.

In Python, interfaces are implicitly defined by a class according to its methods. This is because Python follows the so-called **duck typing** principle.

Traditionally, the idea behind duck typing was that any object is really represented by the methods it has, and by what it is capable of doing. This means that, regardless of the type of the class, its name, docstring, class attributes, or instance attributes, what ultimately defines the essence of the object are the methods it has. The methods defined in a class (what it knows how to do) are what determines what that object will be. It was called duck typing because of the idea that "If it walks like a duck, and quacks like a duck, it must be a duck."

For a long time, duck typing was the sole way interfaces were defined in Python. Later on, PEP-3119 introduced the concept of abstract base classes as a way to define interfaces in a different way. The basic idea of abstract base classes is that they define a basic behavior or interface that some derived classes are responsible for implementing. This is useful in situations where we want to make sure that certain critical methods are actually overridden, and it also works as a mechanism for overriding or extending the functionality of methods such as `isinstance()`.

The introduction of abstract base classes was done to provide a useful and powerful tool for developers to indicate things that must actually be implemented. For example, and considering the previous principle exposed (LSP), if we have a generic Event class, we don't want to use that class itself (because by its own it doesn't mean anything), so we probably want to deal with one of the actual events (the subclasses, like LoginEvent, for example). In this case we could define Event as an abstract base class, to make this explicit. Then the system monitor works with a type of event, and the Event class acts like an interface (as a way of saying "any object that has this kind of behavior"). We can go further and decide that the default implementation of the meets_condition method is not enough (or that sometimes, an implementation can't be provided by the interface), and force each derived class to implement it. For this, we would use an @abstractmethod decorator.

The abc module also contains a way of registering some types as part of a hierarchy, in what is called a virtual subclass. The idea is that this extends the concept of duck typing a little bit further by adding a new criterion—walks like a duck, quacks like a duck, or... it says it is a duck.

These notions of how Python interprets interfaces are important for understanding this principle and the next one.

In abstract terms, the ISP states that when we define an interface that provides multiple methods, it is better to instead break it down into multiple ones, each one containing fewer methods (preferably just one), with a very specific and accurate scope. By separating interfaces into the smallest possible units, to favor code reusability, each class that wants to implement one of these interfaces will most likely be highly cohesive given that it has a quite definite behavior and set of responsibilities.

An interface that provides too much

Now, we want to be able to parse an event from several data sources, in different formats (XML and JSON, for instance). Following good practices, we decide to target an interface as our dependency instead of a concrete class, and something like the following is devised:

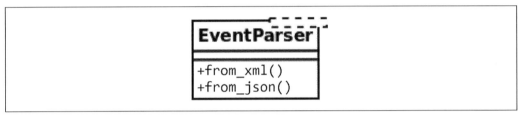

Figure 4.7: An interface providing too many disjoint capabilities

In order to create this as an interface in Python, we would use an abstract base class and define the methods (`from_xml()` and `from_json()`) as abstract, to force derived classes to implement them. Events that derive from this abstract base class and implement these methods would be able to work with their corresponding types.

But what if a particular class does not need the XML method, and can only be constructed from a JSON? It would still carry the `from_xml()` method from the interface, and since it does not need it, it will have to pass. This is not very flexible as it creates coupling and forces clients of the interface to work with methods that they do not need.

The smaller the interface, the better

It would be better to separate this into two different interfaces, one for each method. We can still achieve the same functionality by making our event parser class implement both interfaces (because interfaces or abstract base classes are just regular classes with some enhanced constraints, and Python supports multiple inheritance). The difference now is that we have each method declared in a more specific interface that we can reuse should we need it somewhere else in our code:

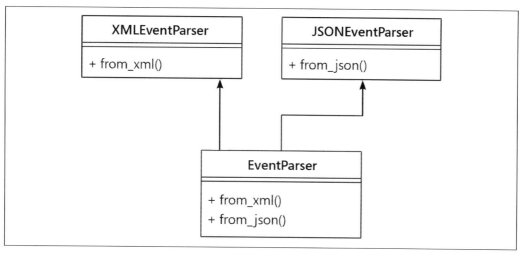

Figure 4.8: The same functionality achieved through separate interfaces

With this design, objects that derive from XMLEventParser and implement the from_xml() method will know how to be constructed from an XML, and the same for a JSON file, but most importantly, we maintain the orthogonality of two independent functions, and preserve the flexibility of the system without losing any functionality that can still be achieved by composing new smaller objects.

This is how the code might look for the representation of *Figure 4.8*:

```python
from abc import ABCMeta, abstractmethod

class XMLEventParser(metaclass=ABCMeta):
    @abstractmethod
    def from_xml(xml_data: str):
        """Parse an event from a source in XML representation."""

class JSONEventParser(metaclass=ABCMeta):
    @abstractmethod
    def from_json(json_data: str):
        """Parse an event from a source in JSON format."""

class EventParser(XMLEventParser, JSONEventParser):
    """An event parser that can create an event from source data either
in XML or JSON format.
    """

    def from_xml(xml_data):
        pass
```

```
def from_json(json_data: str):
    pass
```

Note that the abstract methods required by the interface must be implemented in the concrete class (their actual implementation is not relevant for the example though). If we weren't to implement them, a runtime error would trigger, for example:

```
>>> from src.isp import EventParser
>>> EventParser()
Traceback (most recent call last):
  File "<stdin>", line 1, in <module>
TypeError: Can't instantiate abstract class EventParser with abstract
methods from_json, from_xml
```

There is some resemblance to the SRP, but the main difference is that here we are talking about interfaces, so it is an abstract definition of behavior. There is no reason to change because there is nothing there until the interface is actually implemented. However, failure to comply with this principle will create an interface that will be coupled with orthogonal functionality, and this derived class will also fail to comply with the SRP (it will have more than one reason to change).

How small should an interface be?

The point made in the previous section is valid, but it also needs a warning—avoid a dangerous path if it's misunderstood or taken to the extreme.

A base class (abstract or not) defines an interface for all the other classes to extend it. The fact that this should be as small as possible has to be understood in terms of cohesion—it should do one thing. That doesn't mean it must necessarily have one method. In the previous example, it was by coincidence that both methods were doing disjointed things; hence it made sense to separate them into different classes.

But it could be the case that more than one method rightfully belongs to the same class. Imagine that you want to provide a mixin class that abstracts certain logic in a context manager so that all classes derived from that mixin gain that context manager logic for free. As we already know, a context manager entails two methods: __enter__ and __exit__. They must go together, or the outcome will not be a valid context manager at all!

Failure to place both methods in the same class will result in a broken component that is not only useless but also dangerous. Hopefully, this exaggerated example works as a counterbalance to the one in the previous section, and together you can get a more accurate picture of designing interfaces.

Dependency inversion

This is a really powerful idea that will come up again later when we explore some design patterns in *Chapter 9, Common Design Patterns*, and *Chapter 10, Clean Architecture*.

The **dependency inversion principle (DIP)** proposes an interesting design principle by which we protect our code by making it independent of things that are fragile, volatile, or out of our control. The idea of inverting dependencies is that our code should not adapt to details or concrete implementations, but rather the other way around: we want to force whatever implementation or detail to adapt to our code via a sort of API.

Abstractions have to be organized in such a way that they do not depend on details, but rather the other way around—the details (concrete implementations) should depend on abstractions.

Imagine that two objects in our design need to collaborate, *A* and *B*. *A* works with an instance of *B*, but as it turns out, our module doesn't control *B* directly (it might be an external library, or a module maintained by another team, and so on). If our code heavily depends on *B*, when this changes the code will break. To prevent this, we have to invert the dependency: make *B* have to adapt to *A*. This is done by presenting an interface and forcing our code not to depend on the concrete implementation of *B*, but rather on the interface we have defined. It is then *B*'s responsibility to comply with that interface.

In line with the concepts explored in previous sections, abstractions also come in the form of interfaces (or abstract base classes in Python).

In general, we could expect concrete implementations to change much more frequently than abstract components. It is for this reason that we place abstractions (interfaces) as flexibility points where we expect our system to change, be modified, or extended without the abstraction itself having to be changed.

A case of rigid dependencies

The last part of our event's monitoring system is to deliver the identified events to a data collector to be further analyzed. A naïve implementation of such an idea would consist of having an event streamer class that interacts with a data destination, for example, Syslog:

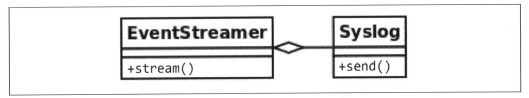

Figure 4.9: A class that has a strong dependency on another

However, this design is not very good, because we have a high-level class (EventStreamer) depending on a low-level one (Syslog is an implementation detail). If something changes in the way we want to send data to Syslog, EventStreamer will have to be modified. If we want to change the data destination for a different one or add new ones at runtime, we are also in trouble because we will find ourselves constantly modifying the stream() method to adapt it to these requirements.

Inverting the dependencies

The solution to these problems is to make EventStreamer work with an interface, rather than a concrete class. This way, implementing this interface is up to the low-level classes that contain the implementation details:

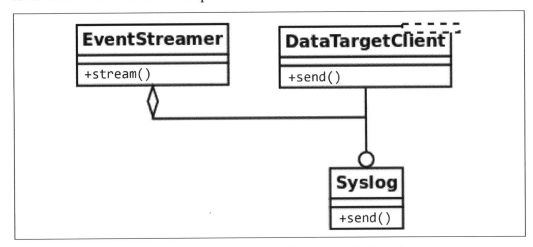

Figure 4.10: The functionality refactored by inverting the dependencies.

Now there is an interface that represents a generic data target where data is going to be sent. Notice how the dependencies have now been inverted since EventStreamer does not depend on a concrete implementation of a particular data target, it does not have to change in line with changes on this one, and it is up to every particular data target to implement the interface correctly and adapt to changes if necessary.

In other words, the original EventStreamer of the first implementation only worked with objects of type Syslog, which was not very flexible. Then we realized that it could work with any object that could respond to a .send() message, and identified this method as the interface that it needed to comply with. Now, in this version, Syslog is actually extending the abstract base class named DataTargetClient, which defines the send() method. From now on, it is up to every new type of data target (email, for instance) to extend this abstract base class and implement the send() method.

We can even modify this property at runtime for any other object that implements a send() method, and it will still work. This is the reason why it is often called **dependency injection**: because the dependency can be provided (injected) dynamically.

The astute reader might be wondering why this is necessary. Python is flexible enough (sometimes too flexible) and will allow us to provide an object like EventStreamer with any particular data target object, without this one having to comply with any interface because it is dynamically typed. The question is this: why do we need to define the abstract base class (interface) at all when we can simply pass an object with a send() method to it?

In all fairness, this is true; there is actually no need to do that, and the program will work just the same. After all, polymorphism does not mean (or require) inheritance has to work. However, defining the abstract base class is a good practice that comes with some advantages, the first one being duck typing. Together with duck typing, we can mention the fact that the models become more readable—remember that inheritance follows the rule of **is a**, so by declaring the abstract base class and extending from it, we are saying that, for instance, Syslog is DataTargetClient, which is something users of your code can read and understand (again, this is duck typing).

All in all, it is not mandatory to define the abstract base class, but it is desirable in order to achieve a cleaner design. This is one of the things this book is for—to help programmers avoid easy-to-make mistakes, just because Python is too flexible, and we can get away with it.

Dependency injection

The concept explored in the previous section gave us a powerful idea: instead of making our code dependent on a specific and concrete implementation, let's create a powerful abstraction that acts as a layer in between. In the example, we discussed how depending on Syslog would lead to a rigid design, so we created an interface for all clients, and decided that Syslog just happens to be one of them, because it implements the DataTargetClient interface. This opens up the door to more clients we want to add in the future: just create a new class that implements the interface and defines the send method. The design is now open for extension and closed for modification (we're starting to see how the principles relate to each other).

Now, how would the collaboration among these objects be? In this part, we explore how the dependency is provided to the object that actually needs it.

One way of doing it would be to just declare that the event streamer works by directly creating the object it needs, in this case a Syslog:

```python
class EventStreamer:
    def __init__(self):
        self._target = Syslog()

    def stream(self, events: list[Event]) -> None:
        for event in events:
            self._target.send(event.serialise())
```

However, this is not a very flexible design, and it doesn't take full advantage of the interface we have created. Note that this design is also harder to test: if you were to write a unit test for this class you would have to either patch the creation of the Syslog object or override it after it has just been created. If the Syslog has side effects at creation time (not good practice in general, but okay in some cases, for example, when you might want to establish a connection), then these side effects are carried to this initialization as well. It's true that this can be overcome by using a lazy property, but the inflexibility of actually controlling the object we provide is still there.

A better design will use dependency injection, and let the target be provided to the event streamer:

```python
class EventStreamer:
    def __init__(self, target: DataTargetClient):
        self._target = target

    def stream(self, events: list[Event]) -> None:
        for event in events:
            self._target.send(event.serialise())
```

This makes use of the interface and enables polymorphism. Now we can pass any object that implements this interface at initialization time, and it also makes it more explicit that an event streamer works with this kind of object.

As opposed to the previous case, this version is also simpler to test. If we don't want to deal with Syslog in our unit tests, we can provide a test double (just a new class that complies with the interface and is useful for whatever we need to test).

Don't force the creation of dependencies in the initialization method. Instead, let your users define the dependencies in a more flexible way, by using an argument in the __init__ method.

In some cases, when the objects have a more complicated initialization (more arguments), or there are many of them, it could be a good idea to declare the interaction between your objects in a dependency graph, and then let a library do the actual creation of the objects for you (that is, to remove the boilerplate of the glue code that binds different objects).

An example of such a library can be pinject (https://github.com/google/pinject), which lets you declare how the objects interact. In our simple example, one possibility would be to write the code like this:

```python
class EventStreamer:
    def __init__(self, target: DataTargetClient):
        self.target = target

    def stream(self, events: list[Event]) -> None:
        for event in events:
            self.target.send(event.serialise())

class _EventStreamerBindingSpec(pinject.BindingSpec):
    def provide_target(self):
        return Syslog()

object_graph = pinject.new_object_graph(
    binding_specs=[_EventStreamerBindingSpec()])
```

With the same definition of our class as before, we can define a binding specification, which is an object that knows how the dependencies are injected. In this object, any method named as provide_<dependency> should return the dependency with that name as the suffix (we settled for Syslog in our simple example).

Then we create the graph object, which we will use to get objects with the dependencies already provided; for example

```
event_streamer = object_graph.provide(EventStreamer)
```

will give us an `event_streamer` object, whose target is an instance of `Syslog`.

When you have multiple dependencies or interrelations among objects, it's probably a good idea to write them declarative and let a tool handle the initialization for you. In this case, the idea is that for these kinds of objects, we define how they're created in a single place, and let the tool do that for us (in that sense it is similar to a factory object).

Keep in mind that this doesn't lose the flexibility originally obtained from our design. The object graph is an object that knows how to build other entities based on the definitions made, but we still are in full control of the `EventStreamer` class we've created, and can use it just as before, by passing any object in the initialization method that complies with the required interface.

Summary

The SOLID principles are key guidelines for good object-oriented software design.

Building software is an incredibly hard task — the logic of the code is complex, its behavior at runtime is hard (if even possible, sometimes) to predict, requirements change constantly as well as the environment, and there are multiple things that can go wrong.

In addition, there are multiple ways of constructing software with different techniques, paradigms, or tools, which can work together to solve a particular problem in a specific manner. However, not all of these approaches will prove to be correct as time passes, and requirements change or evolve. However, by this time, it will already be too late to do something about an incorrect design, as it is rigid, inflexible, and therefore hard to change a refactor into the proper solution.

This means that, if we get the design wrong, it will cost us a lot in the future. How can we then achieve a good design that will eventually pay off? The answer is that we do not know for sure. We are dealing with the future, and the future is uncertain — there is no way to determine if our design will be correct and if our software will be flexible and adaptable for years to come. It is precisely for that reason that we have to stick to principles.

This is where the SOLID principles come into play. They are not a magic rule (after all, there are no silver bullets in software engineering), but they provide good guidelines to follow that have been proven to work in past projects and will make our software much more likely to succeed. The idea isn't to get all the requirements right from the very first version, but to achieve a design that's extensible and flexible enough to change, so that we can adapt it as needed.

In this chapter, we have explored the SOLID principles with the goal of understanding clean design. In the following chapters, we will continue to explore details of the language, and see in some cases how these tools and features can be used with these principles.

Chapter 5, Using Decorators to Improve Our Code, explores how we can improve our code by taking advantage of decorators. Unlike this chapter, which was more focused on abstract ideas of software engineering, *Chapter 5, Using Decorators to Improve Our Code*, will be more Python-focused, but we'll use the principles we've just learned.

References

Here is a list of information you may refer to:

- *SRP 01: The Single Responsibility Principle* (https://8thlight.com/blog/uncle-bob/2014/05/08/SingleReponsibilityPrinciple.html)

- *PEP-3119: Introducing Abstract Base Classes* (https://www.python.org/dev/peps/pep-3119/)

- *Object-Oriented Software Construction, Second Edition,* written by *Bertrand Meyer*

- *LISKOV 01:* A paper written by *Barbara Liskov* called *Data Abstraction and Hierarchy* (https://www.cs.tufts.edu/~nr/cs257/archive/barbara-liskov/data-abstraction-and-hierarchy.pdf)

5
Using Decorators to Improve Our Code

In this chapter, we will explore decorators and see how they are useful in many situations where we want to improve our design. We will start by first exploring what decorators are, how they work, and how they are implemented.

With this knowledge, we will then revisit concepts that we learned in previous chapters regarding general good practices for software design and see how decorators can help us comply with each principle.

The goals of this chapter are as follows:

- To understand how decorators work in Python
- To learn how to implement decorators that apply to functions and classes
- To effectively implement decorators, avoiding common implementation mistakes
- To analyze how to avoid code duplication (the DRY principle) with decorators
- To study how decorators contribute to the separation of concerns
- To analyze examples of good decorators
- To review common situations, idioms, or patterns for when decorators are the right choice

What are decorators in Python?

Decorators were introduced in Python a long time ago, in PEP-318, as a mechanism to simplify the way functions and methods are defined when they have to be modified after their original definition.

We first have to understand that in Python, functions are regular objects just like pretty much anything else. That means you can assign them to variables, pass them around by parameters, or even apply other functions to them. It was typical to want to write a small function, and then apply some transformations to it, generating a new modified version of that function (similar to how function composition works in mathematics).

One of the original motivations for introducing decorators was that because functions such as classmethod and staticmethod were used to transform the original definition of the method, they required an extra line, modifying the original definition of the function in a separate statement.

More generally speaking, every time we had to apply a transformation to a function, we had to call it with the modifier function, and then reassign it to the same name the function was originally defined with.

For instance, if we have a function called original, and then we have a function that changes the behavior of original on top of it, called modifier, we have to write something like the following:

```python
def original(...):
    ...
original = modifier(original)
```

Notice how we change the function and reassign it to the same name. This is confusing, error-prone (imagine that someone forgets to reassign the function, or does reassign it but not in the line immediately after the function definition but much farther away), and cumbersome. For this reason, some syntax support was added to the language.

The previous example could be rewritten like so:

```python
@modifier
def original(...):
    ...
```

This means that decorators are just syntactic sugar for calling whatever is after the decorator as a first parameter of the decorator itself, and the result would be whatever the decorator returns.

The syntax for decorators improves the readability significantly, because now the reader of that code can find the whole definition of the function in a single place. Keep in mind that manually modifying functions as before is still allowed.

 In general, try to avoid re-assigning values to a function already designed without using the decorator syntax. Particularly, if the function gets reassigned to something else and this happens in a remote part of the code (far from where the function was originally defined), this will make your code harder to read.

In line with the Python terminology, and our example, `modifier` is what we call the **decorator**, and `original` is the decorated function, often also called a **wrapped** object.

While the functionality was originally thought of for methods and functions, the actual syntax allows any kind of object to be decorated, so we are going to explore decorators applied to functions, methods, generators, and classes.

One final note is that while the name decorator is correct (after all, the decorator is making changes, extending, or working on top of the wrapped function), it is not to be confused with the decorator design pattern.

Function decorators

Functions are probably the simplest representation of a Python object that can be decorated. We can use decorators on functions to apply all sorts of logic to them—we can validate parameters, check preconditions, change the behavior entirely, modify its signature, cache results (create a memoized version of the original function), and more.

As an example, we will create a basic decorator that implements a `retry` mechanism, controlling a particular domain-level exception and retrying a certain number of times:

```
# decorator_function_1.py
class ControlledException(Exception):
    """A generic exception on the program's domain."""


def retry(operation):
    @wraps(operation)
    def wrapped(*args, **kwargs):
        last_raised = None
        RETRIES_LIMIT = 3
        for _ in range(RETRIES_LIMIT):
```

```
            try:
                return operation(*args, **kwargs)
            except ControlledException as e:
                logger.info("retrying %s", operation.__qualname__)
                last_raised = e
        raise last_raised

    return wrapped
```

The use of @wraps can be ignored for now, as it will be covered in the *Effective decorators – avoiding common mistakes* section.

 The use of _ in the for loop means that the number is assigned to a variable we are not interested in at the moment, because it's not used inside the for loop (it's a common idiom in Python to name _ values that are ignored).

The retry decorator doesn't take any parameters, so it can be easily applied to any function, as follows:

```
@retry
def run_operation(task):
    """Run a particular task, simulating some failures on its
execution."""
    return task.run()
```

The definition of @retry on top of run_operation is just syntactic sugar that Python provides to execute run_operation = retry(run_operation).

In this limited example, we can see how decorators can be used to create a generic retry operation that, under certain conditions (in this case, represented as exceptions that could be related to timeouts), will allow calling the decorated code multiple times.

Decorators for classes

Classes are also objects in Python (frankly, pretty much everything is an object in Python, and it's hard to find a counter-example; however, there are some technical nuances). That means the same considerations apply; they can also be passed by parameters, assigned to variables, asked some methods, or be transformed (decorated).

Class decorators were introduced in PEP-3129, and they have very similar considerations to the function decorators we just explored. The only difference is that when writing the code for this kind of decorator, we have to take into consideration that we are receiving a class as a parameter of the wrapped method, not another function.

We have seen how to use a class decorator when we saw the `dataclasses.dataclass` decorator in *Chapter 2, Pythonic Code*. In this chapter, we will learn how to write our own class decorators.

Some practitioners might argue that decorating a class is something rather convoluted and that such a scenario might jeopardize readability because we would be declaring some attributes and methods in the class, but behind the scenes, the decorator might be applying changes that would render a completely different class.

This assessment is true, but only if this technique is heavily abused. Objectively, this is no different from decorating functions; after all, classes are just another type of object in the Python ecosystem, as functions are. We will review the pros and cons of this issue with decorators in the section titled *Decorators and separation of concerns*, but for now, we'll explore the benefits of decorators that apply particularly to classes:

- All the benefits of reusing code and the DRY principle. A valid case of a class decorator would be to enforce that multiple classes conform to a certain interface or criteria (by writing these checks only once in a decorator that is going to be applied to many classes).

- We could create smaller or simpler classes that will be enhanced later on by decorators.

- The transformation logic we need to apply to a certain class will be much easier to maintain if we use a decorator, as opposed to more complicated (and often rightfully discouraged) approaches such as meta-classes.

Among all the possible applications of decorators, we will explore a simple example to show the sorts of things they can be useful for. Keep in mind that this is not the only application type for class decorators, and also that the code I show you can have many other solutions as well, all with their pros and cons, but I've chosen decorators for the purpose of illustrating their usefulness.

Recalling our event systems for the monitoring platform, we now need to transform the data for each event and send it to an external system. However, each type of event might have its own particularities when selecting how to send its data.

In particular, the event for a login might contain sensitive information such as credentials that we want to hide. Other fields such as timestamp might also require some transformations since we want to show them in a particular format. A first attempt at complying with these requirements would be as simple as having a class that maps to each particular event and knows how to serialize it:

```python
class LoginEventSerializer:
    def __init__(self, event):
        self.event = event

    def serialize(self) -> dict:
        return {
            "username": self.event.username,
            "password": "**redacted**",
            "ip": self.event.ip,
            "timestamp": self.event.timestamp.strftime("%Y-%m-%d
            %H:%M"),
        }


@dataclass
class LoginEvent:
    SERIALIZER = LoginEventSerializer

    username: str
    password: str
    ip: str
    timestamp: datetime

    def serialize(self) -> dict:
        return self.SERIALIZER(self).serialize()
```

Here, we declare a class that is going to map directly with the login event, containing the logic for it—hide the password field, and format the timestamp as required.

While this works and might look like a good option to start with, as time passes and we want to extend our system, we will find some issues:

- **Too many classes**: As the number of events grows, the number of serialization classes will grow in the same order of magnitude, because they are mapped one to one.

- **The solution is not flexible enough**: If we need to reuse parts of the components (for example, we need to hide the password in another type of event that also has it), we will have to extract this into a function, but also call it repeatedly from multiple classes, meaning that we are not reusing that much code after all.

- **Boilerplate**: The serialize() method will have to be present in all event classes, calling the same code. Although we can extract this into another class (creating a mixin), it does not seem like a good use of inheritance.

An alternative solution is to dynamically construct an object that, given a set of filters (transformation functions) and an event instance, can serialize it by applying the filters to its fields. We then only need to define the functions to transform each type of field, and the serializer is created by composing many of these functions.

Once we have this object, we can decorate the class in order to add the serialize() method, which will just call these Serialization objects with itself:

```python
from dataclasses import dataclass


def hide_field(field) -> str:
    return "**redacted**"


def format_time(field_timestamp: datetime) -> str:
    return field_timestamp.strftime("%Y-%m-%d %H:%M")


def show_original(event_field):
    return event_field


class EventSerializer:
    def __init__(self, serialization_fields: dict) -> None:
        self.serialization_fields = serialization_fields

    def serialize(self, event) -> dict:
        return {
            field: transformation(getattr(event, field))
            for field, transformation
            in self.serialization_fields.items()
        }
```

```
class Serialization:

    def __init__(self, **transformations):
        self.serializer = EventSerializer(transformations)

    def __call__(self, event_class):
        def serialize_method(event_instance):
            return self.serializer.serialize(event_instance)
        event_class.serialize - serialize_method
        return event_class

@Serialization(
    username=str.lower,
    password=hide_field,
    ip=show_original,
    timestamp=format_time,
)
@dataclass
class LoginEvent:
    username: str
    password: str
    ip: str
    timestamp: datetime
```

Notice how the decorator makes it easier for the user to know how each field is going to be treated without having to look into the code of another class. Just by reading the arguments passed to the class decorator, we know that the username and IP address will be left unmodified, the password will be hidden, and the timestamp will be formatted.

Now, the code of the class does not need the serialize() method defined, nor does it need to extend from a mixin that implements it, since the decorator will add it. This is probably the only part that justifies the creation of the class decorator because otherwise, the Serialization object could have been a class attribute of LoginEvent, but the fact that it is altering the class by adding a new method to it makes it impossible.

Other types of decorator

Now that we know what the @ syntax for decorators means, we can conclude that it isn't just functions, methods, or classes that can be decorated; actually, anything that can be defined, such as generators, coroutines, and even objects that have already been decorated, can be decorated, meaning that decorators can be stacked.

The previous example showed how decorators can be chained. We first defined the class, and then applied @dataclass to it, which converted it into a data class, acting as a container for those attributes. After that, @Serialization will apply the logic to that class, resulting in a new class with the new serialize() method added to it.

Now that we know the fundamentals of decorators, and how to write them, we can move on to more complex examples. In the next sections, we'll see how to have more flexible decorators with parameters, and different ways of implementing them.

More advanced decorators

With the introduction we've just had, we now know the basics of decorators: what they are, and their syntax and semantics.

Now we're interested in more advanced uses of decorators that will help us structure our code more cleanly.

We'll see that we can use decorators to separate concerns into smaller functions, and reuse code, but in order to so do effectively, we'd like to parametrize the decorators (otherwise, we'd end up repeating code). For this, we'll explore different options on how to pass arguments to decorators.

After that, we can see some examples of good uses of decorators.

Passing arguments to decorators

At this point, we already regard decorators as a powerful tool in Python. However, they could be even more powerful if we could just pass parameters to them so that their logic is abstracted even more.

There are several ways of implementing decorators that can take arguments, but we will go over the most common ones. The first one is to create decorators as nested functions with a new level of indirection, making everything in the decorator fall one level deeper. The second approach is to use a class for the decorator (that is, to implement a callable object that still acts as a decorator).

In general, the second approach favors readability more, because it is easier to think in terms of an object than three or more nested functions working with closures. However, for completeness, we will explore both, and you can decide what is best for the problem at hand.

Decorators with nested functions

Roughly speaking, the general idea of a decorator is to create a function that returns another function (in functional programming, functions that take other functions as parameters are called higher-order functions, and it refers to the same concept we're talking about here). The internal function defined in the body of the decorator is going to be the one being called.

Now, if we wish to pass parameters to it, we then need another level of indirection. The first function will take the parameters, and inside that function, we will define a new one, which will be the decorator, which in turn will define yet another new function, namely the one to be returned as a result of the decoration process. This means that we will have at least three levels of nested functions.

Don't worry if this didn't seem clear so far. After reviewing the examples that are about to come, everything will become clear.

One of the first examples we saw of decorators implemented the retry functionality over some functions. This is a good idea, except it has a problem; our implementation did not allow us to specify the number of retries, and instead, this was a fixed number inside the decorator.

Now, we want to be able to indicate how many retries each instance is going to have, and perhaps we could even add a default value to this parameter. In order to do this, we need another level of nested functions—first for the parameters, and then for the decorator itself.

This is because we are now going to have something in the form of the following:

```
@retry(arg1, arg2,... )
```

And that has to return a decorator because the @ syntax will apply the result of that computation to the object to be decorated. Semantically, it would translate to something like the following:

```
<original_function> = retry(arg1, arg2, ....)(<original_function>)
```

Besides the number of desired retries, we can also indicate the types of exceptions we wish to control. The new version of the code supporting the new requirements might look like this:

```
_DEFAULT_RETRIES_LIMIT = 3


    def with_retry(
        retries_limit: int = _DEFAULT_RETRIES_LIMIT,
        allowed_exceptions: Optional[Sequence[Exception]] = None,
    ):
        allowed_exceptions = allowed_exceptions or
        (ControlledException,) # type: ignore

        def retry(operation):
            @wraps(operation)
            def wrapped(*args, **kwargs):
                last_raised = None
                for _ in range(retries_limit):
                    try:
                        return operation(*args, **kwargs)
                    except allowed_exceptions as e:
                        logger.warning(
                            "retrying %s due to %s",
                            operation.__qualname__, e
                        )
                        last_raised = e
                raise last_raised

            return wrapped

        return retry
```

Here are some examples of how this decorator can be applied to functions, showing the different options it accepts:

```
# decorator_parametrized_1.py
@with_retry()
def run_operation(task):
    return task.run()


@with_retry(retries_limit=5)
def run_with_custom_retries_limit(task):
    return task.run()
```

```
@with_retry(allowed_exceptions=(AttributeError,))
def run_with_custom_exceptions(task):
    return task.run()


@with_retry(
    retries_limit=4, allowed_exceptions=(ZeroDivisionError,
AttributeError)
)
def run_with_custom_parameters(task):
    return task.run()
```

Using nested functions to implement decorators is probably the first thing we'd think of. This works well for most cases, but as you might have noticed, the indentation keeps adding up, for every new function we create, so soon it might lead to too many nested functions. Also, functions are stateless, so decorators written in this way won't necessarily hold internal data, as objects can.

There's a different way of implementing decorators, which instead of using nested functions uses objects, as we explore in the next section.

Decorator objects

The previous example requires three levels of nested functions. The first is going to be a function that receives the parameters of the decorator we want to use. Inside this function, the rest of the functions are closures that use these parameters, along with the logic of the decorator.

A cleaner implementation of this would be to use a class to define the decorator. In this case, we can pass the parameters in the __init__ method, and then implement the logic of the decorator on the magic method named __call__.

The code for the decorator will look like it does in the following example:

```
_DEFAULT_RETRIES_LIMIT = 3
class WithRetry:
    def __init__(
        self,
        retries_limit: int = _DEFAULT_RETRIES_LIMIT,
        allowed_exceptions: Optional[Sequence[Exception]] = None,
    ) -> None:
        self.retries_limit = retries_limit
        self.allowed_exceptions = allowed_exceptions or
```

```
    (ControlledException,)

        def __call__(self, operation):
            @wraps(operation)
            def wrapped(*args, **kwargs):
                last_raised = None

                for _ in range(self.retries_limit):
                    try:
                        return operation(*args, **kwargs)
                    except self.allowed_exceptions as e:
                    logger.warning(
                        "retrying %s due to %s",
                        operation.__qualname__, e
                    )
                        last_raised = e
                raise last_raised

        return wrapped
```

And this decorator can be applied pretty much like the previous one, like so:

```
@WithRetry(retries_limit=5)
def run_with_custom_retries_limit(task):
    return task.run()
```

It is important to note how the Python syntax takes effect here. First, we create the object, so before the @ operation is applied, the object is created with its parameters passed to it. This will create a new object and initialize it with these parameters, as defined in the init method. After this, the @ operation is invoked, so this object will wrap the function named run_with_custom_reries_limit, meaning that it will be passed to the call magic method.

Inside this call magic method, we defined the logic of the decorator as we normally do—we wrap the original function, returning a new one with the logic we want instead.

Decorators with default values

In the previous example, we saw a decorator that takes parameters, but those arguments have default values. The way the previous decorators were written will make sure that they work as long as users don't forget the parentheses to make the function call when using the decorator.

For example, if we only wanted the default values, this would work:

```
@retry()
def my function(): ...
```

But this wouldn't:

```
@retry
def my function(): ...
```

You might argue whether this is necessary and accept (perhaps with proper documentation) that the first example is how the decorator is meant to be used, and the second one is incorrect. And that would be fine, but it requires paying close attention, or runtime errors will occur.

Of course, if the decorator takes parameters that don't have default values, then the second syntax doesn't make sense, and there's only one possibility, which might make things simpler.

Alternatively, you can make the decorator work with both syntaxes. As you might have guessed, this takes extra effort, and as always you should balance whether it's worth it.

Let's illustrate this with a simple example that uses a decorator with parameters to inject arguments into a function. We define a function that takes two parameters, and a decorator that does the same, and the idea is to call the function without arguments and let it work with the parameters passed by the decorator:

```
@decorator(x=3, y=4)
def my_function(x, y):
    return x + y
my_function()  # 7
```

But of course, we define default values for the arguments of the decorator, so we can call it without values. And we'd like to also call it without the parentheses.

The simplest and most naïve way of writing it would be separating both cases with a conditional:

```
def decorator(function=None, *, x=DEFAULT_X, y=DEFAULT_Y):
    if function is None:  # called as `@decorator(...)`

        def decorated(function):
            @wraps(function)
            def wrapped():
```

```
        return function(x, y)

    return wrapped

    return decorated
else:  # called as `@decorator`

    @wraps(function)
    def wrapped():
        return function(x, y)

    return wrapped
```

Note something important about the signature of the decorator: the parameters are keyword-only. This simplifies the definition of the decorator a lot because we can assume the function is None when it's being called without arguments (otherwise, if we were to pass the values by position, the first of the parameters we passed would be confused with the function). If we wanted to be more careful, instead of using None (or any sentinel value), we could inspect the parameter type, assert a function object of the type we expect, and then shift the parameters accordingly, but that would make the decorator much more complicated.

Another alternative would be to abstract part of the wrapped decorator, and then apply a partial application of the function (using functools.partial). To explain this better, let's take an intermediate state, and use a lambda function that shows how the parameters to the decorator are applied, and how the decorator's arguments are "shifted":

```
def decorator(function=None, *, x=DEFAULT_X, y=DEFAULT_Y):
    if function is None:
        return lambda f: decorator(f, x=x, y=y)

    @wraps(function)
    def wrapped():
        return function(x, y)

    return wrapped
```

This is analogous to the previous example, in the sense that we have the definition of the wrapped function (how it's being decorated). Then, if no function is provided, we return a new function that takes a function as a parameter (f) and returns the decorator with that function applied and the rest of the parameters bound. Then, in the second recursive call, the function will exist, and the regular decorator function (wrapped) will be returned instead.

You can achieve the same result by changing the `lambda` definition for a partial application of the function:

```
return partial(decorator, x=x, y=y)
```

If this is too complex for our use cases, we can always decide to make the parameters of our decorators take mandatory values.

In any case, it's probably a good idea to define the parameters of the decorators to be keyword-only (regardless of whether they have default values or not). This is because, in general, when applying a decorator, there isn't that much context about what each value is doing, and using positional values might not yield a very meaningful expression, so it's better to be more expressive and pass the name of the parameter along with the value.

> If you're defining decorators with arguments, prefer to make them keyword-only.

Similarly, if our decorator does not intend to take parameters, and we want to be explicit about it, we can use the syntax we learned in *Chapter 2, Pythonic Code*, to define the function that our decorator receives as a single positional-only parameter.

For our first example, the syntax would be:

```
def retry(operation, /): ...
```

But keep in mind, this is not strictly recommended, just a way to make it explicit to you how the decorator is supposed to be invoked.

Decorators for coroutines

As explained in the introduction, since pretty much everything in Python is an object, then pretty much anything can be decorated, and this includes coroutines as well.

However, there's a caveat here, and that is, as explained in previous chapters, asynchronous programming in Python introduces some differences in syntax. Therefore, these syntax differences will also be carried to the decorator.

Simply speaking, if we were to write a decorator for a coroutine, we could simply adapt to the new syntax (remember to await the wrapped coroutine and define the wrapped object as a coroutine itself, meaning the internal function will likely have to use 'async def' instead of just 'def').

The problem is if we want to have a decorator widely applicable to functions and coroutines. In most cases, creating two decorators would be the simplest (and perhaps best) approach, but if we wanted to expose a simpler interface for our users (by having fewer objects to remember), we could create a thin wrapper, acting like a dispatcher to two internal (not exposed) decorators. This would be like creating a *facade* but with a decorator.

There is no general rule about how hard it would be to create a decorator for functions and coroutines, because that depends on the logic we want to put in the decorator itself. For example, in the code below there is a decorator that changes the parameters of the functions it receives, and this will work both for a regular function or a coroutine:

```
X, Y = 1, 2

def decorator(callable):
    """Call <callable> with fixed values"""

    @wraps(callable)
    def wrapped():
        return callable(X, Y)

    return wrapped

@decorator
def func(x, y):
    return x + y

@decorator
async def coro(x, y):
    return x + y
```

It's important to make one distinction about the coroutine though. The decorator will receive the coroutine as its callable argument, and then invoke it with the parameters. This creates the coroutine object (the task that will go to the event loop), but it doesn't await it, meaning that whoever calls await coro() will end up awaiting the coroutine resulting from what the decorator wrapped. This means, in simple cases like this one, we don't need to replace the coroutine with another coroutine (although this is generally recommended).

But again, this depends on what we need to do. If we need a `timing` function, then we have to wait for the function or coroutine to complete to measure the time, and for this we'll have to call `await` on it, which means that the wrapper object will in turn have to be a coroutine (but not the main decorator, though).

The code below illustrates this example using a decorator that selectively decides how to wrap the caller function:

```python
import inspect

def timing(callable):
    @wraps(callable)
    def wrapped(*args, **kwargs):
        start = time.time()
        result = callable(*args, **kwargs)
        latency = time.time() - start
        return {"latency": latency, "result": result}

    @wraps(callable)
    async def wrapped_coro(*args, **kwargs):
        start = time.time()
        result = await callable(*args, **kwargs)
        latency = time.time() - start
        return {"latency": latency, "result": result}

    if inspect.iscoroutinefunction(callable):
        return wrapped_coro

    return wrapped
```

The second wrapper is required for coroutines. If we didn't have it, then the code would have two problems. First, the call to `callable` (without `await`) would not actually wait for the operation to complete, meaning the results would be incorrect. And even worse, the value for the `result` key on the dictionary wouldn't be the result itself, but the coroutine created. As a consequence, the response would be a dictionary, and whoever tries to call that will try to await a dictionary, which will cause an error.

As a general rule, you should replace a decorated object with another one of the same kind, that is, a function with a function, and a coroutine with another coroutine.

We're still due to study one last enhancement that was recently added to Python, and it lifts some of the restrictions its syntax had.

Extended syntax for decorators

Python 3.9 introduced a novelty for decorators, with PEP-614 (`https://www.python.org/dev/peps/pep-0614/`), because a more general grammar is allowed. Before this enhancement, the syntax for invoking decorators (after the @) was restricted to very limited expressions, and not every single Python expression was allowed.

With these restrictions lifted, we can now write more complex expressions and use them in our decorators, if we think that can save us some lines of code (but as always, be careful not to over-complicate and get a more compact but much harder-to-read line).

As an example, we can simplify some of the nested functions we typically have for a simple decorator that logs a function call along with its parameters. Here (and for illustration purposes only), I replaced the nested function definitions, typical of decorators, with two `lambda` expressions:

```python
def _log(f, *args, **kwargs):
    print(f"calling {f.__qualname__!r} with {args=} and {kwargs=}")
    return f(*args, **kwargs)


@(lambda f: lambda *args, **kwargs: _log(f, *args, **kwargs))
def func(x):
    return x + 1
```

```
>>> func(3)
calling 'func' with args=(3,) and kwargs={}
```

The PEP document cites some examples for when this feature can be useful (like simplifying no-op functions to evaluate other expressions, or avoiding the use of the eval function).

The recommendation of this book for this feature is consistent with all the cases in which a more compact statement can be achieved: write the more compact version of the code as long as it doesn't hurt readability. If the decorator expression becomes hard to read, prefer the more verbose but simpler alternative of writing two or more functions.

Good uses for decorators

In this section, we will take a look at some common patterns that make good use of decorators. These are common situations for when decorators are a good choice.

From all the countless applications decorators can be used for, we will enumerate a few, the most common or relevant ones:

- **Transforming parameters**: Changing the signature of a function to expose a nicer API, while encapsulating details on how the parameters are treated and transformed underneath. We must be careful with this use of decorators, because it's only a good trait when it's intentional. That means, if we are explicitly using decorators to provide a good signature for functions that had a rather convoluted one, then it's a great way of achieving cleaner code by means of decorators. If, on the other hand, the signature of a function changed inadvertently because of a decorator, then that's something we would want to avoid (and we'll discuss how toward the end of the chapter).

- **Tracing code**: Logging the execution of a function with its parameters. You might be familiar with multiple libraries that provide tracing capabilities, and often expose such functionality as decorators to add to our functions. This is a nice abstraction, and a good interface to provide, as a way of integrating the code with external parties without too much disruption. In addition, it's a great source of inspiration, so we can write our own logging or tracing functionality as decorators.

- **Validating parameters**: Decorators can be used to validate parameter types (against expected values or their annotations, for example) in a transparent way. With the use of decorators, we could enforce preconditions for our abstractions, following the ideas of designing by contract.

- **Implementing retry operations**: In a similar way to the example we've explored in the previous section.

- **Simplifying classes by moving some (repetitive) logic into decorators**: This is related to the DRY principle, which we'll revisit toward the end of the chapter.

In the following sections, I'll discuss some of these topics in more detail.

Adapting function signatures

In object-oriented design, sometimes there's the case of having objects with different interfaces that need to interact. A solution to this problem is the adapter design pattern, which we shall discuss in *Chapter 7, Generators, Iterators, and Asynchronous Prpgramming*, when we review some of the main design patterns.

The topic of this section is, however, similar, in the sense that sometimes we need to adapt not objects, but function signatures.

Imagine a scenario in which you're working with legacy code, and there's a module that contains lots of functions defined with a complex signature (lots of parameters, boilerplate, etc.). It would be nice to have a cleaner interface to interact with these definitions but changing lots of functions implies a major refactor.

We can use decorators to keep the differences in the changes to a minimum.

Sometimes we can use decorators as an adapter between our code and a framework we're using, if, for example, that framework has the aforementioned considerations.

Imagine the case of a framework that expects to call functions defined by us, maintaining a certain interface:

```
def resolver_function(root, args, context, info): ...
```

Now, we have that signature everywhere, and decide that it's better for us to create an abstraction from all those parameters that encapsulates them and exposes the behavior we need in our application.

So now we have lots of functions whose first line repeats the boilerplate of creating the same object again and again, and then the rest of the function only interacts with our domain object:

```
def resolver_function(root, args, context, info):
    helper = DomainObject(root, args, context, info)
    ...
    helper.process()
```

In this example, we could have a decorator changing the signature of the function, so that we can write our functions assuming the `helper` object is passed directly. In this case, the task of the decorator would be to intercept the original parameters, create the domain object, and then pass the `helper` object to our function. We then define our functions assuming we only receive the object we need, already initialized.

Namely, we would like to write our code in this form:

```
@DomainArgs
def resolver_function(helper):
    helper.process()
    ...
```

This works the other way around too, for example, if the legacy code we have is the one taking too many parameters, and we're always deconstructing an object that's already created, because refactoring the legacy code would be risky, then we can do that with a decorator as an intermediate layer.

The idea is that this use of decorators can help you write functions with simpler, more compact signatures.

Validating parameters

We have mentioned before that decorators can be used to validate parameters (and even enforce some preconditions or postconditions under the idea of **Design by Contract (DbC)**), so from this, you probably have got the idea that it is somewhat common to use decorators when dealing with or manipulating parameters.

In particular, there are some cases where we find ourselves repeatedly creating similar objects or applying similar transformations that we would wish to abstract away. Most of the time, we can achieve this by simply using a decorator.

Tracing code

When talking about **tracing** in this section, we will refer to something more general that has to do with dealing with the execution of a function that we wish to monitor. This could refer to scenarios in which we want to:

- Trace the execution of a function (for example, by logging the lines it executes)
- Monitor some metrics over a function (such as CPU usage or memory footprint)
- Measure the running time of a function
- Log when a function was called, and the parameters that were passed to it

In the next section, we will explore a simple example of a decorator that logs the execution of a function, including its name and the time it took to run.

Effective decorators – avoiding common mistakes

While decorators are a great feature of Python, they are not exempt from issues if used incorrectly. In this section, we will see some common issues to avoid in order to create effective decorators.

Preserving data about the original wrapped object

One of the most common problems when applying a decorator to a function is that some of the properties or attributes of the original function are not maintained, leading to undesired, and hard-to-track, side effects.

To illustrate this, we show a decorator that is in charge of logging when the function is about to run:

```python
# decorator_wraps_1.py

def trace_decorator(function):
    def wrapped(*args, **kwargs):
        logger.info("running %s", function.__qualname__)
        return function(*args, **kwargs)

    return wrapped
```

Now, let's imagine we have a function with this decorator applied to it. We might initially think that nothing of that function is modified with respect to its original definition:

```python
@trace_decorator
def process_account(account_id: str):
    """Process an account by Id."""
    logger.info("processing account %s", account_id)
    ...
```

But maybe there are changes.

The decorator is not supposed to alter anything from the original function, but, as it turns out, since it contains a flaw, it's actually modifying its name and docstring, among other properties.

Let's try to get help for this function:

```
>>> help(process_account)
Help on function wrapped in module decorator_wraps_1:

wrapped(*args, **kwargs)
```

And let's check how it's called:

```
>>> process_account.__qualname__
'trace_decorator.<locals>.wrapped'
```

And also, the annotations for the original function were lost:

```
>>> process_account.__annotations__
{}
```

We can see that, since the decorator is actually changing the original function for a new one (called `wrapped`), what we actually see are the properties of this function instead of those from the original function.

If we apply a decorator like this one to multiple functions, all with different names, they will all end up being called `wrapped`, which is a major concern (for example, if we want to log or trace the function, this will make debugging even harder).

Another problem is that if we placed docstrings with tests on these functions, they would be overridden by those of the decorator. As a result, the docstrings with the test we want will not run when we call our code with the `doctest` module (as we saw in *Chapter 1*, *Introduction, Code Formatting, and Tools*).

The fix is simple, though. We just have to apply the wraps decorator in the internal function (`wrapped`), telling it that it is actually a wrapping function:

```python
# decorator_wraps_2.py
def trace_decorator(function):
    @wraps(function)
    def wrapped(*args, **kwargs):
        logger.info("running %s", function.__qualname__)
        return function(*args, **kwargs)

    return wrapped
```

Now, if we check the properties, we will obtain what we expected in the first place. Check help for the function, like so:

```
>>> from decorator_wraps_2 import process_account
>>> help(process_account)
Help on function process_account in module decorator_wraps_2:

process_account(account_id)
    Process an account by Id.
```

And verify that its qualified name is correct, like so:

```
>>> process_account.__qualname__
'process_account'
```

Most importantly, we recovered the unit tests we might have had on the docstrings! By using the `wraps` decorator, we can also access the original, unmodified function under the `__wrapped__` attribute. Although it should not be used in production, it might come in handy in some unit tests when we want to check the unmodified version of the function.

In general, for simple decorators, the way we would use `functools.wraps` would typically follow the following general formula or structure:

```
def decorator(original_function):
    @wraps(original_function)
    def decorated_function(*args, **kwargs):
        # modifications done by the decorator ...
        return original_function(*args, **kwargs)

    return decorated_function
```

 Always use `functools.wraps` applied over the wrapped function, when creating a decorator, as shown in the preceding formula.

Dealing with side effects in decorators

In this section, we will learn that it is advisable to avoid side effects in the body of the decorator. There are cases where this might be acceptable, but the bottom line is that if in doubt, decide against it, for the reasons that are explained ahead. Everything that the decorator needs to do aside from the function that it's decorating should be placed in the innermost function definition, or there will be problems when it comes to importing. Nonetheless, sometimes these side effects are required (or even desired) to run at import time, and the obverse applies.

We will see examples of both, and where each one applies. If in doubt, err on the side of caution, and delay all side effects until the very last moment, right after the `wrapped` function is going to be called.

Next, we will see when it's not a good idea to place extra logic outside the `wrapped` function.

Incorrect handling of side effects in a decorator

Let's imagine the case of a decorator that was created with the goal of logging when a function started running and then logging its running time:

```
def traced_function_wrong(function):
    logger.info("started execution of %s", function)
    start_time = time.time()

    @wraps(function)
    def wrapped(*args, **kwargs):
        result = function(*args, **kwargs)
        logger.info(
            "function %s took %.2fs",
            function,
            time.time() - start_time
        )
        return result
    return wrapped
```

Now we will apply the decorator to a regular function, thinking that it will work just fine:

```
@traced_function_wrong
def process_with_delay(callback, delay=0):
    time.sleep(delay)
    return callback()
```

This decorator has a subtle yet critical bug in it.

First, let's import the function, call it several times, and see what happens:

```
>>> from decorator_side_effects_1 import process_with_delay
INFO:started execution of <function process_with_delay at 0x...>
```

Just by importing the function, we will notice that something's amiss. The logging line should not be there, because the function was not invoked.

Now, what happens if we run the function, and see how long it takes to run? Actually, we would expect that calling the same function multiple times will give similar results:

```
>>> main()
...
INFO:function <function process_with_delay at 0x> took 8.67s
```

```
>>> main()
...
INFO:function <function process_with_delay at 0x> took 13.39s

>>> main()
...
INFO:function <function process_with_delay at 0x> took 17.01s
```

Every time we run the same function, it takes increasingly longer! At this point, you have probably already noticed the (now obvious) error.

Remember the syntax for decorators. `@traced_function_wrong` actually means the following:

```
process_with_delay = traced_function_wrong(process_with_delay)
```

And this will run when the module is imported. Therefore, the time that is set in the function will be the time the module was imported. Successive calls will compute the time difference from the running time until that original starting time. It will also log at the wrong moment, and not when the function is actually called.

Luckily, the fix is also very simple—we just have to move the code inside the wrapped function in order to delay its execution:

```
def traced_function(function):
    @functools.wraps(function)
    def wrapped(*args, **kwargs):
        logger.info("started execution of %s", function.__qualname__)
        start_time = time.time()
        result = function(*args, **kwargs)
        logger.info(
            "function %s took %.2fs",
            function.__qualname__,
            time.time() - start_time
        )
        return result
    return wrapped
```

With this new version, the previous problems are resolved.

If the actions of the decorator had been different, the results could have been much more disastrous. For instance, if it requires that you log events and send them to an external service, it will certainly fail unless the configuration has been run right before this has been imported, which we cannot guarantee. Even if we could, it would be bad practice. The same applies if the decorator has any other sort of side effect, such as reading from a file, parsing a configuration, and many more.

Requiring decorators with side effects

Sometimes, side effects on decorators are necessary, and we should not delay their execution until the last possible minute, because that's part of the mechanism that is required for them to work.

One common scenario for when we don't want to delay the side effect of decorators is when we need to register objects to a public registry that will be available in the module.

For instance, going back to our previous event system example, we now want to only make some events available in the module, but not all of them. In the hierarchy of events, we might want to have some intermediate classes that are not actual events we want to process on the system, but some of their derivative classes instead.

Instead of flagging each class based on whether it's going to be processed or not, we could explicitly register each class through a decorator.

In this case, we have a class for all events that relate to the activities of a user. However, this is just an intermediate table for the types of events we actually want, namely `UserLoginEvent` and `UserLogoutEvent`:

```
EVENTS_REGISTRY = {}


def register_event(event_cls):
    """Place the class for the event into the registry to make it
    accessible in the module.
    """
    EVENTS_REGISTRY[event_cls.__name__] = event_cls
    return event_cls


class Event:
    """A base event object"""
```

```
class UserEvent:
    TYPE = "user"


@register_event
class UserLoginEvent(UserEvent):
    """Represents the event of a user when it has just accessed the
system."""


@register_event
class UserLogoutEvent(UserEvent):
    """Event triggered right after a user abandoned the system."""
```

When we look at the preceding code, it seems that EVENTS_REGISTRY is empty, but after importing something from this module, it will get populated with all of the classes that are under the register_event decorator:

```
>>> from decorator_side_effects_2 import EVENTS_REGISTRY
>>> EVENTS_REGISTRY
{'UserLoginEvent': decorator_side_effects_2.UserLoginEvent,
 'UserLogoutEvent': decorator_side_effects_2.UserLogoutEvent}
```

This might seem like it's hard to read, or even misleading, because EVENTS_REGISTRY will have its final value at runtime, right after the module was imported, and we cannot easily predict its value by just looking at the code.

While that is true, in some cases this pattern is justified. In fact, many web frameworks or well-known libraries use this to work and expose objects or make them available. That said, be aware of this risk, if you are to implement something similar in your own projects: most of the time, an alternative solution would be preferred.

It is also true that in this case, the decorator is not changing the wrapped object or altering the way it works in any way. However, the important note here is that if we were to do some modifications and define an internal function that modifies the wrapped object, we would still probably want the code that registers the resulting object outside it.

Notice the use of the word *outside*. It does not necessarily mean before, it's just not part of the same closure; but it's in the outer scope, so it's not delayed until runtime.

Creating decorators that will always work

There are several different scenarios to which decorators might apply. It can also be the case that we need to use the same decorator for objects that fall into these different multiple scenarios, for instance, if we want to reuse our decorator and apply it to a function, a class, a method, or a static method.

If we create the decorator, just thinking about supporting only the first type of object we want to decorate, we might notice that the same decorator does not work equally well on a different type of object. A typical example is where we create a decorator to be used on a function, and then we want to apply it to a method of a class, only to realize that it does not work. A similar scenario might occur if we designed our decorator for a method, and then we want it to also apply for static methods or class methods.

When designing decorators, we typically think about reusing code, so we will want to use that decorator for functions and methods as well.

Defining our decorators with the signature *args and **kwargs will make them work in all cases because it's the most generic kind of signature that we can have. However, sometimes we might want not to use this, and instead define the decorator-wrapping function according to the signature of the original function, mainly because of two reasons:

- It will be more readable since it resembles the original function.
- It actually needs to do something with the arguments, so receiving *args and **kwargs wouldn't be convenient.

Consider the case in which we have many functions in our code base that require a particular object to be created from a parameter. For instance, we pass a string, and initialize a driver object with it, repeatedly. Then we think we can remove the duplication by using a decorator that will take care of converting this parameter accordingly.

In the next example, we pretend that DBDriver is an object that knows how to connect and run operations on a database, but it needs a connection string. The methods we have in our code are designed to receive a string with the information of the database and require us to create an instance of DBDriver always. The idea of the decorator is that it's going to take the place of this conversion automatically—the function will continue to receive a string, but the decorator will create a DBDriver and pass it to the function, so internally we can assume that we receive the object we need directly.

An example of using this in a function is shown in the next listing:

```python
# src/decorator_universal_1.py
from functools import wraps
from log import logger


class DBDriver:
    def __init__(self, dbstring: str) -> None:
        self.dbstring = dbstring

    def execute(self, query: str) -> str:
        return f"query {query} at {self.dbstring}"


def inject_db_driver(function):
    """This decorator converts the parameter by creating a ``DBDriver``
    instance from the database dsn string.
    """
    @wraps(function)
    def wrapped(dbstring):
        return function(DBDriver(dbstring))
    return wrapped


@inject_db_driver
def run_query(driver):
    return driver.execute("test_function")
```

It's easy to verify that if we pass a string to the function, we get the result done by an instance of `DBDriver`, so the decorator works as expected:

```
>>> run_query("test_OK")
'query test_function at test_OK'
```

But now, we want to reuse this same decorator in a class method, where we find the same problem:

```python
class DataHandler:
    @inject_db_driver
    def run_query(self, driver):
        return driver.execute(self.__class__.__name__)
```

We try to use this decorator, only to realize that it doesn't work:

```
>>> DataHandler().run_query("test_fails")
Traceback (most recent call last):
  ...
TypeError: wrapped() takes 1 positional argument but 2 were given
```

What is the problem?

The method in the class is defined with an extra argument—self.

Methods are just a particular kind of function that receive self (the object they're defined upon) as the first parameter.

Therefore, in this case, the decorator (designed to work with only one parameter, named dbstring) will interpret that self is said parameter, and call the method passing the string in the place of self, and nothing in the place of the second parameter, namely the string we are passing.

To fix this issue, we need to create a decorator that will work equally for methods and functions, and we do so by defining this as a decorator object that also implements the protocol descriptor.

Descriptors are fully explained in *Chapter 7, Generators, Iterators, and Asynchronous Programming*, so for now, we can just take this as a recipe that will make the decorator work.

The solution is to implement the decorator as a class object and make this object a description, by implementing the __get__ method:

```python
from functools import wraps
from types import MethodType


class inject_db_driver:
    """Convert a string to a DBDriver instance and pass this to the
       wrapped function."""

    def __init__(self, function) -> None:
        self.function = function
        wraps(self.function)(self)

    def __call__(self, dbstring):
        return self.function(DBDriver(dbstring))
```

```
def __get__(self, instance, owner):
    if instance is None:
        return self
    return self.__class__(MethodType(self.function, instance))
```

Details on descriptors will be explained in *Chapter 6, Getting More Out of Our Objects with Descriptors*, but for the purposes of this example, we can now say that what it does is actually rebind the callable it's decorating to a method, meaning that it will bind the function to the object, and then recreate the decorator with this new callable.

For functions, it still works, because it won't call the __get__ method at all.

Decorators and clean code

Now that we know more about decorators, how to write them, and avoiding common issues, it's time to take them to the next level and see how we can leverage what we have learned to achieve better software.

We have briefly touched on this subject throughout the previous sections, but those were closer-to-the-code examples, as the suggestions referred to how to make specific lines (or sections) of the code more readable.

The topics discussed from now relate to more general design principles. Some of these ideas we have already visited in previous chapters, but the outlook here is to understand how we use decorators for such purposes.

Composition over inheritance

We have already discussed briefly that in general, it's better to have composition rather than inheritance because the latter carries some problems of making components of the code more coupled.

In the book *Design Patterns: Elements of Reusable Object-Oriented Software* (DESIG01), most of the ideas around the design pattern are based on the following idea:

> *Favor composition over class inheritance*

In *Chapter 2, Pythonic Code*, I introduced the idea of using the magic method __getattr__ to resolve attributes dynamically on objects. I also gave the example that this could be used to automatically resolve attributes based on a naming convention should this be required by an external framework, for example. Let's explore two different versions of solving this problem.

For this example, let's assume we're interacting with a framework that has the naming convention of calling attributes with the prefix "resolve_" to resolve an attribute, but our domain objects only have those attributes without the "resolve_" prefix.

Clearly, we don't want to write a lot of repetitive methods named "resolve_x" for every attribute we have, so the first idea is to take advantage of the aforementioned __getattr__ magic method, and place it in a base class:

```
class BaseResolverMixin:
    def __getattr__(self, attr: str):
        if attr.startswith("resolve_"):
            *_, actual_attr = attr.partition("resolve_")
        else:
            actual_attr = attr
        try:
            return self.__dict__[actual_attr]
        except KeyError as e:
            raise AttributeError from e


@dataclass
class Customer(BaseResolverMixin):
    customer_id: str
    name: str
    address: str
```

This will do the trick, but can we do better?

We could devise a class decorator to set this method directly:

```
from dataclasses import dataclass

def _resolver_method(self, attr):
    """The resolution method of attributes that will replace __getattr__."""
    if attr.startswith("resolve_"):
        *_, actual_attr = attr.partition("resolve_")
    else:
        actual_attr = attr
    try:
        return self.__dict__[actual_attr]
    except KeyError as e:
        raise AttributeError from e
```

```
def with_resolver(cls):
    """Set the custom resolver method to a class."""
    cls.__getattr__ = _resolver_method
    return cls


@dataclass
@with_resolver
class Customer:
    customer_id: str
    name: str
    address: str
```

Both versions would comply with the following behavior:

```
>>> customer = Customer("1", "name", "address")
>>> customer.resolve_customer_id
'1'
>>> customer.resolve_name
'name'
```

First, we have the resolve method as a standalone function that respects the signature of how the original __getattr__ would look like (that's why I even preserved self as the name of the first parameter, to be intentional about that function becoming a method).

The rest of the code seems rather simple. Our decorator only sets the method to the class it receives by parameter, and then we apply the decorator to our class without having to use inheritance anymore.

How is this a little bit better than the previous example? For starters, we can argue the use of the decorator implies we're using composition (take a class, modify it, and return a new one) over inheritance, so our code is less coupled with the base class we had at the beginning.

Additionally, we can say that the use of inheritance (via a mixin class) in the first example was rather fictitious. We were not using inheritance to create a more specialized version of the class, only to take advantage of the __getattr__ method. This would be bad for two (complementary) reasons: first, inheritance is not the best way to reuse code. Good code is reused by having small, cohesive abstractions, not creating hierarchies.

Second, remember from previous chapters that creating a subclass should follow with the idea of specialization, the "is a" kind of relation. Think whether, from a conceptual point of view, a customer is indeed a `BaseResolverMivin` (and what is, by the way?).

To shed some more light on this second point, imagine you have a hierarchy like this one:

```
class Connection: pass
class EncryptedConnection(Connection): pass
```

In this case, the use of inheritance is arguably correct, after all, an encrypted connection is a more specific kind of connection. But what would be a more specific kind of `BaseResolverMixin`? This is a mixin class, so it's expected to be mixed in the hierarchy along with other classes (using multiple inheritance). The use of this mix-in class is purely pragmatic, and for implementational purposes. Don't get me wrong, this is a pragmatic book, so you'll have to deal with mix-in classes in your professional experience, and it's perfectly fine to use them, but if we can avoid this purely implementational abstraction, and replace it with something that doesn't compromise our domain objects (in this case the `Customer` class), that's even better.

There's another exciting capability of the new design, which is extensibility. We have seen how decorators can be parametrized. Imagine the flexibility we could achieve in our design if we allowed the decorator to set any resolver function, not just the one we defined.

The DRY principle with decorators

We have seen how decorators allow us to abstract away certain logic into a separate component. The main advantage of this is that we can then apply the decorator multiple times to different objects in order to reuse code. This follows the **Don't Repeat Yourself (DRY)** principle since we define certain knowledge once and only once.

The `retry` mechanism implemented in the previous sections is a good example of a decorator that can be applied multiple times to reuse code. Instead of making each particular function include its own `retry` logic, we create a decorator and apply it several times. This makes sense once we have made sure that the decorator can work with methods and functions equally.

The class decorator that defined how events are to be represented also complies with the DRY principle in the sense that it defines one specific place for the logic for serializing an event, without needing to duplicate code scattered among different classes. Since we expect to reuse this decorator and apply it to many classes, its development (and complexity) pay off.

This last remark is important to bear in mind when trying to use decorators in order to reuse code—we have to be absolutely sure that we will actually be saving code.

Any decorator (especially if it is not carefully designed) adds another level of indirection to the code, and hence more complexity. Readers of the code might want to follow the path of the decorator to fully understand the logic of the function (although these considerations are addressed in the following section), so keep in mind that this complexity has to pay off. If there is not going to be too much reuse, then do not go for a decorator and opt for a simpler option (maybe just a separate function or another small class is enough).

But how do we know what too much reuse is? Is there a rule to determine when to refactor existing code into a decorator? There is nothing specific to decorators in Python, but we could apply a general rule of thumb in software engineering (GLASS 01) that states that a component should be tried out at least three times before considering creating a generic abstraction in the sort of a reusable component. From the same reference (GLASS 01) (I encourage all readers to read *Facts and Fallacies of Software Engineering* because it is a great reference) also comes the idea that creating reusable components is three times harder than creating simple ones.

The bottom line is that reusing code through decorators is acceptable, but only when you take into account the following considerations:

- Do not create the decorator in the first place from scratch. Wait until the pattern emerges and the abstraction for the decorator becomes clear, and then refactor.
- Consider that the decorator has to be applied several times (at least three times) before implementing it.
- Keep the code in the decorators to a minimum.

As we have revisited the DRY principle from the point of view of decorators, we can still discuss the separation of concerns applied to decorators, as explored in the next section.

Decorators and separation of concerns

The last point in the previous list is so important that it deserves a section of its own. We have already explored the idea of reusing code and noticed that a key element of reusing code is having components that are cohesive. This means that they should have the minimum level of responsibility—do one thing, one thing only, and do it well. The smaller our components, the more reusable, and the more they can be applied in a different context without carrying extra behavior that will cause coupling and dependencies, which will make the software rigid.

To show you what this means, let's reprise one of the decorators that we used in a previous example. We created a decorator that traced the execution of certain functions with code similar to the following:

```
def traced_function(function):
    @functools.wraps(function)
    def wrapped(*args, **kwargs):
        logger.info("started execution of %s", function.__qualname__)
        start_time = time.time()
        result = function(*args, **kwargs)
        logger.info(
            "function %s took %.2fs",
            function.__qualname__,
            time.time() - start_time
        )
        return result
    return wrapped
```

Now, this decorator, while it works, has a problem—it is doing more than one thing. It logs that a particular function was just invoked, and also logs how much time it took to run. Every time we use this decorator, we are carrying these two responsibilities, even if we only wanted one of them.

This should be broken down into smaller decorators, each one with a more specific and limited responsibility:

```
def log_execution(function):
    @wraps(function)
    def wrapped(*args, **kwargs):
        logger.info("started execution of %s", function.__qualname__)
        return function(*kwargs, **kwargs)
    return wrapped


def measure_time(function):
    @wraps(function)
    def wrapped(*args, **kwargs):
        start_time = time.time()
        result = function(*args, **kwargs)

        logger.info(
            "function %s took %.2f",
            function.__qualname__,
            time.time() - start_time,
        )
```

```
        return result
    return wrapped
```

Notice that the same functionality that we had previously can be achieved by simply combining both of them:

```
@measure_time
@log_execution
def operation():
    ....
```

Notice how the order in which the decorators are applied is also important.

 Do not place more than one responsibility in a decorator. The **single responsibility principle (SRP)** applies to decorators as well.

Finally, we can analyze good decorators to get an idea of how they're used in practice. The next section starts wrapping up what we've learned in this chapter, by analyzing decorators.

Analysis of good decorators

As a closing note for this chapter, let's review some examples of good decorators and how they are used both in Python itself, as well as in popular libraries. The idea is to get guidelines on how good decorators are created.

Before jumping into examples, let's first identify traits that good decorators should have:

- **Encapsulation, or separation of concerns**: A good decorator should effectively separate different responsibilities between what it does and what it is decorating. It cannot be a leaky abstraction, meaning that a client of the decorator should only invoke it in black-box mode, without knowing how it is actually implementing its logic.

- **Orthogonality**: What the decorator does should be independent, and as decoupled as possible from the object it is decorating.

- **Reusability**: It is desirable that the decorator can be applied to multiple types, and not that it just appears on one instance of one function, because that means that it could just have been a function instead. It has to be generic enough.

A nice example of decorators can be found in the Celery project, where a task is defined by applying the decorator of the task from the application to a function:

```
@app.task
def mytask():
    ....
```

One of the reasons why this is a good decorator is because it is very good at something—encapsulation. The user of the library only needs to define the function body and the decorator will convert that into a task automatically. The @app.task decorator surely wraps a lot of logic and code, but none of that is relevant to the body of mytask(). It is complete encapsulation and separation of concerns—nobody will have to take a look at what that decorator does, so it is a correct abstraction that does not leak any details.

Another common use of decorators is in web frameworks (Pyramid, Flask, and Sanic, just to name a few), on which the handlers for views are registered to the URLs through decorators:

```
@route("/", method=["GET"])
def view_handler(request):
    ...
```

These sorts of decorators have the same considerations as before; they also provide total encapsulation because a user of the web framework rarely (if ever) needs to know what the @route decorator is doing. In this case, we know that the decorator is doing something more, such as registering these functions to a mapper to the URL, and also that it is changing the signature of the original function to provide us with a nicer interface that receives a request object with all the information already set.

The previous two examples are enough to make us notice something else about this use of decorators. They conform to an API. These libraries of frameworks are exposing their functionality to users through decorators, and it turns out that decorators are an excellent way of defining a clean programming interface.

This is probably the best way we should think about decorators. Much like in the example of the class decorator that tells us how the attributes of the event are going to be handled, a good decorator should provide a clean interface so that users of the code know what to expect from the decorator, without needing to know how it works, or any of its details for that matter.

Summary

Decorators are powerful tools in Python that can be applied to many things such as classes, methods, functions, generators, and many more. We have demonstrated how to create decorators in different ways, and for different purposes, and drew some conclusions along the way.

When creating a decorator for functions, try to make its signature match the original function being decorated. Instead of using the generic *args and **kwargs, making the signature match the original one will make it easier to read and maintain, and it will resemble the original function more closely, so it will be more familiar to readers of that code.

Decorators are a very useful tool for reusing code and following the DRY principle. However, their usefulness comes at a cost, and if they are not used wisely, the complexity can do more harm than good. For that reason, we emphasize that decorators should be used when they are going to be applied multiple times (three or more times). In the same way as the DRY principle, we embrace the idea of separation of concerns, with the goal of keeping the decorators as small as possible.

Another good use of decorators is to create cleaner interfaces, for instance, simplifying the definition of a class by extracting part of its logic into a decorator. In this sense, decorators also help readability by providing the users with information about what that particular component will be doing, without needing to know how (encapsulation).

In the next chapter, we will take a look at another advanced feature of Python—descriptors. In particular, we will see how with the help of descriptors, we can create even better decorators and solve some of the issues we encountered in this chapter.

References

Here is a list of information you can refer to:

- *PEP-318*: *Decorators for Functions and Methods* (`https://www.python.org/dev/peps/pep-0318/`)

- *PEP-3129*: *Class Decorators* (`https://www.python.org/dev/peps/pep-3129/`)

- *WRAPT 01*: `https://pypi.org/project/wrapt/`

- *WRAPT 02*: `https://wrapt.readthedocs.io/en/latest/decorators.html#universal-decorators`

- *The Functools module: The wraps function in the functools module of Python's standard library* (`https://docs.python.org/3/library/functools.html#functools.wrap`)

- *ATTRS 01: The attrs library* (`https://pypi.org/project/attrs/`)

- *PEP-557: Data Classes* (`https://www.python.org/dev/peps/pep-0557/`)

- *GLASS 01*: The book written by *Robert L. Glass* called *Facts and Fallacies of Software Engineering*

- *DESIG01*: The book written by *Erich Gamma* called *Design Patterns: Elements of Reusable Object-Oriented Software*

- *PEP-614: Relaxing Grammar Restrictions On Decorators* (`https://www.python.org/dev/peps/pep-0614/`)

6
Getting More Out of Our Objects with Descriptors

This chapter introduces a new concept that is more advanced in Python development since it features descriptors. Moreover, descriptors are not something programmers of other languages are familiar with, so there are no easy analogies or parallelisms to make.

Descriptors are another distinctive feature of Python that take object-oriented programming to another level, and their potential allows users to build more powerful and reusable abstractions. Most of the time, the full potential of descriptors is observed in libraries or frameworks.

In this chapter, we will achieve the following goals that relate to descriptors:

- Understand what descriptors are, how they work, and how to implement them effectively
- Analyze the two types of descriptors (data and non-data descriptors) in terms of their conceptual differences and implementation details
- Reuse code effectively through descriptors
- Analyze examples of good uses of descriptors, and how to take advantage of them for our API libraries

A first look at descriptors

First, we will explore the main idea behind descriptors to understand their mechanics and internal workings. Once this is clear, it will be easier to assimilate how the different types of descriptors work, which we will explore in the next section.

Once we have a general understanding of the idea behind descriptors, we will look at an example where their use gives us a cleaner and more Pythonic implementation.

The machinery behind descriptors

The way descriptors work is not all that complicated, but the problem with them is that there are a lot of caveats to take into consideration, so the implementation details are of the utmost importance here.

To implement descriptors, we need at least two classes. For this generic example, the `client` class will take advantage of the functionality we want to implement in the `descriptor` (this is generally just a domain model class, a regular abstraction we create for our solution), and the `descriptor` class will implement the logic of the descriptor itself.

A descriptor is, therefore, just an object that is an instance of a class that implements the descriptor protocol. This means that the interface of this class must contain at least one of the following magic methods (part of the descriptor protocol as of Python 3.6+):

- `__get__`
- `__set__`
- `__delete__`
- `__set_name__`

For the purposes of this initial high-level introduction, the following naming conventions will be used:

Name	Meaning
`ClientClass`	The domain-level abstraction that will take advantage of the functionality to be implemented by the descriptor. This class is said to be a client of the descriptor. This class contains a class attribute (named `descriptor` by this convention), which is an instance of `DescriptorClass`.

DescriptorClass	The class that implements the descriptor itself. This class should implement some of the aforementioned magic methods that entail the descriptor protocol.
client	An instance of ClientClass. client = ClientClass().
descriptor	An instance of DescriptorClass. descriptor = DescriptorClass(). This object is a class attribute that is placed in ClientClass.

Table 6.1: Descriptor naming conventions used in this chapter

This relationship is illustrated in *Figure 6.1*:

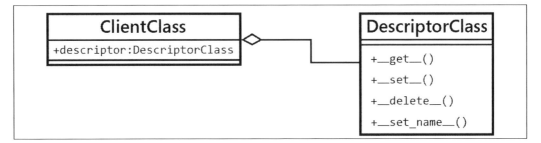

Figure 6.1: The relationship between ClientClass and DescriptorClass

A very important observation to keep in mind is that for this protocol to work, the descriptor object has to be defined as a class attribute. Creating this object as an instance attribute will not work, so it must be in the body of the class, and not in the __init__ method.

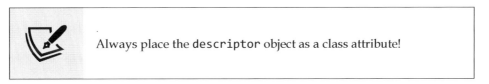

Always place the descriptor object as a class attribute!

On a slightly more critical note, readers can also note that it is possible to implement the descriptor protocol partially—not all methods must always be defined; instead, we can implement only those we need, as we will see shortly.

So, now we have the structure in place—we know what elements are set and how they interact. We need a class for the descriptor, another class that will consume the logic of the descriptor, which, in turn, will have a descriptor object (an instance of DescriptorClass) as a class attribute, and instances of ClientClass that will follow the descriptor protocol when we call for the attribute named descriptor. But now what? How does all of this fit into place at runtime?

Normally, when we have a regular class and we access its attributes, we simply obtain the objects as we expect them, and even their properties, as in the following example:

```
>>> class Attribute:
...         value = 42
...
...
>>> class Client:
...         attribute = Attribute()
...
>>> Client().attribute
<__main__.Attribute object at 0x...>
>>> Client().attribute.value
42
```

But, in the case of descriptors, something different happens. When an object is defined as a class attribute (and this one is a descriptor), when a client requests this attribute, instead of getting the object itself (as we would expect from the previous example), we get the result of having called the __get__ magic method.

Let's start with some simple code that only logs information about the context, and returns the same client object:

```
class DescriptorClass:
    def __get__(self, instance, owner):
        if instance is None:
            return self
        logger.info(
            "Call: %s.__get__(%r, %r)",
            self.__class__.__name__,
            instance,
            owner
        )
        return instance


class ClientClass:
    descriptor = DescriptorClass()
```

When running this code, and requesting the descriptor attribute of an instance of ClientClass, we will discover that we are, in fact, not getting an instance of DescriptorClass, but whatever its __get__() method returns instead:

```
>>> client = ClientClass()
>>> client.descriptor
INFO:Call: DescriptorClass.__get__(<ClientClass object at 0x...>,
<class 'ClientClass'>)
<ClientClass object at 0x...>
>>> client.descriptor is client
INFO:Call: DescriptorClass.__get__(ClientClass object at 0x...>, <class
'ClientClass'>)
True
```

Notice how the logging line, placed under the __get__ method, was called instead of just returning the object we created. In this case, we made that method return the `client` itself, hence making a true comparison of the last statement. The parameters of this method are explained in more detail in the following subsections, so don't worry about them for now. The crux of this example is to understand that the lookup of attributes behaves differently when one of those attributes is a descriptor (in this case, because it has a __get__ method).

Starting from this simple, yet demonstrative, example, we can start creating more complex abstractions and better decorators because the important note here is that we have a new (powerful) tool to work with. Notice how this changes the control flow of the program in a completely different way. With this tool, we can abstract all sorts of logic behind the __get__ method, and make the `descriptor` transparently run all sorts of transformations without clients even noticing. This takes encapsulation to a new level.

Exploring each method of the descriptor protocol

Up until now, we have seen quite a few examples of descriptors in action, and we got the idea of how they work. These examples gave us a first glimpse of the power of descriptors, but you might be wondering about some implementation details and idioms whose explanations we failed to address.

Since descriptors are just objects, these methods take `self` as the first parameter. For all of them, this just means the `descriptor` object itself.

In this section, we will explore each method of the descriptor protocol in full detail, explaining what each parameter signifies, and how they are intended to be used.

The get method

The signature of this magic method is as follows:

```
__get__(self, instance, owner)
```

The first parameter, `instance`, refers to the object from which the `descriptor` is being called. In our first example, this would mean the `client` object.

The `owner` parameter is a reference to the class of that object, which, following our example (from *Figure 6.1*), would be `ClientClass`.

From the previous paragraph, we can conclude that the parameter named `instance` in the signature of `__get__` is the object over which the descriptor is taking action, and `owner` is the class of `instance`. The astute reader might be wondering why the signature is defined like this. After all, the class can be taken from `instance` directly (`owner = instance.__class__`). There is an edge case—when the `descriptor` is called from the class (`ClientClass`), and not from the instance (`client`), then the value of `instance` is `None`, but we might still want to do some processing in that case. That's why Python chooses to pass the class as a different parameter.

With the following simple code, we can demonstrate the difference between a descriptor being called from the `class` or from an `instance`. In this case, the `__get__` method is doing two separate things for each case:

```python
# descriptors_methods_1.py

class DescriptorClass:
    def __get__(self, instance, owner):
        if instance is None:
            return f"{self.__class__.__name__}.{owner.__name__}"
        return f"value for {instance}"


class ClientClass:
    descriptor = DescriptorClass()
```

When we call it from `ClientClass` directly, it will do one thing, which is composing a namespace with the names of the classes:

```
>>> ClientClass.descriptor
'DescriptorClass.ClientClass'
```

And then if we call it from an object we have created, it will return the other message instead:

```
>>> ClientClass().descriptor
'value for <descriptors_methods_1.ClientClass object at 0x...>'
```

In general, unless we really need to do something with the owner parameter, the most common idiom is to just return the descriptor itself when instance is None. This is because when users are calling the descriptor from the class, they're probably expecting to get the descriptor itself, so it makes sense. But of course, it really depends on the example (later in the chapter, we'll see different usages with their explanations).

The set method

The signature of this method is as follows:

```
__set__(self, instance, value)
```

This method is called when we try to assign something to a descriptor. It is activated with statements such as the following, in which a descriptor is an object that implements __set__ (). The instance parameter, in this case, would be client, and the value would be the "value" string:

```
client.descriptor = "value"
```

You can note some similarity between this behavior and the @property.setter decorator from previous chapters, on which the argument of the setter function was the right-hand-side value of the statement (in this case the string "value"). We'll revisit this later in the chapter.

If client.descriptor doesn't implement __set__(), then "value" (any object on the right-hand side of the statement) will override the descriptor entirely.

> Be careful when assigning a value to an attribute that is a descriptor. Make sure it implements the __set__ method, and that we are not causing an undesired side effect.

By default, the most common use of this method is just to store data in an object. Nevertheless, we have seen how powerful descriptors are so far, and that we can take advantage of them, for example, if we were to create generic validation objects that can be applied multiple times (again, this is something that if we don't abstract, we might end up repeating multiple times in setter methods of properties).

The following listing illustrates how we can take advantage of this method in order to create generic validation objects for attributes, which can be created dynamically with functions to validate on the values before assigning them to the object:

```python
class Validation:

    def __init__(
        self, validation_function: Callable[[Any], bool], error_msg: str
    ) -> None:
        self.validation_function = validation_function
        self.error_msg = error_msg

    def __call__(self, value):
        if not self.validation_function(value):
            raise ValueError(f"{value!r} {self.error_msg}")


class Field:

    def __init__(self, *validations):
        self._name = None
        self.validations = validations

    def __set_name__(self, owner, name):
        self._name = name

    def __get__(self, instance, owner):
        if instance is None:
            return self
        return instance.__dict__[self._name]

    def validate(self, value):
        for validation in self.validations:
            validation(value)

    def __set__(self, instance, value):
        self.validate(value)
        instance.__dict__[self._name] = value
```

```
class ClientClass:
    descriptor = Field(
        Validation(lambda x: isinstance(x, (int, float)), "is not a
        number"),
        Validation(lambda x: x >= 0, "is not >= 0"),
    )
```

We can see this object in action in the following listing:

```
>>> client = ClientClass()
>>> client.descriptor = 42
>>> client.descriptor
42
>>> client.descriptor = -42
Traceback (most recent call last):
    ...
ValueError: -42 is not >= 0
>>> client.descriptor = "invalid value"
    ...
ValueError: 'invalid value' is not a number
```

The idea is that something that we would normally place in a property can be abstracted away into a descriptor, and be reused multiple times. In this case, the __ set__() method would be doing what the @property.setter would have been doing.

This is a more generic mechanism than using properties, because, as we'll see later, properties are a particular case of descriptors.

The delete method

The signature for the delete method is simpler, and it looks like this:

```
__delete__(self, instance)
```

This method is called upon with the following statement, in which self would be the descriptor attribute, and instance would be the client object in this example:

```
>>> del client.descriptor
```

In the following example, we use this method to create a `descriptor` with the goal of preventing you from removing attributes from an object without the required administrative privileges. Notice how, in this case, the `descriptor` has logic that is used to predicate with the values of the object that is using it, instead of different related objects:

```python
# descriptors_methods_3.py

class ProtectedAttribute:
    def __init__(self, requires_role=None) -> None:
        self.permission_required = requires_role
        self._name = None

    def __set_name__(self, owner, name):
        self._name = name

    def __set__(self, user, value):
        if value is None:
            raise ValueError(f"{self._name} can't be set to None")
        user.__dict__[self._name] = value

    def __delete__(self, user):
        if self.permission_required in user.permissions:
            user.__dict__[self._name] = None
        else:
            raise ValueError(
                f"User {user!s} doesn't have {self.permission_required}
"
                "permission"
            )


class User:
    """Only users with "admin" privileges can remove their email
address."""

    email = ProtectedAttribute(requires_role="admin")

    def __init__(self, username: str, email: str, permission_list: list
= None) -> None:
        self.username = username
        self.email = email
        self.permissions = permission_list or []
```

```
def __str__(self):
    return self.username
```

Before seeing examples of how this object works, it's important to remark on some of the criteria of this descriptor. Notice the User class requires the username and email as mandatory parameters. According to its __init__ method, it cannot be a user if it doesn't have an email attribute. If we were to delete that attribute and extract it from the object entirely, we would be creating an inconsistent object, with some invalid intermediate state that does not correspond to the interface defined by the class User. Details like this one are really important, in order to avoid issues. Some other object is expecting to work with this User, and it also expects that it has an email attribute.

For this reason, it was decided that the "deletion" of an email will just simply set it to None, and that is the part of the code listing that is in bold. For the same reason, we must forbid someone from trying to set a None value to it, because that would bypass the mechanism we placed in the __delete__ method.

Here, we can see it in action, assuming a case where only users with "admin" privileges can remove their email address:

```
>>> admin = User("root", "root@d.com", ["admin"])
>>> user = User("user", "user1@d.com", ["email", "helpdesk"])
>>> admin.email
'root@d.com'
>>> del admin.email
>>> admin.email is None
True
>>> user.email
'user1@d.com'
>>> user.email = None
...
ValueError: email can't be set to None
>>> del user.email
...
ValueError: User user doesn't have admin permission
```

Here, in this simple descriptor, we see that we can delete the email from users that contain the "admin" permission only. As for the rest, when we try to call del on that attribute, we will get a ValueError exception.

In general, this method of the descriptor is not as commonly used as the two previous ones, but it is shown here for completeness.

The set name method

This is a relatively new method that was added in Python 3.6, and has this structure:

```
__set_name__(self, owner, name)
```

When we create the descriptor object in the class that is going to use it, we generally need the descriptor to know the name of the attribute it is going to be handling.

This attribute name is the one we use to read from and write to __dict__ in the __get__ and __set__ methods, respectively.

Before Python 3.6, the descriptor couldn't take this name automatically, so the most general approach was to just pass it explicitly when initializing the object. This works fine, but it has an issue in that it requires that we duplicate the name every time we want to use the descriptor for a new attribute.

This is what a typical descriptor would look like if we didn't have this method:

```python
class DescriptorWithName:
    def __init__(self, name):
        self.name = name

    def __get__(self, instance, value):
        if instance is None:
            return self
        logger.info("getting %r attribute from %r", self.name,
instance)
        return instance.__dict__[self.name]

    def __set__(self, instance, value):
        instance.__dict__[self.name] = value


class ClientClass:
    descriptor = DescriptorWithName("descriptor")
```

We can see how the descriptor uses this value:

```
>>> client = ClientClass()
>>> client.descriptor = "value"
>>> client.descriptor
INFO:getting 'descriptor' attribute from <ClientClass object at 0x...>
'value'
```

Now, if we wanted to avoid writing the name of the attribute twice (once for the variable assigned inside the class, and once again as the name of the first parameter of the `descriptor`), we'd have to resort to a few tricks, like using a class decorator, or (even worse) using a meta-class.

In Python 3.6, the new method `__set_name__` was added, and it receives the class where that descriptor is being created, and the name that is being given to that `descriptor`. The most common idiom is to use this method for the `descriptor` so that it can store the required name in this method.

For compatibility, it is generally a good idea to keep a default value in the `__init__` method but still take advantage of `__set_name__`.

With this method, we can rewrite the previous `descriptor` as follows:

```
class DescriptorWithName:
    def __init__(self, name=None):
        self.name = name

    def __set_name__(self, owner, name):
        self.name = name
    ...
```

`__set_name__` is useful to get the name of the attribute the descriptor was assigned, but if we wanted to override the value, the `__init__` method would still take precedence, so we retain flexibility.

Even though we're free to name our descriptors however we like, we generally use the name of the descriptor (the attribute name) as a key of the `__dict__` of the client object, which means it'll be interpreted as an attribute. For this reason, try to name the descriptors you use as valid Python identifiers.

 If you're setting a bespoke name for your descriptor, use a valid Python identifier.

Types of descriptors

Based on the methods we have just explored, we can make an important distinction among descriptors in terms of how they work. Understanding this distinction plays an important role in working effectively with descriptors and will also help to avoid caveats or common errors at runtime.

If a descriptor implements the __set__ or __delete__ methods, it is called a **data descriptor**. Otherwise, a descriptor that solely implements __get__ is a **non-data descriptor**. Notice that __set_name__ does not affect this classification at all.

When trying to resolve an attribute of an object, a data descriptor will always take precedence over the dictionary of the object, whereas a non-data descriptor will not. That means that in a non-data descriptor if the object has a key on its dictionary with the same name as the descriptor, then that will always be called, and the descriptor itself will never run.

Conversely, in a data descriptor, even if there is a key in the dictionary with the same name as the descriptor, this one will never be used since the descriptor itself will always end up being called.

The following two sections explain this in more detail, with examples, to get a deeper idea of what to expect from each type of descriptor.

Non-data descriptors

We will start with a descriptor that only implements the __get__ method, and see how it is used:

```
class NonDataDescriptor:
    def __get__(self, instance, owner):
        if instance is None:
            return self
        return 42


class ClientClass:
    descriptor = NonDataDescriptor()
```

As usual, if we ask for the descriptor, we get the result of its __get__ method:

```
>>> client = ClientClass()
>>> client.descriptor
42
```

But if we change the descriptor attribute to something else, we lose access to this value, and get what was assigned to it instead:

```
>>> client.descriptor = 43
>>> client.descriptor
43
```

Now, if we delete the `descriptor` and ask for it again, let's see what we get:

```
>>> del client.descriptor
>>> client.descriptor
42
```

Let's rewind what just happened. When we first created the `client` object, the `descriptor` attribute lay in the class, not the instance, so if we ask for the dictionary of the `client` object, it will be empty:

```
>>> vars(client)
{}
```

And then, when we request the `.descriptor` attribute, it doesn't find any key in `client.__dict__` named "descriptor", so it goes to the class, where it will find it ... but only as a descriptor, hence why it returns the result of the __get__ method.

But then, we change the value of the `.descriptor` attribute to something else, and what this does is sets the value 99 into the dictionary of the `instance`, meaning that this time it won't be empty:

```
>>> client.descriptor = 99
>>> vars(client)
{'descriptor': 99}
```

So, when we ask for the `.descriptor` attribute here, it will look for it in the object (and this time it will find it because there is a key named `descriptor` in the __dict__ attribute of the object, as the `vars` result shows us), and return it without having to look for it in the class. For this reason, the `descriptor` protocol is never invoked, and the next time we ask for this attribute, it will instead return the value we have overridden it with (99).

Afterward, we delete this attribute by calling `del`, and what this does is to remove the key named "descriptor" from the dictionary of the object, leaving us back in the first scenario, where it's going to default to the class where the descriptor protocol will be triggered:

```
>>> del client.descriptor
>>> vars(client)
{}
>>> client.descriptor
42
```

This means that if we set the attribute of the `descriptor` to something else, we might accidentally break it. Why? Because the `descriptor` doesn't handle the delete action (some of them don't need to).

This is called a non-data descriptor because it doesn't implement the __set__ magic method, as we will see in the next example.

Data descriptors

Now, let's look at the difference in using a data descriptor. For this, we are going to create another simple `descriptor` that does implement the __set__ method:

```
class DataDescriptor:

    def __get__(self, instance, owner):
        if instance is None:
            return self
        return 42

    def __set__(self, instance, value):
        logger.debug("setting %s.descriptor to %s", instance, value)
        instance.__dict__["descriptor"] = value


class ClientClass:
    descriptor = DataDescriptor()
```

Let's see what the value of the `descriptor` returns:

```
>>> client = ClientClass()
>>> client.descriptor
42
```

Now, let's try to change this value to something else, and see what it returns instead:

```
>>> client.descriptor = 99
>>> client.descriptor
42
```

The value returned by the `descriptor` didn't change. But when we assign a different value to it, it must be set to the dictionary of the object (as it was previously):

```
>>> vars(client)
{'descriptor': 99}

>>> client.__dict__["descriptor"]
99
```

So, the __set__() method was called, and indeed it did set the value to the dictionary of the object, only this time, when we request this attribute, instead of using the __dict__ attribute of the dictionary, the descriptor takes precedence (because it's an overriding descriptor).

One more thing—deleting the attribute will not work anymore:

```
>>> del client.descriptor
Traceback (most recent call last):
  ...
AttributeError: __delete__
```

The reason is as follows—given that now the descriptor always takes precedence, calling del on an object doesn't try to delete the attribute from its dictionary (__dict__), but instead it tries to call the __delete__() method of the descriptor (which is not implemented in this example, hence the attribute error).

This is the difference between data and non-data descriptors. If the descriptor implements __set__(), then it will always take precedence, no matter what attributes are present in the dictionary of the object. If this method is not implemented, then the dictionary will be looked up first, and then the descriptor will run.

An interesting observation you might have noticed is this line on the set method:

```
instance.__dict__["descriptor"] = value
```

There are a lot of things to question about that line, but let's break it down into parts.

First, why is it altering just the name of a "descriptor" attribute? This is just a simplification for this example, but, as it happens, the descriptor doesn't know at this point the name of the attribute it was assigned to, so we just used the one from the example, knowing that it was going to be "descriptor". This is a simplification to make the example use less code, but it could be easily resolved by using the __set_name__ method we studied in the previous section.

In a real example, you would do one of two things—either receive the name as a parameter and store it internally in the init method, so that this one will just use the internal attribute, or, even better, use the __set_name__ method.

Why is it accessing the __dict__ attribute of the instance directly? Another good question, which also has at least two explanations. First, you might be thinking why not just do the following?

```
setattr(instance, "descriptor", value)
```

Remember that this method (__set__) is called when we try to assign something to the attribute that is a descriptor. So, using setattr() will call this descriptor again, which, in turn, will call it again, and so on and so forth. This will end up in an infinite recursion.

 Do not use setattr() or the assignment expression directly on the descriptor inside the __set__ method because that will trigger an infinite recursion.

Why, then, is the descriptor not able to book-keep the values of the properties for all of its objects?

The client class already has a reference to the descriptor. If we add a reference from the descriptor back to the client object, we are creating circular dependencies, and these objects will never be garbage-collected. Since they are pointing at each other, their reference counts will never drop below the threshold for removal, and that will cause memory leaks in our program.

 Watch out for potential memory leaks when working with descriptors (or objects in general). Make sure you don't create circular dependencies.

A possible alternative here is to use weak references, with the weakref module, and create a weak reference key dictionary if we want to do that. This implementation is explained later on in this chapter, but for the implementations within this book, we prefer to use this idiom (and not weakref), since it is fairly common and accepted when writing descriptors.

As of now, we have studied the different kinds of descriptors, what they are, and how they work, and we even got a first idea of how we can use them to our advantage. The next section emphasizes precisely that last point: we'll see descriptors in action. From now on, we'll take a more practical approach, and see how we can use descriptors to achieve better code. After that, we'll even explore examples of good descriptors.

Descriptors in action

Now that we have seen what descriptors are, how they work, and what the main ideas behind them are, we can see them in action. In this section, we will be exploring some situations that can be elegantly addressed through descriptors.

Here, we will look at some examples of working with descriptors, and we will also cover implementation considerations for them (different ways of creating them, with their pros and cons), and finally, we will discuss what the most suitable scenarios for descriptors are.

An application of descriptors

We will start with a simple example that works but will lead to some code duplication. Later on, we will devise a way of abstracting the repeated logic into a descriptor, which will address the duplication problem, and we will observe that the code on our client classes will reduce drastically.

A first attempt without using descriptors

The problem we want to solve now is that we have a regular class with some attributes, but we wish to track all of the different values a particular attribute has over time, for example, in a list. The first solution that comes to mind is to use a property, and every time a value is changed for that attribute in the setter method of the property, we add it to an internal list that will keep this trace as we want it.

Imagine that our class represents a traveler in our application that has a current city, and we want to keep track of all the cities that user has visited throughout the running of the program. The following code is a possible implementation that addresses these requirements:

```
class Traveler:

    def __init__(self, name, current_city):
        self.name = name
        self._current_city = current_city
        self._cities_visited = [current_city]

    @property
    def current_city(self):
        return self._current_city

    @current_city.setter
```

```
    def current_city(self, new_city):
        if new_city != self._current_city:
            self._cities_visited.append(new_city)
        self._current_city = new_city


    @property
    def cities_visited(self):
        return self._cities_visited
```

We can easily check that this code works according to our requirements:

```
>>> alice = Traveler("Alice", "Barcelona")
>>> alice.current_city = "Paris"
>>> alice.current_city = "Brussels"
>>> alice.current_city = "Amsterdam"

>>> alice.cities_visited
['Barcelona', 'Paris', 'Brussels', 'Amsterdam']
```

So far, this is all we need and nothing else has to be implemented. For the purposes of this problem, the property would be more than enough. What happens if we need the exact same logic in multiple places of the application? This would mean that this is actually an instance of a more generic problem—tracing all the values of an attribute in another one. What would happen if we want to do the same with other attributes, such as keeping track of all the tickets Alice bought, or all the countries she has been to? We would have to repeat the logic in all of these places.

Moreover, what would happen if we need this same behavior in different classes? We would have to repeat the code or come up with a generic solution (maybe a decorator, a property builder, or a descriptor). Since property builders are a particular (and more convoluted) case of descriptors, they are beyond the scope of this book, and instead, descriptors are suggested as a cleaner way of proceeding.

As another solution to this problem, we can use the __setattr__ magic method that was introduced in *Chapter 2, Pythonic Code*. We have already seen solutions of this kind in the previous chapter when we discussed class decorators as an alternative to using __getattr__. The considerations of these solutions are analogous: we would need to create a new base class that implements this generic method, then define some class attributes to signal the attributes that need to be traced, and finally implement this logic in the method. This class would be a mixin that could be added to the hierarchy of the classes, but that also has the same problems that were previously discussed (a stronger coupling and potential problems with a hierarchy that is not conceptually right).

As we saw in the previous chapter, we analyzed the differences, and we saw how a class decorator was better than using this magic method in a base class; here, I also assume descriptors will provide a cleaner solution, so the magic method will be avoided, and we'll explore how to solve this problem with descriptors in the next section. That said, the reader is more than welcome to implement the solution that uses __setattr__ to compare and a similar analysis.

The idiomatic implementation

We will now look at how to address the questions of the previous section by using a descriptor that is generic enough to be applied in any class. Again, this example is not really needed because the requirements do not specify such generic behavior (we haven't even followed the rule of three instances of the similar pattern previously creating the abstraction), but it is shown with the goal of portraying descriptors in action.

Do not implement a descriptor unless there is actual evidence of the repetition we are trying to solve, and the complexity is proven to have paid off.

Now, we will create a generic descriptor that, given a name for the attribute to hold the traces of another one, will store the different values of the attribute in a list.

As we mentioned previously, the code is more than what we need for the problem, but its intention is just to show how a descriptor would help us in this case. Given the generic nature of descriptors, the reader will notice that the logic on it (the name of their method and attributes) does not relate to the domain problem at hand (a Traveler object). This is because the idea of the descriptor is to be able to use it in any type of class, probably in different projects, with the same outcomes.

In order to address this gap, some parts of the code are annotated, and the respective explanation for each section (what it does, and how it relates to the original problem) is described in the following code:

```python
class HistoryTracedAttribute:
    def __init__(self, trace_attribute_name: str) -> None:
        self.trace_attribute_name = trace_attribute_name  # [1]
        self._name = None

    def __set_name__(self, owner, name):
        self._name = name
```

```
    def __get__(self, instance, owner):
        if instance is None:
            return self
        return instance.__dict__[self._name]

    def __set__(self, instance, value):
        self._track_change_in_value_for_instance(instance, value)
        instance.__dict__[self._name] = value

    def _track_change_in_value_for_instance(self, instance, value):
        self._set_default(instance)    # [2]
        if self._needs_to_track_change(instance, value):
            instance.__dict__[self.trace_attribute_name].append(value)

    def _needs_to_track_change(self, instance, value) -> bool:
        try:
            current_value = instance.__dict__[self._name]
        except KeyError:    # [3]
            return True
        return value != current_value  # [4]

    def _set_default(self, instance):
        instance.__dict__.setdefault(self.trace_attribute_name, [])   #
[6]


class Traveler:

    current_city = HistoryTracedAttribute("cities_visited")  # [1]

    def __init__(self, name: str, current_city: str) -> None:
        self.name = name
        self.current_city = current_city  # [5]
```

The idea behind the descriptor is that it will create a new attribute that is in charge of keeping track of the changes that have been happening to some other attribute. For the purposes of this explanation, we can call them tracer and traced attributes, respectively.

Some annotations and comments on the code are as follows (the numbers in the list correspond to the number annotations in the previous listing):

1. The name of the attribute is one of the variables assigned to the descriptor, in this case, current_city (the traced attribute). We pass to the descriptor the name of the variable in which it will store the trace for the variable of the descriptor. In this example, we are telling our object to keep track of all the values that current_city has had in the attribute named cities_visited (the tracer).

2. The first time we call the descriptor, in __init__, the attribute for tracing values will not exist, in which case we initialize it to an empty list to later append values to it.

3. In the __init__ method, the name of the attribute current_city will not exist either, so we want to keep track of this change as well. This is the equivalent of initializing the list with the first value in the previous example.

4. Only track changes when the new value is different from the one that is currently set.

5. In the __init__ method, the descriptor already exists, and this assignment instruction triggers the actions from *step 2* (create the empty list to start tracking values for it), and *step 3* (append the value to this list, and set it to the key in the object for retrieval later).

6. The setdefault method in a dictionary is used to avoid a KeyError. In this case, an empty list will be returned for those attributes that aren't still available (see https://docs.python.org/3/library/stdtypes.html#dict. setdefault for reference).

It is true that the code in the descriptor is rather complex. On the other hand, the code in the client class is considerably simpler. Of course, this balance only pays off if we are going to use this descriptor multiple times, which is a concern we have already covered.

What might not be so clear at this point is that the descriptor is indeed completely independent from the client class. Nothing in it suggests anything about the business logic. That makes it perfectly suitable to apply it in any other class; even if it does something completely different, the descriptor will have the same effect.

That is the true Pythonic nature of descriptors. They are more appropriate for defining libraries, frameworks, and internal APIs, but less so for business logic.

Now that we have seen some first descriptors implemented, we can take a look at different ways of writing descriptors. So far, the examples have used a single form, but as anticipated earlier in the chapter, there are different ways in which we can implement descriptors, as we shall see.

Different forms of implementing descriptors

We have to first understand a common issue that's specific to the nature of descriptors before thinking of ways of implementing them. First, we will discuss the problem of a global shared state, and afterward, we will move on and look at different ways descriptors can be implemented while taking this into consideration.

The issue of shared state

As we have already mentioned, descriptors need to be set as class attributes in order to work. This should not be a problem most of the time, but it does come with some warnings that need to be taken into consideration.

The problem with class attributes is that they are shared across all instances of that class. Descriptors are not an exception here, so if we try to keep data in a descriptor object, keep in mind that all of them will have access to the same value.

Let's see what happens when we incorrectly define a descriptor that keeps the data itself, instead of storing it in each object:

```
class SharedDataDescriptor:
    def __init__(self, initial_value):
        self.value = initial_value

    def __get__(self, instance, owner):
        if instance is None:
            return self
        return self.value

    def __set__(self, instance, value):
        self.value = value

class ClientClass:
    descriptor = SharedDataDescriptor("first value")
```

In this example, the descriptor object stores the data itself. This carries with it the inconvenience that when we modify the value for an instance, all other instances of the same classes are also modified with this value as well. The following code listing puts that theory into action:

```
>>> client1 = ClientClass()
>>> client1.descriptor
'first value'
```

```
>>> client2 = ClientClass()
>>> client2.descriptor
'first value'

>>> client2.descriptor = "value for client 2"
>>> client2.descriptor
'value for client 2'

>>> client1.descriptor
'value for client 2'
```

Notice how we change one object, and suddenly all of them are from the same class, and we can see that this value is reflected. This is because `ClientClass.descriptor` is unique; it's the same object for all of them.

In some cases, this might be what we actually want (for instance, if we were to create a sort of Borg pattern implementation, on which we want to share state across all objects from a class), but in general, that is not the case, and we need to differentiate between objects. Such a pattern is discussed in more detail in *Chapter 9, Common Design Patterns*.

To achieve this, the descriptor needs to know the value for each `instance` and return it accordingly. That is the reason we have been operating with the dictionary (`__dict__`) of each `instance` and setting and retrieving the values from there.

This is the most common approach. We have already covered why we cannot use `getattr()` and `setattr()` on those methods, so modifying the `__dict__` attribute is the last standing option, and, in this case, is acceptable.

Accessing the dictionary of the object

The way we implement descriptors throughout this book is making the `descriptor` object store the values in the dictionary of the object, `__dict__`, and retrieve the parameters from there as well.

 Always store and return the data from the `__dict__` attribute of the instance.

All of the examples we have seen so far use this approach, but in the following section, we will take a look at some alternatives.

Using weak references

Another alternative (if we don't want to use __dict__) is to make the descriptor object keep track of the values for each instance itself, in an internal mapping, and return values from this mapping as well.

There is a caveat, though. This mapping cannot just be any dictionary. Since the client class has a reference to the descriptor, and now the descriptor will keep references to the objects that use it, this will create circular dependencies, and, as a result, these objects will never be garbage-collected because they are pointing at each other.

In order to address this, the dictionary has to be a weak key one, as defined in the weakref (WEAKREF 01) module.

In this case, the code for the descriptor might look like the following:

```python
from weakref import WeakKeyDictionary


class DescriptorClass:
    def __init__(self, initial_value):
        self.value = initial_value
        self.mapping = WeakKeyDictionary()

    def __get__(self, instance, owner):
        if instance is None:
            return self
        return self.mapping.get(instance, self.value)

    def __set__(self, instance, value):
        self.mapping[instance] = value
```

This addresses the issues, but it does come with some considerations:

- The objects no longer hold their attributes — the descriptor does instead. This is somewhat controversial, and it might not be entirely accurate from a conceptual point of view. If we forget this detail, we might ask the object, by inspecting its dictionary, to find things that just aren't there (for example, calling vars(client) will not return the complete data,).

- It poses the requirement that the objects need to be hashable. If they aren't, they can't be part of the mapping. This might be too demanding a requirement for some applications (or it might force us to implement custom __hash__ and __eq__ magic methods).

For these reasons, we prefer the implementation that has been shown so far in this book, which uses the dictionary of each instance. However, for completeness, we have shown this alternative as well.

More considerations about descriptors

Here, we will discuss general considerations about descriptors in terms of what we can do with them, when it is a good idea to use them, and also how things that we might have initially conceived as having been resolved by means of another approach can be improved through descriptors. We will then analyze the pros and cons of the original implementation versus the one after descriptors have been used.

Reusing code

Descriptors are a generic tool and a powerful abstraction that we can use to avoid code duplication.

A good scenario where descriptors might be useful is if we find ourselves in a situation where we need to write properties (as in a method decorated with @ property @<property>.setter or @<property>.deleter), but we need to do the same property logic multiple times. That is, if we needed something like a generic property, or else we'll find ourselves writing multiple properties with the same logic and repeating boilerplate. Properties are just a particular case of descriptors (the @property decorator is a descriptor that implements the full descriptor protocol to define its get, set, and delete actions), which means that we can even use descriptors to accomplish far more complex tasks.

Another powerful type we have seen for reusing code was decorators, as explained in *Chapter 5, Using Decorators to Improve Our Code*. Descriptors can help us create better decorators by making sure that they will be able to work correctly for class methods as well.

When it comes to decorators, we could say that it is safe to always implement the __get__() method on them, and also make it a descriptor. When trying to decide whether the decorator is worth creating, consider the three-problems rule we stated in *Chapter 5, Using Decorators to Improve Our Code*, but note that there are no extra considerations toward descriptors.

As for generic descriptors, besides the aforementioned three-instances rule that applies to decorators (and, in general, any reusable component), it is advisable to also keep in mind that you should use descriptors for cases where you want to define an internal API, which is some code that will have clients consuming it. This is a feature oriented more towards designing libraries and frameworks, rather than one-time solutions.

Unless there is a very good reason to, or the code will look significantly better, we should avoid putting business logic in a descriptor. Instead, the code of a descriptor will contain more implementational code rather than business code. It is more similar to defining a new data structure or object that another part of our business logic will use as a tool.

> In general, descriptors will contain implementation logic, and not so much business logic.

An alternative to class decorators

If we recall the class decorator we used in *Chapter 5, Using Decorators to Improve Our Code*, to determine how an event object is going to be serialized, we ended up with an implementation that (for Python 3.7+) relied on two class decorators:

```
@Serialization(
    username=show_original,
    password=hide_field,
    ip=show_original,
    timestamp=format_time,
)
@dataclass
class LoginEvent:
    username: str
    password: str
    ip: str
    timestamp: datetime
```

The first one takes the attributes from the annotations to declare the variables, whereas the second one defines how to treat each file. Let's see whether we can change these two decorators for descriptors instead.

The idea is to create a descriptor that will apply the transformation over the values of each attribute, returning the modified version according to our requirements (for example, hiding sensitive information, and formatting dates correctly):

```
from dataclasses import dataclass
from datetime import datetime
from functools import partial
from typing import Callable
```

```python
class BaseFieldTransformation:

    def __init__(self, transformation: Callable[[], str]) -> None:
        self._name = None
        self.transformation = transformation

    def __get__(self, instance, owner):
        if instance is None:
            return self
        raw_value = instance.__dict__[self._name]
        return self.transformation(raw_value)

    def __set_name__(self, owner, name):
        self._name = name

    def __set__(self, instance, value):
        instance.__dict__[self._name] = value


ShowOriginal = partial(BaseFieldTransformation, transformation=lambda
x: x)
HideField = partial(
    BaseFieldTransformation, transformation=lambda x: "**redacted**"
)
FormatTime = partial(
    BaseFieldTransformation,
    transformation=lambda ft: ft.strftime("%Y-%m-%d %H:%M"),
)
```

This descriptor is interesting. It was created with a function that takes one argument and returns one value. This function will be the transformation we want to apply to the field. From the base definition that defines generically how it is going to work, the rest of the descriptor classes are defined, simply by changing the particular function each one needs.

The example uses functools.partial (https://docs.python.org/3/library/functools.html#functools.partial) as a way of simulating sub-classes, by applying a partial application of the transformation function for that class, leaving a new callable that can be instantiated directly.

In order to keep the example simple, we will implement the __init__() and serialize() methods, although they could be abstracted away as well. Under these considerations, the class for the event will now be defined as follows:

```python
@dataclass
class LoginEvent:
    username: str = ShowOriginal()
    password: str = HideField()
    ip: str = ShowOriginal()
    timestamp: datetime = FormatTime()

    def serialize(self) -> dict:
        return {
            "username": self.username,
            "password": self.password,
            "ip": self.ip,
            "timestamp": self.timestamp,
        }
```

We can see how the object behaves at runtime:

```
>>> le = LoginEvent("john", "secret password", "1.1.1.1", datetime.
utcnow())
>>> vars(le)
{'username': 'john', 'password': 'secret password', 'ip': '1.1.1.1',
'timestamp': ...}
>>> le.serialize()
{'username': 'john', 'password': '**redacted**', 'ip': '1.1.1.1',
'timestamp': '...'}
>>> le.password
'**redacted**'
```

There are some differences with respect to the previous implementation that used a decorator. This example added the serialize() method and hid the fields before presenting them to its resulting dictionary, but if we asked for any of these attributes from an instance of the event in memory at any point, it would still give us the original value, without any transformation applied to it (we could have chosen to apply the transformation when setting the value, and return it directly on __get__(), as well).

Depending on the sensitivity of the application, this may or may not be acceptable, but in this case, when we ask the object for its `public` attributes, the descriptor will apply the transformation before presenting the results. It is still possible to access the original values by asking for the dictionary of the object (by accessing __dict__), but when we ask for the value, by default, it will return it converted.

In this example, all descriptors follow a common logic, which is defined in the base class. The descriptor should store the value in the object and then ask for it, applying the transformation it defines. We could create a hierarchy of classes, each one defining its own conversion function, in a way that the template method design pattern works. In this case, since the changes in the derived classes are relatively small (just one function), we opted for creating the derived classes as partial applications of the base class. Creating any new transformation field should be as simple as defining a new class that will be the base class, which is partially applied with the function we need. This can even be done ad hoc, so there might be no need to set a name for it.

Regardless of this implementation, the point is that since descriptors are objects, we can create models, and apply all rules of object-oriented programming to them. Design patterns also apply to descriptors. We could define our hierarchy, set the custom behavior, and so on. This example follows the **Open/Closed Principle (OCP)**, which we introduced in *Chapter 4, The SOLID Principles*, because adding a new type of conversion method would just be about creating a new class, derived from the base one with the function it needs, without having to modify the base class itself (to be fair, the previous implementation with decorators was also OCP-compliant, but there were no classes involved for each transformation mechanism).

Let's take an example where we create a base class that implements the __init__() and `serialize()` methods so that we can define the `LoginEvent` class simply by deriving from it, as follows:

```
class LoginEvent(BaseEvent):
    username = ShowOriginal()
    password = HideField()
    ip = ShowOriginal()
    timestamp = FormatTime()
```

Once we achieve this code, the class looks cleaner. It only defines the attributes it needs, and its logic can be quickly analyzed by looking at the class for each attribute. The base class will abstract only the common methods, and the class of each event will look simpler and more compact.

Not only do the classes for each event look simpler, but the descriptor itself is very compact and a lot simpler than the class decorators. The original implementation with class decorators was good, but descriptors made it even better.

Analysis of descriptors

We have seen how descriptors work so far and explored some interesting situations in which they contribute to clean design by simplifying their logic and leveraging more compact classes.

Up to this point, we know that by using descriptors, we can achieve cleaner code, abstracting away repeated logic and implementation details. But how do we know our implementation of the descriptors is clean and correct? What makes a good descriptor? Are we using this tool properly or over-engineering with it?

In this section, we will analyze descriptors in order to answer these questions.

How Python uses descriptors internally

What makes a good descriptor? A simple answer would be that a good descriptor is pretty much like any other good Python object. It is consistent with Python itself. The idea that follows this premise is that analyzing how Python uses descriptors will give us a good idea of good implementations so that we know what to expect from the descriptors we write.

We will see the most common scenarios where Python itself uses descriptors to solve parts of its internal logic, and we will also discover elegant descriptors and that have been there in plain sight all along.

Functions and methods

The most resonating case of an object that is a descriptor is probably a function. Functions implement the __get__ method, so they can work as methods when defined inside a class.

In Python, methods are just regular functions, only they take an extra argument. By convention, the first argument of a method is named self, and it represents an instance of the class that the method is being defined in. Then, whatever the method does with self would be the same as any other function receiving the object and applying modifications to it.

In order words, when we define something like this:

```
class MyClass:
    def method(self, ...):
        self.x = 1
```

It is actually the same as if we define this:

```
class MyClass: pass

def method(myclass_instance: MyClass, ...):
    myclass_instance.x = 1

method(MyClass())
```

So, it is just another function, modifying the object, only it's defined inside the class, and it is said to be bound to the object.

When we call something in the form of this:

```
instance = MyClass()
instance.method(...)
```

Python is, in fact, doing something equivalent to this:

```
instance = MyClass()
MyClass.method(instance, ...)
```

Note that this is just a syntax conversion that is handled internally by Python. The way this works is by means of descriptors.

Since functions implement the descriptor protocol (see the following listing) before calling the method, the __get__() method is invoked first (as we saw at the beginning of the chapter, this is part of the descriptor protocol: when the object being retrieved implements __set__, this is invoked and its result is returned instead). Then within this __get__ method, some transformations happen before running the code on the internal callable:

```
>>> def function(): pass
...
>>> function.__get__
<method-wrapper '__get__' of function object at 0x...>
```

In the `instance.method(...)` statement, before processing all the arguments of the callable inside the parentheses, the `"instance.method"` part is evaluated.

Since `method` is an object defined as a class attribute, and it has a __get__ method, this is called. What this does is convert the function into a method, which means binding the callable to the instance of the object it is going to work with.

Let's see this with an example so that we can get an idea of what Python might be doing internally.

We will define a callable object inside a class that will act as a sort of function or method that we want to define to be invoked externally. An instance of the Method class is supposed to be a function or method to be used inside a different class. This function will just print its three parameters — the instance that it received (which would be the self parameter on the class it's being defined in), and two more arguments. In the __call__() method, the self parameter does not represent an instance of MyClass, but instead an instance of Method. The parameter named instance is meant to be a MyClass type of object:

```python
class Method:
    def __init__(self, name):
        self.name = name

    def __call__(self, instance, arg1, arg2):
        print(f"{self.name}: {instance} called with {arg1} and {arg2}")

class MyClass:
    method = Method("Internal call")
```

Under these considerations and, after creating the object, the following two calls should be equivalent, based on the preceding definition:

```python
instance = MyClass()
Method("External call")(instance, "first", "second")
instance.method("first", "second")
```

However, only the first one works as expected, as the second one gives an error:

```
Traceback (most recent call last):
File "file", line , in <module>
    instance.method("first", "second")
TypeError: __call__() missing 1 required positional argument: 'arg2'
```

We are seeing the same error we faced with a decorator in *Chapter 5, Using Decorators to Improve Our Code*. The arguments are being shifted to the left by one: instance is taking the place of self, "first" is being passed in the place of instance, and "second" in the place of arg1. There is nothing to provide for arg2.

In order to fix this, we need to make `Method` a descriptor.

This way, when we call `instance.method` first, we are going to call its `__get__()`, on which we bind this callable to the object accordingly (bypassing the object as the first parameter), and then proceed:

```
from types import MethodType

class Method:
    def __init__(self, name):
        self.name = name

    def __call__(self, instance, arg1, arg2):
        print(f"{self.name}: {instance} called with {arg1} and {arg2}")

    def __get__(self, instance, owner):
        if instance is None:
            return self
        return MethodType(self, instance)
```

Now, both calls work as expected:

```
External call: <MyClass object at 0x...> called with first and second
Internal call: <MyClass object at 0x...> called with first and second
```

What we did is convert the `function` (actually the callable object we defined instead) into a method by using `MethodType` from the `types` module. The first parameter of this class should be a callable (`self`, in this case, is one by definition because it implements `__call__`), and the second one is the object to bind this function to.

Something similar to this is what function objects use in Python so they can work as methods when they are defined inside a class. In this example, the `MyClass` abstraction was trying to simulate a function object because in the actual interpreter, this is implemented in C, so it would be harder to experiment with, but with this illustration, we can get an idea of what Python is internally doing when calling methods of our objects.

Since this is a very elegant solution, it's worth exploring it to keep it in mind as a Pythonic approach when defining our own objects. For instance, if we were to define our own callable, it would be a good idea to also make it a descriptor so that we can use it in classes as class attributes as well.

Built-in decorators for methods

As you might have known from looking at the official documentation (PYDESCR-02), all @property, @classmethod, and @staticmethod decorators are descriptors.

We have mentioned several times that the idiom makes the descriptor return itself when it's being called from a class directly. Since properties are actually descriptors, that is the reason why, when we ask it from the class, we don't get the result of computing the property, but the entire property object instead:

```
>>> class MyClass:
... @property
... def prop(self): pass
...
>>> MyClass.prop
<property object at 0x...>
```

For class methods, the __get__ function in the descriptor will make sure that the class is the first parameter to be passed to the function being decorated, regardless of whether it's called from the class directly or from an instance. For static methods, it will make sure that no parameters are bound other than those defined by the function, namely undoing the binding done by __get__() on functions that make self the first parameter of that function.

Let's take an example; we create a @classproperty decorator that works like the regular @property decorator, but for classes instead. With a decorator like this one, the following code should be able to solve our use case:

```
class TableEvent:
    schema = "public"
    table = "user"

    @classproperty
    def topic(cls):
        prefix = read_prefix_from_config()
        return f"{prefix}{cls.schema}.{cls.table}"
```

```
>>> TableEvent.topic
'public.user'
>>> TableEvent().topic
'public.user'
```

The code for making this work is compact and relatively straightforward:

```
class classproperty:
    def __init__(self, fget):
        self.fget = fget

    def __get__(self, instance, owner):
        return self.fget(owner)
```

As we saw in the previous chapter, the initialization method takes the function that is going to be decorated when the decorator syntax is used. The interesting bit here is that we take advantage of the __get__ magic method to call that function with the class as a parameter when it's being called.

You can appreciate how this example is different from the general boilerplate of the __get__ method when called from a class: in these cases, most of the time, we ask if instance is None, and return self, but not here. In this case, we actually expect the instance to be None (because it's being called from a class and not an object), so we do need the owner parameter (namely the class being acted upon).

Slots

__slots__ is a class attribute to define a fixed set of fields an object of that class can have.

From the examples that have been given so far, the reader might have already noticed that in Python the internal representation for objects is done with dictionaries. This is why the attributes of an object are stored as strings in its __dict__ attribute. This is the reason why we can dynamically add new attributes to an object or remove current ones. There is no such thing as a "frozen" definition of attributes to be declared for objects. We can also inject methods dynamically (and we have done so in previous examples).

All of this changes with the __slots__ class attribute. In this attribute, we define as a string what the names of the attributes that are allowed in a class are. And from that moment on, we will not be able to dynamically add any new attributes to instances of this class. Trying to add extra attributes dynamically to a class that defines __slots__ will result in an AttributeError. By defining this attribute, the class becomes static, so it will not have a __dict__ attribute where you can add more objects dynamically.

How, then, are its attributes retrieved if not from the dictionary of the object? By using descriptors. Each name defined in a slot will have its own descriptor that will store the value for retrieval later:

```python
from dataclasses import dataclass


@dataclass
class Coordinate2D:
    __slots__ = ("lat", "long")

    lat: float
    long: float

    def __repr__(self):
        return f"{self.__class__.__name__}({self.lat}, {self.long})"
```

With the use of __slots__, Python will only reserve enough memory for the attributes defined on it on the new objects as they're created. This will make the objects not have a __dict__ attribute, so they can't be changed dynamically, and any attempt to use its dictionary (for example, by using the function vars(...)) would result in a TypeError.

And because there is no __dict__ attribute to store the values of the instance variables, what Python does instead is to create a descriptor for each slot and store the value there. This has the side effect that we cannot mix class attributes with instance ones (for example, if a common idiom for us would be to use a class attribute as a default value for an instance attribute, with this approach we would not be able to, because values would get overridden).

While this is an interesting feature, it has to be used with caution because it takes away the dynamic nature of Python. In general, this ought to be reserved only for objects that we know are static, and if we are absolutely sure we are not adding any attributes to them dynamically in other parts of the code.

As an upside of this, objects defined with slots use less memory, since they only need a fixed set of fields to hold values and not an entire dictionary.

Implementing descriptors in decorators

We now understand how Python uses descriptors in functions to make them work as methods when they are defined inside a class. We have also seen examples of cases where we can make decorators work by making them comply with the descriptor protocol by using the __get__() method of the interface to adapt the decorator to the object it is being called with. This solves the problem for our decorators in the same way that Python solves the issue of functions as methods in objects.

The general recipe for adapting a decorator in such a way is to implement the __get__() method on it and use `types.MethodType` to convert the callable (the decorator itself) into a method bound to the object it is receiving (the `instance` parameter received by __get__).

For this to work, we will have to implement the decorator as an object, because otherwise, if we are using a function, it will already have a __get__() method, which will be doing something different that will not work unless we adapt it. The cleaner way to proceed is to define a class for the decorator.

> Use a decorator class when defining a decorator that we want to apply to class methods, and implement the __get__() method on it.

Final remarks about descriptors

To wrap up our analysis on descriptors, I would like to share some thoughts in terms of clean code and good practices or recommendations from experience.

Interface of descriptors

When we revisited the interface segregation principle in *Chapter 4, The SOLID Principles* (the "I" in SOLID), we said that it's good practice to keep the interfaces small, and for that reason, we might want to separate them into smaller ones.

This idea appears here once again, not in the sense of an interface as in an abstract base class, but as the interface that the descriptor itself will present.

As already mentioned, the descriptor protocol entails four methods, but partial implementation is allowed. That means you don't need to implement all of them all the time. In fact, if you only implement the minimal required methods, that would be better.

Most of the time, you'll find that you can address your requirements by only implementing the __get__ method.

 Do not implement more methods than are necessary. The fewer methods you can implement of the descriptor protocol, the better.

Moreover, you'll find that the __delete__ method is seldom required.

Object-oriented design of the descriptors

With this concept, I don't mean that we can improve our object-oriented design capabilities by merely using descriptors (we have already covered that). But since descriptors are just regular objects, the rules of object-oriented design apply to them as well. For example, we can have base classes of descriptors, make use of inheritance to create more specific ones, etc.

Keep in mind that all the rules and recommendations of good practices apply as well. For example, if you have a base class for a descriptor that only implements the __get__ method, then it wouldn't be a good idea to create a sub-class of it that also implements the __set__ method, as it wouldn't comply with Liskov's substitution principle (because we'd have a more specific type that implements an enhanced interface that the parent doesn't provide).

Type annotations on descriptors

Applying type annotations on descriptors might be complicated most of the time.

There could be issues with circular dependencies (meaning the Python file that contains the definition for the descriptor will have to read from the file of the consumer in order to get the types, but then the client needs to read the file with the definition of the descriptor object to use it). Even if you surmount these issues with the use of strings instead of the actual types, there's another problem.

If you know the exact type to annotate the descriptor methods, that means the descriptor is probably only useful for one type of class. And that generally defeats the purpose of a descriptor: the recommendation of this book is to use descriptors for scenarios in which we know we can benefit from a generalization, and reuse a lot of code. If we're not reusing code, the complexity of having descriptors is not worth it.

For this reason, and even though it is generally good practice to always add annotations to our definitions, for the case of descriptors, it might be simpler just not to. Instead, think of it as a good opportunity for writing useful docstrings that accurately document the behavior of the descriptor.

Summary

Descriptors are a more advanced feature in Python that push the boundaries closer to metaprogramming. One of their most interesting aspects is how they make crystal clear that classes in Python are just regular objects, and, as such, they have properties that we can interact with. Descriptors are, in this sense, the most interesting type of attribute a class can have because their protocol facilitates more advanced, object-oriented possibilities.

We have seen the mechanics of descriptors, their methods, and how all of this fits together, making a more interesting picture of object-oriented software design. By understanding descriptors, we were able to create powerful abstractions that yield clean and compact classes. We have seen how to fix decorators that we want to apply to functions and methods, and we have understood a lot more about how Python works internally, and how descriptors play such a core and critical role in the implementation of the language.

This study of how descriptors are used internally in Python should work as a reference to identify good uses of descriptors in our own code, with the goal of achieving idiomatic solutions.

Despite all of the powerful options that descriptors represent to our advantage, we have to keep in mind when to properly make use of them without over-engineering. In this line, we have suggested that we should reserve the functionality of descriptors for truly generic cases, such as the design of internal development APIs, libraries, or frameworks. Another important consideration along these lines is that, in general, we should not place business logic in descriptors, but rather logic that implements technical functionality to be used by other components that do contain business logic.

Speaking of advanced functionality, the next chapter also covers an interesting and in-depth topic: generators. On the surface, generators are rather simple (and most readers are probably already familiar with them), but what they have in common with descriptors is that they can also be complex, yield a more advanced and elegant design, and make Python a unique language to work with.

References

Here is a list of a few things you can reference for more information:

- Python's official documentation on descriptors: `https://docs.python.org/3/reference/datamodel.html#implementing-descriptors`
- *WEAKREF 01: Python's weakref module* (`https://docs.python.org/3/library/weakref.html`)
- *PYDESCR-02: Built-in decorators as descriptors* (`https://docs.python.org/3/howto/descriptor.html#static-methods-and-class-methods`)

7
Generators, Iterators, and Asynchronous Programming

Generators are another one of those features that makes Python a peculiar language over more traditional ones. In this chapter, we will explore their rationale, why they were introduced in the language, and the problems they solve. We will also cover how to address problems idiomatically by using generators, and how to make our generators (or any iterable, for that matter) Pythonic.

We will understand why iteration (in the form of the iterator pattern) is automatically supported in the language. From there, we will take another journey and explore how generators became such a fundamental feature of Python in order to support other functionality, such as coroutines and asynchronous programming.

The goals of this chapter are as follows:

- To create generators that improve the performance of our programs
- To study how iterators (and the iterator pattern, in particular) are deeply embedded in Python
- To solve problems that involve iteration idiomatically
- To understand how generators work as the basis for coroutines and asynchronous programming
- To explore the syntactic support for coroutines—`yield from`, `await`, and `async def`

Mastering generators will take you a long way in writing idiomatic Python, hence the importance of them for this book. In this chapter, we not only study how to use generators, but we also explore their internals, in order to deeply understand how they work.

Technical requirements

The examples in this chapter will work with any version of Python 3.9 on any platform.

The code used in this chapter can be found at `https://github.com/PacktPublishing/Clean-Code-in-Python-Second-Edition`. The instructions are available in the `README` file.

Creating generators

Generators were introduced in Python a long time ago (PEP-255), with the idea of introducing iteration in Python while improving the performance of the program (by using less memory) at the same time.

The idea of a generator is to create an object that is iterable, and, while it's being iterated, will produce the elements it contains, one at a time. The main use of generators is to save memory—instead of having a very large list of elements in memory, holding everything at once, we have an object that knows how to produce each particular element, one at a time, as it is required.

This feature enables lazy computations of heavyweight objects in memory, in a similar manner to what other functional programming languages (Haskell, for instance) provide. It would even be possible to work with infinite sequences because the lazy nature of generators enables such an option.

A first look at generators

Let's start with an example. The problem at hand now is that we want to process a large list of records and get some metrics and indicators over them. Given a large dataset with information about purchases, we want to process it in order to get the lowest sale, the highest sale, and the average price of a sale.

For the simplicity of this example, we will assume a CSV with only two fields, in the following format:

```
<purchase_date>, <price>
...
```

We are going to create an object that receives all the purchases, and this will give us the necessary metrics. We could get some of these values out of the box by simply using the min() and max() built-in functions, but that would require iterating all of the purchases more than once, so instead, we are using our custom object, which will get these values in a single iteration.

The code that will get the numbers for us looks rather simple. It's just an object with a method that will process all the prices in one go, and, at each step, will update the value of each particular metric we are interested in. First, we will show the first implementation in the following listing, and, later on in this chapter (once we have seen more about iteration), we will revisit this implementation and get a much better (and more compact) version of it. For now, we are settling with the following:

```python
class PurchasesStats:
    def __init__(self, purchases):
        self.purchases = iter(purchases)
        self.min_price: float = None
        self.max_price: float = None
        self._total_purchases_price: float = 0.0
        self._total_purchases = 0
        self._initialize()
    def _initialize(self):
        try:
            first_value = next(self.purchases)
        except StopIteration:
            raise ValueError("no values provided")

        self.min_price = self.max_price = first_value
        self._update_avg(first_value)

    def process(self):
        for purchase_value in self.purchases:
            self._update_min(purchase_value)
            self._update_max(purchase_value)
            self._update_avg(purchase_value)
        return self

    def _update_min(self, new_value: float):
        if new_value < self.min_price:
            self.min_price = new_value

    def _update_max(self, new_value: float):
        if new_value > self.max_price:
```

```
            self.max_price = new_value

    @property
    def avg_price(self):
        return self._total_purchases_price / self._total_purchases

    def _update_avg(self, new_value: float):
        self._total_purchases_price += new_value
        self._total_purchases += 1

    def __str__(self):
        return (
            f"{self.__class__.__name__}({self.min_price}, "
            f"{self.max_price}, {self.avg_price})"
        )
```

This object will receive all the totals for purchases and process the required values. Now, we need a function that loads these numbers into something that this object can process. Here is the first version:

```
def _load_purchases(filename):
    purchases = []
    with open(filename) as f:
        for line in f:
            *_, price_raw = line.partition(",")
            purchases.append(float(price_raw))

    return purchases
```

This code works; it loads all the numbers of the file into a list that, when passed to our custom object, will produce the numbers we want. It has a performance issue, though. If you run it with a rather large dataset, it will take a while to complete, and it might even fail if the dataset is large enough to not fit into the main memory.

If we take a look at our code that consumes this data, it is processing purchases, one at a time, so we might be wondering why our producer fits everything in memory at once. It is creating a list where it puts all of the content of the file, but we know we can do better.

The solution is to create a generator. Instead of loading the entire content of the file in a list, we will produce the results one at a time. The code will now look like this:

```
def load_purchases(filename):
    with open(filename) as f:
        for line in f:
            *_, price_raw = line.partition(",")
            yield float(price_raw)
```

If you measure the process this time, you will notice that the usage of memory has dropped significantly. We can also see how the code looks simpler — there is no need to define the list (therefore, there is no need to append to it), and the return statement has also disappeared.

In this case, the `load_purchases` function is a generator function, or simply a generator.

In Python, the mere presence of the keyword `yield` in any function makes it a generator, and, as a result, when calling it, nothing other than creating an instance of the generator will happen:

```
>>> load_purchases("file")
<generator object load_purchases at 0x...>
```

A generator object is an iterable (we will revisit iterables in more detail later on), which means that it can work with `for` loops. Note how we did not have to change anything on the consumer code — our statistics processor remained the same, with the `for` loop unmodified, after the new implementation.

Working with iterables allows us to create these kinds of powerful abstractions that are polymorphic with respect to `for` loops. As long as we keep the iterable interface, we can iterate over that object transparently.

What we're exploring in this chapter is another case of idiomatic code that blends well with Python itself. In previous chapters, we have seen how we can implement our own context managers to connect our objects into with statements, or how can we create custom container objects to leverage the `in` operator, or booleans for the `if` statement, and so on. Now it's the turn of the `for` operator, and for that, we'll create iterators.

Before going into the details and nuances of generators, we can take a quick look at how generators relate to a concept that we have already seen: comprehensions. A generator in the form of a comprehension is called a generator expression, and we'll discuss it briefly in the next section.

Generator expressions

Generators save a lot of memory, and since they are iterators, they are a convenient alternative to other iterables or containers that require more space in memory such as lists, tuples, or sets.

Much like these data structures, they can also be defined by comprehension, only that they are called a generator expression (there is an ongoing argument about whether they should be called generator comprehensions. In this book, we will just refer to them by their canonical name, but feel free to use whichever you prefer).

In the same way, we would define a list comprehension. If we replace the square brackets with parentheses, we get a generator that results from the expression. Generator expressions can also be passed directly to functions that work with iterables, such as `sum()` and `max()`:

```
>>> [x**2 for x in range(10)]
[0, 1, 4, 9, 16, 25, 36, 49, 64, 81]

>>> (x**2 for x in range(10))
<generator object <genexpr> at 0x...>

>>> sum(x**2 for x in range(10))
285
```

 Always pass a generator expression, instead of a list comprehension, to functions that expect iterables, such as `min()`, `max()`, and `sum()`. This is more efficient and Pythonic.

What the previous recommendation means is to try to avoid passing lists to functions that already work with generators. The example in the next code is something you would want to avoid, and favor the approach from the previous listing:

```
>>> sum([x**2 for x in range(10)])  # here the list can be avoided
```

And, of course, you can assign a generator expression to a variable and use it somewhere else (as with comprehensions). Keep in mind that there is an important distinction in this case, because we're talking about generators here. A list can be reused and iterated multiple times, but a generator will be exhausted after it has been iterated over. For this reason, make sure the result of the expression is consumed only once, or you'll get unexpected results.

Remember that generators are exhausted after they're iterated over, because they don't hold all the data in memory.

A common approach is to create new generator expressions in the code. This way, the first one will be exhausted after is iterated, but then a new one is created. Chaining generator expressions this way is useful and helps to save memory as well as to make the code more expressive because it's resolving different iterations in different steps. One scenario where this is useful is when you need to apply multiple filters on an iterable; you can achieve this by using multiple generator expressions that act as chained filters.

Now that we have a new tool in our toolbox (iterators), let's see how we can use it to write more idiomatic code.

Iterating idiomatically

In this section, we will first explore some idioms that come in handy when we have to deal with iteration in Python. These code recipes will help us get a better idea of the types of things we can do with generators (especially after we have already seen generator expressions), and how to solve typical problems in relation to them.

Once we have seen some idioms, we will move on to exploring iteration in Python in more depth, analyzing the methods that make iteration possible, and how iterable objects work.

Idioms for iteration

We are already familiar with the built-in enumerate() function that, given an iterable, will return another one on which the element is a tuple, whose first element is the index of the second one (corresponding to the element in the original iterable):

```
>>> list(enumerate("abcdef"))
[(0, 'a'), (1, 'b'), (2, 'c'), (3, 'd'), (4, 'e'), (5, 'f')]
```

We wish to create a similar object, but in a more low-level fashion; one that can simply create an infinite sequence. We want an object that can produce a sequence of numbers, from a starting one, without any limits.

An object as simple as the following one can do the trick. Every time we call this object, we get the next number of the sequence ad infinitum:

```python
class NumberSequence:

    def __init__(self, start=0):
        self.current = start

    def next(self):
        current = self.current
        self.current += 1
        return current
```

Based on this interface, we would have to use this object by explicitly invoking its next() method:

```python
>>> seq = NumberSequence()
>>> seq.next()
0
>>> seq.next()
1

>>> seq2 = NumberSequence(10)
>>> seq2.next()
10
>>> seq2.next()
11
```

But with this code, we cannot reconstruct the enumerate() function as we would like to, because its interface does not support being iterated over a regular Python for loop, which also means that we cannot pass it as a parameter to functions that expect something to iterate over. Notice how the following code fails:

```python
>>> list(zip(NumberSequence(), "abcdef"))
Traceback (most recent call last):
  File "...", line 1, in <module>
TypeError: zip argument #1 must support iteration
```

The problem lies in the fact that NumberSequence does not support iteration. To fix this, we have to make the object an iterable by implementing the magic method __iter__(). We have also changed the previous next() method, by using the __next__ magic method, which makes the object an iterator:

```python
class SequenceOfNumbers:
```

```
    def __init__(self, start=0):
        self.current = start

    def __next__(self):
        current = self.current
        self.current += 1
        return current

    def __iter__(self):
        return self
```

This has an advantage—not only can we iterate over the element, but we also don't even need the .next() method anymore because having __next__() allows us to use the next() built-in function:

```
>>> list(zip(SequenceOfNumbers(), "abcdef"))
[(0, 'a'), (1, 'b'), (2, 'c'), (3, 'd'), (4, 'e'), (5, 'f')]
>>> seq = SequenceOfNumbers(100)
>>> next(seq)
100
>>> next(seq)
101
```

This makes use of the iteration protocol. Similar to the context manager protocol we have explored in previous chapters, which consists of the __enter__ and __exit__ methods, this protocol relies on the __iter__ and __next__ methods.

Having these protocols in Python has an advantage: everyone that knows Python will be familiar with this interface already, so there's a sort of "standard contract." This means, instead of having to define your own methods and agree with the team (or any potential reader of the code), that this is the expected standard or protocol your code works with (as with our custom next() method in the first example); Python already provides an interface and has a protocol already. We only have to implement it properly.

The next() function

The next() built-in function will advance the iterable to its next element and return it:

```
>>> word = iter("hello")
>>> next(word)
```

```
'h'
>>> next(word)
'e'   # ...
```

If the iterator does not have more elements to produce, the `StopIteration` exception is raised:

```
>>> ...
>>> next(word)
'o'
>>> next(word)
Traceback (most recent call last):
  File "<stdin>", line 1, in <module>
StopIteration
>>>
```

This exception signals that the iteration is over and that there are no more elements to consume.

If we wish to handle this case, besides catching the `StopIteration` exception, we could provide this function with a default value in its second parameter. Should this be provided, it will be the return value in lieu of throwing `StopIteration`:

```
>>> next(word, "default value")
'default value'
```

It is advisable to use the default value most of the time, to avoid having exceptions at runtime in our programs. If we are absolutely sure that the iterator we're dealing with cannot be empty, it's still better to be implicit (and intentional) about it, and not rely on side effects of built-in functions (that is, to properly assert the case).

The `next()` function can be quite useful in combination with generator expressions, in situations where we want to look for the first elements of an iterable that meets certain criteria. We'll see examples of this idiom throughout the chapter, but the main idea is to use this function instead of creating a list comprehension and then taking its first element.

Using a generator

The previous code can be simplified significantly by simply using a generator. Generator objects are iterators. This way, instead of creating a class, we can define a function that yields the values as needed:

```
def sequence(start=0):
```

```
    while True:
        yield start
        start += 1
```

Remember that from our first definition, the `yield` keyword in the body of the function makes it a generator. Because it is a generator, it's perfectly fine to create an infinite loop like this, because, when this generator function is called, it will run all the code until the next `yield` statement is reached. It will produce its value and suspend there:

```
>>> seq = sequence(10)
>>> next(seq)
10
>>> next(seq)
11

>>> list(zip(sequence(), "abcdef"))
[(0, 'a'), (1, 'b'), (2, 'c'), (3, 'd'), (4, 'e'), (5, 'f')]
```

This difference can be thought of as an analogy of the different ways there are to create a decorator, as we explored in the previous chapter (with an object of functions). Here as well, we can use a generator function, or an iterable object, as in the previous section. Whenever is possible, constructing a generator is recommended, because it's syntactically simpler, and therefore easier to understand.

Itertools

Working with iterable objects has the advantage that the code blends better with Python itself because iteration is a key component of the language. Besides that, we can take full advantage of the `itertools` module (ITER-01). Actually, the `sequence()` generator we just created is fairly similar to `itertools.count()`. However, there is more we can do.

One of the nicest things about iterators, generators, and itertools is that they are composable objects that can be chained together.

For instance, going back to our first example that processed `purchases` in order to get some metrics, what if we want to do the same, but only for those values over a certain threshold? The naïve approach to solving this problem would be to place the condition while iterating:

```
# ...
    def process(self):
        for purchase in self.purchases:
```

```
        if purchase > 1000.0:
            ...
```

This is not only non-Pythonic, but it's also rigid (and rigidity is a trait that denotes bad code). It doesn't handle changes very well. What if the number changes now? Do we pass it by parameter? What if we need more than one? What if the condition is different (less than, for instance)? Do we pass a lambda?

These questions should not be answered by this object, whose sole responsibility is to compute a set of well-defined metrics over a stream of purchases represented as numbers. And, of course, the answer is no. It would be a huge mistake to make such a change (once again, clean code is flexible, and we don't want to make it rigid by coupling this object to external factors). These requirements will have to be addressed elsewhere.

It's better to keep this object independent of its clients. The less responsibility this class has, the more useful it will be for more clients, hence enhancing its chances of being reused.

Instead of changing this code, we're going to keep it as it is and assume that the new data is filtered according to whatever requirements each customer of the class has.

For instance, if we wanted to process only the first 10 purchases that amount to more than 1000, we would do the following:

```
>>> from itertools import islice
>>> purchases = islice(filter(lambda p: p > 1000.0, purchases), 10)
>>> stats = PurchasesStats(purchases).process()  # ...
```

There is no memory penalization for filtering this way because since they are all generators, the evaluation is always lazy. This gives us the power of thinking as if we had filtered the entire set at once and then passed it to the object, but without actually fitting everything in memory.

Keep in mind the trade-off mentioned at the beginning of the chapter, between memory and CPU usage. While the code might use less memory, it could take up more CPU time, but most of the times, this is acceptable, when we have to process lots of objects in memory while keeping the code maintainable.

Simplifying code through iterators

Now, we will briefly discuss some situations that can be improved with the help of iterators, and occasionally the itertools module. After discussing each case, and its proposed optimization, we will close each point with a corollary.

Repeated iterations

Now that we have seen more about iterators, and introduced the `itertools` module, we can show you how one of the first examples of this chapter (the one for computing statistics about some purchases) can be dramatically simplified:

```
def process_purchases(purchases):
    min_, max_, avg = itertools.tee(purchases, 3)
    return min(min_), max(max_), median(avg)
```

In this example, `itertools.tee` will split the original iterable into three new ones. We will use each of these for the different kinds of iterations that we require, without needing to repeat three different loops over `purchases`.

The reader can simply verify that if we pass an iterable object as the `purchases` parameter, this one is traversed only once (thanks to the `itertools.tee` function [TEE]), which was our main requirement. It is also possible to verify how this version is equivalent to our original implementation. In this case, there is no need to manually raise `ValueError` because passing an empty sequence to the `min()` function will do this.

 If you are thinking about running a loop over the same object more than once, stop and think if `itertools.tee` can be of any help.

The `itertools` module contains many useful functions and nice abstractions that come in handy when dealing with iterations in Python. It also contains good recipes about how to solve typical iteration problems in an idiomatic fashion. As general advice, if you're thinking about how to solve a particular problem that involves iteration, go and take a look at this module. Even if the answer isn't literally there, it'll be good inspiration.

Nested loops

In some situations, we need to iterate over more than one dimension, looking for a value, and nested loops come as the first idea. When the value is found, we need to stop iterating, but the `break` keyword doesn't work entirely because we have to escape from two (or more) `for` loops, not just one.

What would be the solution to this? A flag signaling escape? No. Raising an exception? No, this would be the same as the flag, but even worse because we know that exceptions are not to be used for control flow logic. Moving the code to a smaller function and returning it? Close, but not quite.

The answer is, whenever possible, flatten the iteration to a single for loop.

This is the kind of code we would like to avoid:

```python
def search_nested_bad(array, desired_value):
    coords = None
    for i, row in enumerate(array):
        for j, cell in enumerate(row):
            if cell == desired_value:
                coords = (i, j)
                break

        if coords is not None:
            break

    if coords is None:
        raise ValueError(f"{desired_value} not found")

    logger.info("value %r found at [%i, %i]", desired_value, *coords)
    return coords
```

And here is a simplified version of it that does not rely on flags to signal termination, and has a simpler, more compact structure of iteration:

```python
def _iterate_array2d(array2d):
    for i, row in enumerate(array2d):
        for j, cell in enumerate(row):
            yield (i, j), cell

def search_nested(array, desired_value):
    try:
        coord = next(
            coord
            for (coord, cell) in _iterate_array2d(array)
            if cell == desired_value
        )
    except StopIteration as e:
        raise ValueError(f"{desired_value} not found") from e

    logger.info("value %r found at [%i, %i]", desired_value, *coord)
    return coord
```

It's worth mentioning how the auxiliary generator that was created works as an abstraction for the iteration that's required. In this case, we just need to iterate over two dimensions, but if we needed more, a different object could handle this without the client needing to know about it. This is the essence of the iterator design pattern, which, in Python, is transparent, since it supports iterator objects automatically, which is the topic covered in the next section.

 Try to simplify the iteration as much as possible with as many abstractions as are required, flattening the loops wherever possible.

Hopefully, this example serves as inspiration to you to get the idea that we can use generators for something more than just saving memory. We can take advantage of the iteration as an abstraction. That is, we can create abstractions not only by defining classes or functions but also by taking advantage of the syntax of Python. In the same way that we have seen how to abstract away some logic behind a context manager (so we don't know the details of what happens under the `with` statement), we can do the same with iterators (so we can forget the underlying logic of a `for` loop).

That's why we will start exploring how the iterator pattern works in Python, starting with the next section.

The iterator pattern in Python

Here, we will take a small detour from generators to understand iteration in Python more deeply. Generators are a particular case of iterable objects, but iteration in Python goes beyond generators, and being able to create good iterable objects will give us the chance to create more efficient, compact, and readable code.

In the previous code listings, we have been seeing examples of `iterable` objects that are also iterators, because they implement both the `__iter__()` and `__next__()` magic methods. While this is fine in general, it's not strictly required that they always have to implement both methods, and here we'll show the subtle differences between an `iterable` object (one that implements `__iter__`) and an iterator (that implements `__next__`).

We also explore other topics related to iterations, such as sequences and container objects.

The interface for iteration

An `iterable` is an object that supports iteration, which, at a very high level, means that we can run a for .. in ... loop over it, and it will work without any issues. However, `iterable` does not mean the same as iterator.

Generally speaking, an `iterable` is just something we can iterate, and it uses an iterator to do so. This means that in the __iter__ magic method, we would like to return an iterator, namely, an object with a __next__() method implemented.

An iterator is an object that only knows how to produce a series of values, one at a time, when it's being called by the already explored built-in next() function, while the iterator is not called, it's simply frozen, sitting idly by until it's called again for the next value to produce. In this sense, generators are iterators.

Python concept	Magic method	Considerations
Iterable	__iter__	They work with an iterator to construct the iteration logic. These objects can be iterated in a for ... in ...: loop.
Iterator	__next__	Define the logic for producing values one at a time. The StopIteration exception signals that the iteration is over. The values can be obtained one by one via the built-in next() function.

Table 7.1: Iterables and iterators

In the following code, we will see an example of an iterator object that is not iterable — it only supports invoking its values, one at a time. Here, the name sequence refers just to a series of consecutive numbers, not to the sequence concept in Python, which we will explore later on:

```python
class SequenceIterator:
    def __init__(self, start=0, step=1):
        self.current = start
        self.step = step

    def __next__(self):
        value = self.current
        self.current += self.step
        return value
```

Notice that we can get the values of the sequence one at a time, but we can't iterate over this object (this is fortunate because it would otherwise result in an endless loop):

```
>>> si = SequenceIterator(1, 2)
>>> next(si)
1
>>> next(si)
3
>>> next(si)
5
>>> for _ in SequenceIterator(): pass
...
Traceback (most recent call last):
  ...
TypeError: 'SequenceIterator' object is not iterable
```

The error message is clear, as the object doesn't implement __iter__().

Just for explanatory purposes, we can separate the iteration in another object (again, it would be enough to make the object implement both __iter__ and __next__, but doing so separately will help clarify the distinctive point we're trying to make in this explanation).

Sequence objects as iterables

As we have just seen, if an object implements the __iter__() magic method, it means it can be used in a for loop. While this is a great feature, it's not the only possible form of iteration we can achieve. When we write a for loop, Python will try to see if the object we're using implements __iter__, and if it does, it will use that to construct the iteration, but if it doesn't, there are fallback options.

If the object happens to be a sequence (meaning that it implements the __getitem__() and __len__() magic methods), it can also be iterated. If that is the case, the interpreter will then provide values in sequence, until the IndexError exception is raised, which, analogous to the aforementioned StopIteration, also signals the stop for the iteration.

With the sole purpose of illustrating such a behavior, we will run the following experiment that shows a sequence object that implements map() over a range of numbers:

```
# generators_iteration_2.py
```

```python
class MappedRange:
    """Apply a transformation to a range of numbers."""

    def __init__(self, transformation, start, end):
        self._transformation = transformation
        self._wrapped = range(start, end)

    def __getitem__(self, index):
        value = self._wrapped.__getitem__(index)
        result = self._transformation(value)
        logger.info("Index %d: %s", index, result)
        return result

    def __len__(self):
        return len(self._wrapped)
```

Keep in mind that this example is only designed to illustrate that an object such as this one can be iterated with a regular for loop. There is a logging line placed in the __getitem__ method to explore what values are passed while the object is being iterated, as we can see from the following test:

```
>>> mr = MappedRange(abs, -10, 5)
>>> mr[0]
Index 0: 10
10
>>> mr[-1]
Index -1: 4
4
>>> list(mr)
Index 0: 10
Index 1: 9
Index 2: 8
Index 3: 7
Index 4: 6
Index 5: 5
Index 6: 4
Index 7: 3
Index 8: 2
Index 9: 1
Index 10: 0
Index 11: 1
Index 12: 2
```

```
Index 13: 3
Index 14: 4
[10, 9, 8, 7, 6, 5, 4, 3, 2, 1, 0, 1, 2, 3, 4]
```

As a word of caution, it's important to highlight that while it is useful to know this, it's also a fallback mechanism for when the object doesn't implement __iter__, so most of the time we'll want to resort to these methods by thinking about creating proper sequences, and not just objects we want to iterate over.

> When thinking about designing an object for iteration, favor a proper iterable object (with __iter__), rather than a sequence that can coincidentally also be iterated.

Iterables are an important part of Python, not only because of the capabilities they offer to us as software engineers, but also because they play a fundamental role in the internals of Python.

We have seen in *A brief introduction to asynchronous code* in *Chapter 2, Pythonic Code*, how to read asynchronous code. Now that we have also explored iterators in Python, we can see how these two concepts are related. In particular, the next section explores coroutines, and we'll see how iterators are at the core of them.

Coroutines

The idea of a coroutine is to have a function, whose execution can be suspended at a given point in time, to be later resumed. By having this kind of functionality, a program might be able to suspend a part of the code, in order to dispatch something else for processing, and then come back to this original point to resume.

As we already know, generator objects are iterables. They implement __iter__() and __next__(). This is provided by Python automatically so that when we create a generator object function, we get an object that can be iterated or advanced through the next() function.

Besides this basic functionality, they have more methods so that they can work as coroutines (PEP-342). Here, we will explore how generators evolved into coroutines to support the basis of asynchronous programming before we go into more detail in the next section, where we will explore the new features of Python and the syntax that covers programming asynchronously.

The basic methods added in PEP-342 to support coroutines are as follows:

- `.close()`
- `.throw(ex_type[, ex_value[, ex_traceback]])`
- `.send(value)`

Python takes advantage of generators in order to create coroutines. Because generators can naturally suspend, they're a convenient starting point. But generators weren't enough as they were originally thought to be, so these methods were added. This is because typically, it's not enough to just be able to suspend some part of the code; you'd also want to communicate with it (pass data, and signal about changes in the context).

By exploring each method in more detail, we'll be able to learn more about the internals of coroutines in Python. After this, I'll present another recapitulation of how asynchronous programming works, but unlike the one presented in *Chapter 2, Pythonic Code*, this one will relate to the internal concepts we just learned.

The methods of the generator interface

In this section, we will explore what each of the aforementioned methods does, how it works, and how it is expected to be used. By understanding how to use these methods, we will be able to make use of simple coroutines.

Later on, we will explore more advanced uses of coroutines, and how to delegate to sub-generators (coroutines) in order to refactor code, and how to orchestrate different coroutines.

close()

When calling this method, the generator will receive the `GeneratorExit` exception. If it's not handled, then the generator will finish without producing any more values, and its iteration will stop.

This exception can be used to handle a finishing status. In general, if our coroutine does some sort of resource management, we want to catch this exception and use that control block to release all resources being held by the coroutine. It is similar to using a context manager or placing the code in the `finally` block of an exception control, but handling this exception specifically makes it more explicit.

In the following example, we have a coroutine that makes use of a database handler object that holds a connection to a database, and runs queries over it, streaming data by pages of a fixed length (instead of reading everything that is available at once):

```
def stream_db_records(db_handler):
    try:
        while True:
            yield db_handler.read_n_records(10)
    except GeneratorExit:
        db_handler.close()
```

At each call to the generator, it will return 10 rows obtained from the database handler, but when we decide to explicitly finish the iteration and call `close()`, we also want to close the connection to the database:

```
>>> streamer = stream_db_records(DBHandler("testdb"))
>>> next(streamer)
[(0, 'row 0'), (1, 'row 1'), (2, 'row 2'), (3, 'row 3'), ...]
>>> next(streamer)
[(0, 'row 0'), (1, 'row 1'), (2, 'row 2'), (3, 'row 3'), ...]
>>> streamer.close()
INFO:...:closing connection to database 'testdb'
```

 Use the `close()` method on generators to perform finishing-up tasks when needed.

This method is intended to be used for resource cleanup, so you'd typically use it for manually freeing resources when you couldn't do this automatically (for example, if you didn't use a context manager). Next, we'll see how to pass exceptions to the generator.

throw(ex_type[, ex_value[, ex_traceback]])

This method will `throw` the exception at the line where the generator is currently suspended. If the generator handles the exception that was sent, the code in that particular except clause will be called; otherwise, the exception will propagate to the caller.

Here, we are modifying the previous example slightly to show the difference when we use this method for an exception that is handled by the coroutine, and when it's not:

```
class CustomException(Exception):
    """A type of exception that is under control."""
```

```
def stream_data(db_handler):
    while True:
        try:
            yield db_handler.read_n_records(10)
        except CustomException as e:
            logger.info("controlled error %r, continuing", e)
        except Exception as e:
            logger.info("unhandled error %r, stopping", e)
            db_handler.close()
            break
```

Now, it is a part of the control flow to receive a CustomException, and, in such a case, the generator will log an informative message (of course, we can adapt this according to our business logic on each case), and move on to the next yield statement, which is the line where the coroutine reads from the database and returns that data.

This particular example handles all exceptions, but if the last block (except Exception:) wasn't there, the result would be that the generator is raised at the line where the generator is paused (again, yield), and it will propagate from there to the caller:

```
>>> streamer = stream_data(DBHandler("testdb"))
>>> next(streamer)
[(0, 'row 0'), (1, 'row 1'), (2, 'row 2'), (3, 'row 3'), (4, 'row 4'),
...]
>>> next(streamer)
[(0, 'row 0'), (1, 'row 1'), (2, 'row 2'), (3, 'row 3'), (4, 'row 4'),
...]
>>> streamer.throw(CustomException)
WARNING:controlled error CustomException(), continuing
[(0, 'row 0'), (1, 'row 1'), (2, 'row 2'), (3, 'row 3'), (4, 'row 4'),
...]
>>> streamer.throw(RuntimeError)
ERROR:unhandled error RuntimeError(), stopping
INFO:closing connection to database 'testdb'
Traceback (most recent call last):
  ...
StopIteration
```

When our exception from the domain was received, the generator continued. However, when it received another exception that was not expected, the default block caught where we closed the connection to the database and finished the iteration, which resulted in the generator being stopped. As we can see from the `StopIteration` that was raised, this generator can't be iterated further.

send(value)

In the previous example, we created a simple generator that reads rows from a database, and when we wished to finish its iteration, this generator released the resources linked to the database. This is a good example of using one of the methods that generators provide (`close()`), but there is more we can do.

An obvservation of the generator is that it was reading a fixed number of rows from the database.

We would like to parametrize that number (10) so that we can change it throughout different calls. Unfortunately, the `next()` function does not provide us with options for that. But luckily, we have `send()`:

```
def stream_db_records(db_handler):
    retrieved_data = None
    previous_page_size = 10
    try:
        while True:
            page_size = yield retrieved_data
            if page_size is None:
                page_size = previous_page_size

            previous_page_size = page_size

            retrieved_data = db_handler.read_n_records(page_size)
    except GeneratorExit:
        db_handler.close()
```

The idea is that we have now made the coroutine able to receive values from the caller by means of the `send()` method. This method is the one that actually distinguishes a generator from a coroutine because when it's used, it means that the `yield` keyword will appear on the right-hand side of the statement, and its return value will be assigned to something else.

In coroutines, we generally find the `yield` keyword to be used in the following form:

```
receive = yield produced
```

`yield`, in this case, will do two things. It will send `produced` back to the caller, which will pick it up on the next round of iteration (after calling `next()`, for example), and it will suspend there. At a later point, the caller will want to send a value back to the coroutine by using the `send()` method. This value will become the result of the `yield` statement, assigned in this case to the variable named `receive`.

Sending values to the coroutine only works when this one is suspended at a `yield` statement, waiting for something to produce. For this to happen, the coroutine will have to be advanced to that status. The only way to do this is by calling `next()` on it. This means that before sending anything to the coroutine, this has to be advanced at least once via the `next()` method. Failure to do so will result in an exception:

```
>>> def coro():
...     y = yield
...
>>> c = coro()
>>> c.send(1)
Traceback (most recent call last):
  File "<stdin>", line 1, in <module>
TypeError: can't send non-None value to a just-started generator
>>>
```

 Always remember to advance a coroutine by calling `next()` before sending any values to it.

Back to our example. We are changing the way elements are produced or streamed to make it able to receive the length of the records it expects to read from the database.

The first time we call `next()`, the generator will advance up to the line containing `yield`; it will provide a value to the caller (`None`, as set in the variable), and it will suspend there). From there, we have two options. If we choose to advance the generator by calling `next()`, the default value of `10` will be used, and it will go on with this as usual. This is because calling `next()` is technically the same as `send(None)`, but this is covered in the `if` statement that will handle the value that we previously set.

If, on the other hand, we decide to provide an explicit value via `send(<value>)`, this one will become the result of the `yield` statement, which will be assigned to the variable containing the length of the page to use, which, in turn, will be used to read from the database.

Successive calls will have this logic, but the important point is that now we can dynamically change the length of the data to read in the middle of the iteration, at any point.

Now that we understand how the previous code works, most Pythonistas would expect a simplified version of it (after all, Python is also about brevity and clean and compact code):

```
def stream_db_records(db_handler):
    retrieved_data = None
    page_size = 10
    try:
        while True:
            page_size = (yield retrieved_data) or page_size
            retrieved_data = db_handler.read_n_records(page_size)
    except GeneratorExit:
        db_handler.close()
```

This version is not only more compact, but it also illustrates the idea better. The parentheses around `yield` makes it clearer that it's a statement (think of it as if it were a function call), and that we are using the result of it to compare it against the previous value.

This works as we expect it does, but we always have to remember to advance the coroutine before sending any data to it. If we forget to call the first `next()`, we'll get a `TypeError`. This call could be ignored for our purposes because it doesn't return anything we'll use.

It would be good if we could use the coroutine directly, right after it is created, without having to remember to call `next()` the first time, every time we are going to use it. Some authors (PYCOOK) devised an interesting decorator to achieve this. The idea of this decorator is to advance the coroutine, so the following definition works automatically:

```
@prepare_coroutine
def auto_stream_db_records(db_handler):
    retrieved_data = None
    page_size = 10
    try:
```

```
        while True:
            page_size = (yield retrieved_data) or page_size
            retrieved_data = db_handler.read_n_records(page_size)
    except GeneratorExit:
        db_handler.close()
```

```
>>> streamer = auto_stream_db_records(DBHandler("testdb"))
>>> len(streamer.send(5))
5
```

Keep in mind, these are the fundamentals of how coroutines work in Python. By following these examples, you'll get an idea of what's actually going on in Python when working with coroutines. However, in modern Python, you wouldn't typically write these sorts of coroutines by yourself, because there's new syntax available (which we have mentioned, but we'll revisit to see how they relate to the ideas we have just seen).

Before jumping into the new syntactic capabilities, we need to explore the last jump the coroutines took in terms of their added functionality, in order to bridge missing gaps. After that, we'll be able to understand the meaning behind each keyword and statement used in asynchronous programming.

More advanced coroutines

So far, we have a better understanding of coroutines, and we can create simple ones to handle small tasks. We can say that these coroutines are, in fact, just more advanced generators (and that would be right, coroutines are just fancy generators), but, if we actually want to start supporting more complex scenarios, we usually have to go for a design that handles many coroutines concurrently, and that requires more features.

When handling many coroutines, we find new problems. As the control flow of our application becomes more complex, we want to pass values up and down the stack (as well as exceptions), be able to capture values from sub-coroutines we might call at any level, and finally, schedule multiple coroutines to run toward a common goal.

To make things simpler, generators had to be extended once again. That is what PEP-380 addressed by changing the semantics of generators so that they can return values and by introducing the new yield from construction.

Returning values in coroutines

As introduced at the beginning of this chapter, iteration is a mechanism that calls next() on an iterable object many times until a StopIteration exception is raised.

So far, we have been exploring the iterative nature of generators — we produce values one at a time, and, in general, we only care about each value as it's being produced at every step of the for loop. This is a very logical way of thinking about generators, but coroutines have a different idea; even though they are technically generators, they weren't conceived with the idea of iteration in mind, but with the goal of suspending the execution of code until it's resumed later on.

This is an interesting challenge; when we design a coroutine, we usually care more about suspending the state rather than iterating (and iterating a coroutine would be an odd case). The challenge lies in that it is easy to mix them both. This is because of a technical implementation detail; the support for coroutines in Python was built upon generators.

If we want to use coroutines to process some information and suspend its execution, it would make sense to think of them as lightweight threads (or green threads, as they are called in other platforms). In such a case, it would make sense if they could return values, much like calling any other regular function.

But let's remember that generators are not regular functions, so in a generator, the construction value = generator() will do nothing other than create a generator object. What would be the semantics for making a generator return a value? It will have to be after the iteration is done.

When a generator returns a value, its iteration is immediately stopped (it can't be iterated any further). To preserve the semantics, the StopIteration exception is still raised, and the value to be returned is stored inside the exception object. It's the responsibility of the caller to catch it.

In the following example, we are creating a simple generator that produces two values and then returns a third. Notice how we have to catch the exception in order to get this value, and how it's stored precisely inside the exception under the attribute named value:

```
>>> def generator():
...     yield 1
...     yield 2
...     return 3
...
>>> value = generator()
>>> next(value)
1
>>> next(value)
2
>>> try:
```

```
...        next(value)
... except StopIteration as e:
...        print(f">>>>>> returned value: {e.value}")
...
>>>>>> returned value: 3
```

As we'll see later, this mechanism is used to make coroutines return values. Before PEP-380, this didn't make any sense, and any attempt at having a return statement inside a generator was considered a syntax error. But now, the idea is that, when the iteration is over, we want to return a final value, and the way to provide it is to store it in the exception being raised at the end of the iteration (StopIteration). That might not be the cleanest approach, but it's completely backward-compatible, as it doesn't change the interface of the generator.

Delegating into smaller coroutines – the 'yield from' syntax

The previous feature is interesting in the sense that it opens up a lot of new possibilities with coroutines (generators), now that they can return values. But this feature, by itself, would not be so useful without proper syntax support, because catching the returned value this way is a bit cumbersome.

This is one of the main features of the yield from syntax. Among other things (that we'll review in detail), it can collect the value returned by a sub-generator. Remember that we said that returning data in a generator was nice, but that, unfortunately, writing statements as value = generator() wouldn't work? Well, writing them as value = yield from generator() would.

The simplest use of yield from

In its most basic form, the new yield from syntax can be used to chain generators from nested for loops into a single one, which will end up with a single string of all the values in a continuous stream.

A canonical example is about creating a function similar to itertools.chain() from the standard library. This is a very nice function because it allows you to pass any number of iterables and will return them all together in one stream.

The naïve implementation might look like this:

```
def chain(*iterables):
    for it in iterables:
```

```
        for value in it:
            yield value
```

It receives a variable number of `iterables`, traverses through all of them, and since each value is iterable, it supports a `for... in..` construction, so we have another `for` loop to get every value inside each particular iterable, which is produced by the caller function.

This might be helpful in multiple cases, such as chaining generators together or trying to iterate things that it wouldn't normally be possible to compare in one go (such as lists with tuples, and so on).

However, the `yield from` syntax allows us to go further and avoid the nested loop because it's able to produce the values from a sub-generator directly. In this case, we could simplify the code like this:

```
def chain(*iterables):
    for it in iterables:
        yield from it
```

Notice that for both implementations, the behavior of the generator is exactly the same:

```
>>> list(chain("hello", ["world"], ("tuple", " of ", "values.")))
['h', 'e', 'l', 'l', 'o', 'world', 'tuple', ' of ', 'values.']
```

This means that we can use `yield from` over any other iterable, and it will work as if the top-level generator (the one the `yield from` is using) were generating those values itself.

This works with any iterable, and even generator expressions aren't the exception. Now that we're familiar with its syntax, let's see how we could write a simple generator function that will produce all the powers of a number (for instance, if provided with `all_powers(2, 3)`, it will have to produce $2^0, 2^1,... 2^3$):

```
def all_powers(n, pow):
    yield from (n ** i for i in range(pow + 1))
```

While this simplifies the syntax a bit, saving one line of a `for` statement isn't a big advantage, and it wouldn't justify adding such a change to the language.

Indeed, this is actually just a side effect and the real raison d'être of the `yield from` construction is what we are going to explore in the following two sections.

Capturing the value returned by a sub-generator

In the following example, we have a generator that calls another two nested generators, producing values in a sequence. Each one of these nested generators returns a value, and we will see how the top-level generator is able to effectively capture the return value since it's calling the internal generators through yield from:

```python
def sequence(name, start, end):
    logger.info("%s started at %i", name, start)
    yield from range(start, end)
    logger.info("%s finished at %i", name, end)
    return end


def main():
    step1 = yield from sequence("first", 0, 5)
    step2 = yield from sequence("second", step1, 10)
    return step1 + step2
```

This is a possible execution of the code in main while it's being iterated:

```python
>>> g = main()
>>> next(g)
INFO:generators_yieldfrom_2:first started at 0
0
>>> next(g)
1
>>> next(g)
2
>>> next(g)
3
>>> next(g)
4
>>> next(g)
INFO:generators_yieldfrom_2:first finished at 5
INFO:generators_yieldfrom_2:second started at 5
5
>>> next(g)
6
>>> next(g)
7
>>> next(g)
8
>>> next(g)
9
```

```
>>> next(g)
INFO:generators_yieldfrom_2:second finished at 10
Traceback (most recent call last):
  File "<stdin>", line 1, in <module>
StopIteration: 15
```

The first line of main delegates into the internal generator, and produces the values, extracting them directly from it. This is nothing new, as we have already seen. Notice, though, how the sequence() generator function returns the end value, which is assigned in the first line to the variable named step1, and how this value is correctly used at the start of the following instance of that generator.

In the end, this other generator also returns the second end value (10), and the main generator, in turn, returns the sum of them (5+10=15), which is the value we see once the iteration has stopped.

 We can use yield from to capture the last value of a coroutine after it has finished its processing.

With this example and the ones presented in the previous section, you can get an idea of what the yield from construction does in Python. The yield from construction will take the generator, and forward the iteration of it downstream, but once it's done, it'll catch its StopIteration exception, get the value of it, and return that value to the caller function. The value attribute of the StopIteration exception becomes the result of the statement.

This is a powerful construction, because in conjunction with the topic of the next section (how to send and receive contextual information from a sub-generator), this means coroutines can take the shape of something similar to threads.

Sending and receiving data to and from a sub-generator

Now, we will see the other nice feature of the yield from syntax, which is probably what gives it its full power. As we already introduced when we explored generators acting as coroutines, we know that we can send values and throw exceptions at them, and, in such cases, the coroutine will either receive the value for its internal processing, or it will have to handle the exception accordingly.

If we now have a coroutine that delegates into other ones (such as in the previous example), we would also like to preserve this logic. Having to do so manually would be quite complex (you can take a look at the code described in PEP-380 if we didn't have this handled by yield from automatically).

In order to illustrate this, let's keep the same top-level generator (main) unmodified with respect to the previous example (calling other internal generators), but let's modify the internal generators to make them able to receive values and handle exceptions.

The code is probably not idiomatic, only for the purposes of showing how this mechanism works:

```
def sequence(name, start, end):
    value = start
    logger.info("%s started at %i", name, value)
    while value < end:
        try:
            received = yield value
            logger.info("%s received %r", name, received)
            value += 1
        except CustomException as e:
            logger.info("%s is handling %s", name, e)
            received = yield "OK"
    return end
```

Now, we will call the main coroutine, not only by iterating it, but also by providing values and throwing exceptions at it in order to see how they are handled inside sequence:

```
>>> g = main()
>>> next(g)
INFO: first started at 0
0
>>> next(g)
INFO: first received None
1
>>> g.send("value for 1")
INFO: first received 'value for 1'
2
>>> g.throw(CustomException("controlled error"))
INFO: first is handling controlled error
'OK'
... # advance more times
INFO:second started at 5
5
>>> g.throw(CustomException("exception at second generator"))
INFO: second is handling exception at second generator
'OK'
```

This example is telling us a lot of different things. Notice how we never send values to sequence, but only to main, and even so, the code that is receiving those values is the nested generators. Even though we never explicitly send anything to sequence, it's receiving the data as it's being passed along by yield from.

The main coroutine calls two other coroutines internally, producing their values, and it will be suspended at a particular point in time in any of those. When it's stopped at the first one, we can see the logs telling us that it is that instance of the coroutine that received the value we sent. The same happens when we throw an exception to it. When the first coroutine finishes, it returns the value that was assigned in the variable named step1, and passed as input for the second coroutine, which will do the same (it will handle the send() and throw() calls, accordingly).

The same happens for the values that each coroutine produces. When we are at any given step, the return from calling send() corresponds to the value that the sub-coroutine (the one that main is currently suspended at) has produced. When we throw an exception that is being handled, the sequence coroutine produces the value OK, which is propagated to the called coroutine (main), and that in turn will end up at main's caller.

As anticipated, these methods, together with yield from, provide us with a lot of new functionality (something that can resemble threads). This opens up the doors for asynchronous programming, which we will explore next.

Asynchronous programming

With the constructions we have seen so far, we can create asynchronous programs in Python. This means that we can create programs that have many coroutines, schedule them to work in a particular order, and switch between them when they're suspended after a yield from has been called on each of them.

The main advantage that we can take from this is the possibility of parallelizing I/O operations in a non-blocking way. What we would need is a low-level generator (usually implemented by a third-party library) that knows how to handle the actual I/O while the coroutine is suspended. The idea is for the coroutine to effect suspension so that our program can handle another task in the meantime. The way the application would retrieve the control back is by means of the yield from statement, which will suspend and produce a value to the caller (as in the examples we saw previously when we used this syntax to alter the control flow of the program).

This is roughly the way asynchronous programming had been working in Python for quite a few years, until it was decided that better syntactic support was needed.

The fact that coroutines and generators are technically the same causes some confusion. Syntactically (and technically), they are the same, but semantically, they are different. We create generators when we want to achieve efficient iteration. We typically create coroutines with the goal of running non-blocking I/O operations.

While this difference is clear, the dynamic nature of Python would still allow developers to mix these different types of objects, ending up with a runtime error at a very late stage of the program. Remember that in the simplest and most basic form of the yield from syntax, we used this construction over iterable objects (we created a sort of chain function applied over strings, lists, and so on). None of these objects were coroutines, and it still worked. Then, we saw that we can have multiple coroutines, use yield from to send the value (or exceptions), and get some results back. These are clearly two very different use cases; however, if we write something along the lines of the following statement:

```
result = yield from iterable_or_awaitable()
```

It's not clear what iterable_or_awaitable returns. It can be a simple iterable such as a string, and it might still be syntactically correct. Or, it might be an actual coroutine. The cost of this mistake will be paid much later, at runtime.

For this reason, the typing system in Python had to be extended. Before Python 3.5, coroutines were just generators with a @coroutine decorator applied, and they were to be called with the yield from syntax. Now, there is a specific type of object the Python interpreter recognizes as such, that is, a coroutine.

This change heralded syntax changes as well. The await and async def syntax were introduced. The former is intended to be used instead of yield from, and it only works with awaitable objects (which coroutines conveniently happen to be). Trying to call await with something that doesn't respect the interface of an awaitable will raise an exception (this is a good example of how interfaces can help to achieve a more solid design, preventing runtime errors).

async def is the new way of defining coroutines, replacing the aforementioned decorator, and this actually creates an object that, when called, will return an instance of a coroutine. In the same way as when you invoke a generator function, the interpreter will return you a generator object, when you invoke an object defined with async def, it'll give you a coroutine object that has an __await__ method, and therefore can be used in await expressions.

Without going into all the details and possibilities of asynchronous programming in Python, we can say that despite the new syntax and the new types, this is not doing anything fundamentally different from the concepts we have covered in this chapter.

The idea behind programming asynchronously in Python is that there is an event loop (typically `asyncio` because it's the one that is included in the `standard library`, but there are many others that will work just the same) that manages a series of coroutines. These coroutines belong to the event loop, which is going to call them according to its scheduling mechanism. When each one of these runs, it will call our code (according to the logic we have defined inside the coroutine we programmed), and when we want to get control back to the event loop, we call `await <coroutine>`, which will process a task asynchronously. The event loop will resume and another coroutine will take place while that operation is left running.

This mechanism represents the basics of how asynchronous programming works in Python. You can think that the new syntax added for coroutines (`async def` / `await`) is just an API for you to write code in a way that's going to be called by the event loop. By default, that event loop will typically be `asyncio` because it's the one that comes in the `standard library`, but any event loop system that matches the API would work. This means you can use libraries like `uvloop` (`https://github.com/MagicStack/uvloop`) and `trio` (`https://github.com/python-trio/trio`), and the code would work the same. You can even register your own event loop, and it should also work the same (provided compliance with the API, that is).

In practice, there are more particularities and edge cases that are beyond the scope of this book. It is, however, worth mentioning that these concepts are related to the ideas introduced in this chapter and that this arena is another place where generators demonstrate being a core concept of the language, as there are many things constructed on top of them.

Magic asynchronous methods

I've made the case in previous chapters (and hopefully convinced you) that whenever possible, we can take advantage of the magic methods in Python in order to make the abstractions we created blend naturally with the syntax of the language and this way achieve better, more compact, and perhaps cleaner code.

But what happens if on any of these methods we need to call a coroutine? If we have to call `await` in a function, that means the function itself would have to be a coroutine (defined with `async def`), or else there will be a syntax error.

But then, how does this work with the current syntax and magic methods? It doesn't. We need new syntax, and new magic methods, in order to work with asynchronous programming. The good news is that they're analogous to the previous ones.

Here's a summary of the new magic methods and how they relate to the new syntax.

Concept	Magic methods	Syntax usage
Context manager	__aenter__ __aexit__	`async with async_cm() as x:` ...
Iteration	__aiter__ __anext__	`async for e in aiter:` ...

Table 7.2: Asynchronous syntax and their magic methods

This new syntax is mentioned in PEP-492 (`https://www.python.org/dev/peps/pep-0492/`).

Asynchronous context managers

The idea is simple: if we were to use a context manager but needed to call a coroutine on it, we couldn't use the normal __enter__ and __exit__ methods because they're defined as regular functions, so instead we need to use the new __aenter__ and __aexit__ coroutine methods. And instead of calling it merely using with, we'd have to use async with.

There's even an @asynccontextmanager decorator available in the contextlib module, to create an asynchronous context manager in the same way as shown before.

The async with syntax for asynchronous context managers works in a similar way: when the context is entered, the __aenter__ coroutine is called automatically, and when it's being exited, __aexit__ will trigger. It's even possible to group multiple asynchronous context managers in the same async with statement, but it's not possible to mix them with regular ones. An attempt of using a regular context manager with the async with syntax will fail with an AttributeError.

Our example from *Chapter 2*, *Pythonic Code*, would look like the following code if adapted to asynchronous programming:

```
@contextlib.asynccontextmanager
async def db_management():
    try:
        await stop_database()
        yield
    finally:
        await start_database()
```

Moreover, if we had more than one context manager that we wanted to use, we could do, for example:

```
@contextlib.asynccontextmanager
async def metrics_logger():
    yield await create_metrics_logger()


async def run_db_backup():
    async with db_management(), metrics_logger():
        print("Performing DB backup...")
```

As you'd expect, the contextlib module provides the abstract base class AbstractAsyncContextManager, which requires the implementation of the __aenter__ and __aexit__ methods.

Other magic methods

What happens with the rest of the magic methods? Do they all get their asynchronous counterpart? No, but there's something I wanted to point out about that: it shouldn't be needed.

Remember that achieving clean code is in part about making sure you distribute the responsibilities correctly in the code and place things in their proper places. To give an example, if you're thinking about calling a coroutine inside a __getattr__ method, there's something probably amiss in your design, as there should probably be a better place for that coroutine.

Coroutines that we await are used in order to have parts of our code running concurrently, so they typically relate to external resources being managed, whereas the logic we put in the rest of the magic methods (__getitem__, __getattr__, etc.) should be object-oriented code, or code that can be resolved in terms of solely the internal representation of that object.

By the same token (and also following up on good design practices), it wouldn't be good to make __init__ a coroutine, because we typically want lightweight objects that we can initialize safely without side effects. Even better, we have already covered the benefits of using dependency injection, so that's even more reason not to want an asynchronous initialization method: our object should work with dependencies already initialized.

The second case of the previous table, asynchronous iteration, is of more interest for the purposes of this chapter, so we'll explore it in the next section.

The syntax for asynchronous iteration (`async for`) works with any asynchronous iterator, whether it is created by us (as we'll see how to do in the next section), or whether it's an asynchronous generator (which we'll see in the section after that).

Asynchronous iteration

In the same way that we have the iterator objects we saw at the beginning of the chapter (that is, objects that support being iterated over with Python's built-in `for` loop), we can do the same, but in an asynchronous fashion.

Imagine we want to create an iterator to abstract the way in which we read data from an external source (like a database), but the part that extracts the data itself is a coroutine, so we couldn't call it during the already familiar __next__ operation as before. That's why we need to make use of the __anext__ coroutine.

The following example illustrates in a simple way how this can be achieved. Disregarding external dependencies, or any other accidental complexity, we'll focus on the methods that make this type of operation possible, in order to study them:

```python
import asyncio
import random


async def coroutine():
    await asyncio.sleep(0.1)
    return random.randint(1, 10000)


class RecordStreamer:
    def __init__(self, max_rows=100) -> None:
        self._current_row = 0
        self._max_rows = max_rows

    def __aiter__(self):
        return self

    async def __anext__(self):
        if self._current_row < self._max_rows:
            row = (self._current_row, await coroutine())
            self._current_row += 1
            return row
        raise StopAsyncIteration
```

The first method, __aiter__, is used to indicate that the object is an asynchronous iterator. Just as in the synchronous version, most of the time it's enough to return self, and therefore it doesn't need to be a coroutine.

But __anext__, on the other hand, is precisely the part of our code where our asynchronous logic lies, so that needs to be a coroutine for starters. In this case, we're awaiting another coroutine in order to return part of the data to be returned.

It also needs a separate exception in order to signal the end of the iteration, in this case, called StopAsyncIteration.

This exception works in an analogous way, only that it's meant for the async for kind of loops. When encountered, the interpreter will finish the loop.

This sort of object can be used in the following form:

```
async for row in RecordStreamer(10):
    ...
```

You can clearly see how this is analogous to the synchronous version we explored at the beginning of the chapter. One important distinction though is that, as we would expect, the next() function wouldn't work on this object (it doesn't implement __next__ after all), so advancing an asynchronous generator by one place would require a different idiom.

Advancing the asynchronous iterator by one place could be achieved by doing something like the following:

```
await async_iterator.__anext__()
```

But more interesting constructions, like the ones we saw before about using the next() function to work over a generator expression to search for the first value that meets certain conditions, wouldn't be supported, because they're not capable of handling asynchronous iterators.

Inspired by the previous idiom, we can create a generator expression using the asynchronous iteration, and then take the first value from it. Better yet, we can create our own version of this function to work with asynchronous generators, which might look like this:

```
NOT_SET = object()

async def anext(async_generator_expression, default=NOT_SET):
    try:
        return await async_generator_expression.__anext__()
```

```
    except StopAsyncIteration:
        if default is NOT_SET:
            raise
        return default
```

Starting from Python 3.8, the `asyncio` module has a nice capability that allows us to interact with coroutines directly from the REPL. That way, we can test interactively how the previous code would work:

```
$ python -m asyncio
>>> streamer = RecordStreamer(10)
>>> await anext(streamer)
(0, 5017)
>>> await anext(streamer)
(1, 5257)
>>> await anext(streamer)
(2, 3507)
...
>>> await anext(streamer)
(9, 5440)
>>> await anext(streamer)
Traceback (most recent call last):
    ...
    raise StopAsyncIteration
StopAsyncIteration
>>>
```

You'll note that it resembles the original `next()` function both in terms of interface and behavior.

Now we know how to use iteration in asynchronous programming, but we can do better than that. Most of the time we just need a generator and not a whole iterator object. Generators have the advantage that their syntax makes them easier to write and understand, so in the next section, I'll mention how to create generators for asynchronous programs.

Asynchronous generators

Before Python 3.6, the functionality explored in the previous section was the only way to achieve asynchronous iteration in Python. Because of the intricacies of the coroutines and generators we explored in previous sections, trying to use the `yield` statement inside a coroutine was not entirely defined, hence not allowed (for example, would `yield` try to suspend the coroutine, or generate a value for the caller?).

Asynchronous generators were introduced in PEP-525 (`https://www.python.org/dev/peps/pep-0525/`).

The issue with the use of the `yield` keyword inside a coroutine was solved in this PEP, and it's now allowed, but with a different and clear meaning. Unlike the first example of coroutines we have seen, `yield` inside a coroutine properly defined (with `async def`) doesn't mean to suspend or pause the execution of that coroutine, but instead to produce a value for the caller. This is an asynchronous generator: same as the generators we've seen at the very beginning of the chapter, but that can be used in an asynchronous way (meaning they probably await other coroutines inside their definition).

The main advantage of asynchronous generators over iterators is the same advantage regular generators have; they allow us to achieve the same thing but in a more compact way.

As promised, the previous example looks more compact when written with an asynchronous generator:

```
async def record_streamer(max_rows):
    current_row = 0
    while current_row < max_rows:
        row = (current_row, await coroutine())
        current_row += 1
        yield row
```

This feels closer to a regular generator as the structure is the same except for the `async def` / `await` construction. Moreover, you'll have to remember fewer details (as to the methods that need implementation and the right exception that has to be triggered), so I'd recommend that whenever possible you try to favor asynchronous generators over iterators.

This concludes our journey through iteration in Python and asynchronous programming. In particular, this last topic we've just explored is the pinnacle of it, because it relates to all the concepts we've learned in this chapter.

Summary

Generators are everywhere in Python. Since their inception in Python a long time ago, they proved to be a great addition that makes programs more efficient and iteration much simpler.

As time passed by, and more complex tasks needed to be added to Python, generators helped again in supporting coroutines.

And, while in Python coroutines are generators, we still don't have to forget that they're semantically different. Generators are created with the idea of iteration, while coroutines have the goal of asynchronous programming (suspending and resuming the execution of a part of our program at any given time). This distinction became so important that it made Python's syntax (and type system) evolve.

Iteration and asynchronous programming constitute the last of the main pillars of Python programming. Now, it's time to see how everything fits together and to put all of these concepts we have been exploring over the past few chapters into action. This means that by now, you have a complete understanding of Python's capabilities.

It's now time to use this to your advantage, so in the next chapters, we'll see how to put these concepts into action, related to more general ideas of software engineering, such as testing, design patterns, and architecture.

We'll start this new part of our journey by exploring unit testing and refactoring in the next chapter.

References

Here is a list of information you can refer to:

- *PEP-234: Iterators* (`https://www.python.org/dev/peps/pep-0234/`)

- *PEP-255: Simple Generators* (`https://www.python.org/dev/peps/pep-0255/`)

- *ITER-01: Python's itertools module* (`https://docs.python.org/3/library/itertools.html`)

- *GoF*: The book written by *Erich Gamma, Richard Helm, Ralph Johnson,* and *John Vlissides* named *Design Patterns: Elements of Reusable Object-Oriented Software*

- *PEP-342: Coroutines via Enhanced Generators* (`https://www.python.org/dev/peps/pep-0342/`)

- *PYCOOK*: The book written by *Brian Jones* and *David Beazley* named *Python Cookbook: Recipes for Mastering Python 3, Third Edition*

- *PY99: Fake threads (generators, coroutines, and continuations)* (`https://mail.python.org/pipermail/python-dev/1999-July/000467.html`)

- *CORO-01: Co Routine* (`http://wiki.c2.com/?CoRoutine`)

- *CORO-02: Generators Are Not Coroutines* (`http://wiki.c2.com/?GeneratorsAreNotCoroutines`)

- *PEP-492: Coroutines with async and await syntax* (`https://www.python.org/dev/peps/pep-0492/`)

- *PEP-525: Asynchronous Generators* (`https://www.python.org/dev/peps/pep-0525/`)

- *TEE: The itertools.tee function* (`https://docs.python.org/3/library/itertools.html#itertools.tee`)

8

Unit Testing and Refactoring

The ideas explored in this chapter are fundamental pillars in the global context of the book because of their importance to our ultimate goal: to write better and more maintainable software.

Unit tests (and any form of automatic tests, for that matter) are critical to software maintainability, and therefore something that cannot be missing from any quality project. It is for that reason that this chapter is dedicated exclusively to aspects of automated testing as a key strategy, to safely modify the code, and iterate over it, in incrementally better versions.

After this chapter, we will have gained more insight into the following:

- Why automated tests are critical for a project's success
- How unit tests work as a heuristic of the quality of the code
- What frameworks and tools are available to develop automated tests and set up quality gates
- Taking advantage of unit tests to understand the domain problem better and document code
- Concepts related to unit testing, such as test-driven development

In the previous chapters, we have seen Python-specific traits and how we can leverage them to achieve more maintainable code. We have also explored how general design principles of software engineering can be applied to Python using its peculiarities. Here we'll also revisit an important concept of software engineering, such as automatic testing, but with the use of tools, some of them available in the standard library (such as the `unittest` module), and some others that are external packages (such as `pytest`). We begin this journey by exploring how software design relates to unit testing.

Design principles and unit testing

In this section, we are first going to take a look at unit testing from a conceptual point of view. We will revisit some of the software engineering principles we discussed in the previous chapter to get an idea of how this is related to clean code.

After that, we will discuss in more detail how to put these concepts into practice (at the code level), and what frameworks and tools we can make use of.

First, we quickly define what unit testing is about. Unit tests are code in charge of validating other parts of the code. Normally, anyone would be tempted to say that unit tests validate the "core" of the application, but such a definition regards unit tests as secondary, which is not the way they are thought of in this book. Unit tests are core, and a critical component of the software and they should be treated with the same considerations as the business logic.

A unit test is a piece of code that imports parts of the code with the business logic, and exercises its logic, asserting several scenarios with the idea of guaranteeing certain conditions. There are some traits that unit tests must have, such as:

- Isolation: Unit tests should be completely independent from any other external agent, and they have to focus only on the business logic. For this reason, they do not connect to a database, they don't perform HTTP requests, and so on. Isolation also means that the tests are independent among themselves: they must be able to run in any order, without depending on any previous state.

- Performance: Unit tests must run quickly. They are intended to be run multiple times, repeatedly.

- Repeatability: Unit tests should be able to objectively assess the status of the software in a deterministic way. This means the results yielded by the tests should be repeatable. Unit tests assess the status of the code: if a test fails, it must keep on failing until the code is fixed. If a test passes, and no changes in the code are made, it should continue to pass. Tests shouldn't be flaky or randomized.

- Self-validating: The execution of a unit test determines its result. There should be no extra step required to interpret the unit test (much less manual intervention).

More concretely, in Python, this means that we will have new `*.py` files where we are going to place our unit tests, and they are going to be called by some tool. These files will have `import` statements, to take what we need from our business logic (what we intend to test), and inside this file, we program the tests themselves. Afterward, a tool will collect our unit tests and run them, giving a result.

This last part is what self-validation actually means. When the tool calls our files, a Python process will be launched, and our tests will be running on it. If the tests fail, the process will have exited with an error code (in a Unix environment, this can be any number other than 0). The standard is that the tool runs the test, and prints a dot (.) for every successful test; an F if the test failed (the condition of the test was not satisfied), and an E if there was an exception.

A note about other forms of automated testing

Unit tests are intended to verify very small units of code, for example, a function, or a method. We want our unit tests to reach a very detailed level of granularity, testing as much code as possible. To test something bigger, such as a class, we would not want to use just unit tests, but rather a test suite, which is a collection of unit tests. Each one of them will be testing something more specific, like a method of that class.

Unit tests aren't the only available mechanism of automatic testing, and we shouldn't expect them to catch all possible errors. There are also *acceptance* and *integration* tests, both beyond the scope of this book.

In an integration test, we want to test multiple components at once. In this case, we want to validate if collectively, they work as expected. In this case, it is acceptable (more than that, desirable) to have side effects, and to forget about isolation, meaning that we will want to issue HTTP requests, connect to databases, and so on. While we'd want our integration tests to actually run as the production code would, there are some dependencies we would still want to avoid. For example, if your service connects to another external dependency via the Internet, then that part would indeed be omitted.

Let's say you have your application that uses a database and connects to some other internal services. The application will have different configuration files for different environments, and of course, in production you'll have the configuration set for the real services. However, for an integration test, you'll want to mock the database with a Docker container that's built specifically for those tests, and this will be configured in a specific configuration file. As for the dependencies, you'll want to mock them with Docker services, whenever that's possible.

Mocking as part of unit testing will be covered later on in this chapter. When it comes to mocking dependencies to perform *component* testing, this will be covered in *Chapter 10, Clean Architecture*, when we mention components in the context of software architecture.

An acceptance test is an automated form of testing that tries to validate the system from the perspective of a user, typically executing use cases.

These last two forms of testing lose another nice trait compared to unit tests: speed. As you can imagine, they will take more time to run, and therefore they will be run less frequently.

In a good development environment, the programmer will have the entire test suite and will run unit tests all the time, repeatedly, while making changes to the code, iterating, refactoring, and so on. Once the changes are ready, and the pull request is open, the continuous integration service will run the build for that branch, where the unit tests will run as long as the integration or acceptance tests that might exist. Needless to say, the status of the build should be successful (green) before merging, but the important part is the difference between the kinds of tests: we want to run unit tests all the time, and those tests that take longer less frequently.

For this reason, we want to have a lot of small unit tests, and a few automated tests, strategically designed to cover as much as possible of where the unit tests could not reach (the use of the database, for instance).

Finally, a word to the wise. Remember that this book encourages pragmatism. Besides these definitions given, and the points made about unit tests at the beginning of the section, the reader has to keep in mind that the best solution according to your criteria and context should predominate. Nobody knows your system better than you, which means if, for some reason, you have to write a unit test that needs to launch a Docker container to test against a database, go for it. As we have repeatedly remembered throughout the book, *practicality beats purity*.

Unit testing and agile software development

In modern software development, we want to deliver value constantly, and as quickly as possible. The rationale behind these goals is that the earlier we get feedback, the less the impact, and the easier it will be to change. These are not new ideas at all; some of them resemble principles from decades ago, and others (such as the idea of getting feedback from stakeholders as soon as possible and iterating upon it) you can find in essays such as **The Cathedral and the Bazaar** (abbreviated as **CatB**).

Therefore, we want to be able to respond effectively to changes, and for that, the software we write will have to change. As I mentioned in previous chapters, we want our software to be adaptable, flexible, and extensible.

The code alone (regardless of how well written and designed it is) cannot guarantee us that it's flexible enough to be changed, if there's no formal proof that it will keep on running correctly after it was modified.

Let's say we design a piece of software following the SOLID principles, and in one part we actually have a set of components that comply with the open/ closed principle, meaning that we can easily extend them without affecting too much existing code. Assume further that the code is written in a way that favors refactoring, so we could change it as required. What's to say that when we make these changes, we aren't introducing any bugs? How do we know that existing functionality is preserved (and there are no regressions)? Would you feel confident enough releasing that to your users? Will they believe that the new version works just as expected?

The answer to all of these questions is that we can't be sure unless we have a formal proof of it. And unit tests are just that: formal proof that the program works according to the specifications.

Unit (or automated) tests, therefore, work as a safety net that gives us the confidence to work on our code. Armed with these tools, we can efficiently work on our code, and therefore this is what ultimately determines the velocity (or capacity) of the team working on the software product. The better the tests, the more likely it is that we can deliver value quickly without being stopped by bugs every now and then.

Unit testing and software design

This is the other face of the coin when it comes to the relationship between the main code and unit testing. Besides the pragmatic reasons explored in the previous section, it comes down to the fact that good software is testable software.

Testability (the quality attribute that determines how easy to test software is) is not just nice to have, but a driver for clean code.

Unit tests aren't just something complementary to the main code base, but rather something that has a direct impact and real influence on how the code is written. There are many levels of this, from the very beginning, when we realize that the moment we want to add unit tests for some parts of our code, we have to change it (resulting in a better version of it), to its ultimate expression (explored near the end of this chapter) when the entire code (the design) is driven by the way it's going to be tested via **test-driven design**.

Starting off with a simple example, I'll show you a small use case in which tests (and the need to test our code) lead to improvements in the way our code ends up being written.

In the following example, we will simulate a process that requires sending metrics to an external system about the results obtained at each particular task (as always, details won't make any difference as long as we focus on the code). We have a Process object that represents a task on the domain problem, and it uses a metrics client (an external dependency and therefore something we don't control) to send the actual metrics to the external entity (this could be sending data to syslog, or statsd, for instance):

```python
class MetricsClient:
    """3rd-party metrics client"""

    def send(self, metric_name, metric_value):
        if not isinstance(metric_name, str):
            raise TypeError("expected type str for metric_name")

        if not isinstance(metric_value, str):
            raise TypeError("expected type str for metric_value")

        logger.info("sending %s = %s", metric_name, metric_value)


class Process:

    def __init__(self):
        self.client = MetricsClient()  # A 3rd-party metrics client

    def process_iterations(self, n_iterations):
        for i in range(n_iterations):
            result = self.run_process()
            self.client.send(f"iteration.{i}", str(result))
```

In the simulated version of the third-party client, we put the requirement that the parameters provided must be of string type. Therefore, if the result of the run_process method is not a string, we might expect it to fail, and indeed it does:

```
Traceback (most recent call last):
...
    raise TypeError("expected type str for metric_value")
TypeError: expected type str for metric_value
```

Remember that this validation is out of our hands and we cannot change the code, so we must provide the method with parameters of the correct type before proceeding. But since this is a bug we detected, we first want to write a unit test to make sure it will not happen again. We do this to prove that we fixed the issue, and to protect against this bug in the future, regardless of how many times the code is changed.

It would be possible to test the code as is by mocking the client of the Process object (we will see how to do so in the *Mock objects* section, when we explore the tools for unit testing), but doing so runs more code than is needed (notice how the part we want to test is nested in the code). Moreover, it's good that the method is relatively small, because if it weren't, the test would have to run even more undesired parts that we might also need to mock. This is another example of good design (small, cohesive functions or methods), that relates to testability.

Finally, we decide not to go to much trouble and test just the part that we need to, so instead of interacting with the client directly on the main method, we delegate to a wrapper method, and the new class looks like this:

```
class WrappedClient:

    def __init__(self):
        self.client = MetricsClient()

    def send(self, metric_name, metric_value):
        return self.client.send(str(metric_name), str(metric_value))

class Process:
    def __init__(self):
        self.client = WrappedClient()

    ... # rest of the code remains unchanged
```

In this case, we opted for creating our own version of the client for metrics, that is, a wrapper around the third-party library one we used to have. To do this, we place a class that (with the same interface) will make the conversion of the types accordingly.

This way of using composition resembles the adapter design pattern (we'll explore design patterns in the next chapter, so, for now, it's just an informative message), and since this is a new object in our domain, it can have its respective unit tests. Having this object will make things simpler to test, but more importantly, now that we look at it, we realize that this is probably the way the code should have been written in the first place. Trying to write a unit test for our code made us realize that we were missing an important abstraction entirely!

Now that we have separated the method as it should be, let's write the actual unit test for it. The details pertaining to the `unittest` module used in this example will be explored in more detail in the part of the chapter where we explore testing tools and libraries, but for now, reading the code will give us a first impression on how to test it, and it will make the previous concepts a little less abstract:

```python
import unittest
from unittest.mock import Mock

class TestWrappedClient(unittest.TestCase):
    def test_send_converts_types(self):
        wrapped_client = WrappedClient()
        wrapped_client.client = Mock()
        wrapped_client.send("value", 1)

        wrapped_client.client.send.assert_called_with("value", "1")
```

`Mock` is a type that's available in the `unittest.mock` module, which is a convenient object to ask about all sorts of things. For example, in this case, we're using it in place of the third-party library (mocked into the boundaries of the system, as commented on in the next section) to check that it's called as expected (and once again, we're not testing the library itself, only that it is called correctly). Notice how we run a call like the one in our `Process` object, but we expect the parameters to be converted to strings.

This is an example of how a unit test helps us in terms of the design of our code: by trying to test the code, we came up with a better version of it. We can go even further and say that this test isn't good enough, because of how the unit test is overriding an internal collaborator of the wrapper client in the second line. In an attempt to fix this, we might say that the actual client must be provided by a parameter (using dependency injection), instead of creating it in its initialization method. And once again, the unit test made us think of a better implementation.

The corollary of the previous example should be that the testability of a piece of code also speaks to its quality. In other words, if the code is hard to test, or its tests are complicated, then it probably needs to be improved.

> *"There are no tricks to writing tests; there are only tricks to writing testable code"*
>
> – *Miško Hevery*

Defining the boundaries of what to test

Testing requires effort. And if we are not careful when deciding what to test, we will never end testing, hence wasting a lot of effort without achieving much.

We should scope the testing to the boundaries of our code. If we don't, we would have to also test the dependencies (external/third-party libraries or modules) in our code, and then their respective dependencies, and so on in a never-ending journey. It's not our responsibility to test dependencies, so we can assume that these projects have tests of their own. It would be enough just to test that the correct calls to external dependencies are done with the correct parameters (and that might even be an acceptable use of patching), but we shouldn't put more effort in than that.

This is another instance where good software design pays off. If we have been careful in our design, and clearly defined the boundaries of our system (that is, we designed toward interfaces, instead of concrete implementations that will change, hence inverting the dependencies over external components to reduce temporal coupling), then it will be much easier to mock these interfaces when writing unit tests.

In good unit testing, we want to patch on the boundaries of our system and focus on the core functionality to be exercised. We don't test external libraries (third-party tools installed via `pip`, for instance), but instead, we check that they are called correctly. When we explore `mock` objects later on in this chapter, we will review techniques and tools for performing these types of assertion.

Tools for testing

There are a lot of tools we can use for writing our unit tests, all of them with pros and cons and serving different purposes. I'll present the two most common libraries used for unit testing in Python. They cover most (if not all) use cases, and they're very popular, so knowing how to use them comes in handy.

Along with testing frameworks and test running libraries, it's often common to find projects that configure code coverage, which they use as quality metrics. Since coverage (when used as a metric) is misleading, after seeing how to create unit tests, we'll discuss why it's not to be taken lightly.

The next section starts by introducing the main libraries we're going to use in this chapter for unit testing.

Frameworks and libraries for unit testing

In this section, we will discuss two frameworks for writing and running unit tests. The first one, unittest, is available in the standard library of Python, while the second one, pytest, has to be installed externally via pip:

- unittest: https://docs.python.org/3/library/unittest.html

- pytest: https://docs.pytest.org/en/latest/

When it comes to covering testing scenarios for our code, unittest alone will most likely suffice, since it has plenty of helpers. However, for more complex systems on which we have multiple dependencies, connections to external systems, and probably the need to patch objects, define fixtures, and parameterize test cases, then pytest looks like a more complete option.

We will use a small program as an example to show you how it could be tested using both options, which, in the end, will help us to get a better picture of how the two of them compare.

The example demonstrating testing tools is a simplified version of a version control tool that supports code reviews in merge requests. We will start with the following criteria:

- A merge request is rejected if at least one person disagrees with the changes.

- If nobody has disagreed, and the merge request is good for at least two other developers, it's approved.

- In any other case, its status is pending.

And here is what the code might look like:

```python
from enum import Enum

class MergeRequestStatus(Enum):
    APPROVED = "approved"
    REJECTED = "rejected"
    PENDING = "pending"

class MergeRequest:
    def __init__(self):
        self._context = {
```

```
        "upvotes": set(),
        "downvotes": set(),
    }

@property
def status(self):
    if self._context["downvotes"]:
        return MergeRequestStatus.REJECTED
    elif len(self._context["upvotes"]) >= 2:
        return MergeRequestStatus.APPROVED
    return MergeRequestStatus.PENDING

def upvote(self, by_user):
    self._context["downvotes"].discard(by_user)
    self._context["upvotes"].add(by_user)

def downvote(self, by_user):
    self._context["upvotes"].discard(by_user)
    self._context["downvotes"].add(by_user)
```

Using this code as a base, let's see how it can be unit tested using both of the libraries presented in this chapter. The idea is not only to learn about how to use each library, but also to identify some differences.

unittest

The unittest module is a great option with which to start writing unit tests because it provides a rich API to write all kinds of testing conditions, and since it's available in the standard library, it's quite versatile and convenient.

The unittest module is based on the concepts of JUnit (from Java), which, in turn, is also based on the original ideas of unit testing that come from Smalltalk (perhaps this is the reason behind the naming convention of the methods on this module), so it's object-oriented in nature. For this reason, tests are written through classes, where the checks are verified by methods, and it's common to group tests by scenarios in classes.

To start writing unit tests, we have to create a test class that inherits from unittest. TestCase, and define the conditions we want to stress on its methods. These methods should start with test_*, and can internally use any of the methods inherited from unittest.TestCase to check conditions that must hold true.

Some examples of conditions we might want to verify for our case are as follows:

```python
class TestMergeRequestStatus(unittest.TestCase):

    def test_simple_rejected(self):
        merge_request = MergeRequest()
        merge_request.downvote("maintainer")
        self.assertEqual(merge_request.status, MergeRequestStatus.
REJECTED)

    def test_just_created_is_pending(self):
        self.assertEqual(MergeRequest().status, MergeRequestStatus.
PENDING)

    def test_pending_awaiting_review(self):
        merge_request = MergeRequest()
        merge_request.upvote("core-dev")
        self.assertEqual(merge_request.status, MergeRequestStatus.
PENDING)

    def test_approved(self):
        merge_request = MergeRequest()
        merge_request.upvote("dev1")
        merge_request.upvote("dev2")

        self.assertEqual(merge_request.status, MergeRequestStatus.
APPROVED)
```

The API for unit testing provides many useful methods for comparison, the most common one being assertEqual(<actual>, <expected>[, message]), which can be used to compare the result of the operation against the value we were expecting, optionally using a message that will be shown in the case of an error.

I named the parameters using the order (<actual>, <expected>), because that's the order I've found most of the times in my experience. Even though I believe this is the most common form (as a convention) to use in Python, there are no recommendations or guidelines regarding this. In fact, some projects (such as gRPC) use the inverse form (<expected>, <actual>), and this is actually a convention in other languages (for example, Java and Kotlin). The key is to be consistent and respect the form that's already been used in your project.

Another useful testing method allows us to check whether a certain exception was raised or not (assertRaises).

When something exceptional happens, we raise an exception in our code to prevent further processing under the wrong assumptions, and also to inform the caller that something is wrong with the call as it was performed. This is the part of the logic that ought to be tested, and that's what this method is for.

Imagine that we are now extending our logic a little bit further to allow users to close their merge requests, and once this happens, we don't want any more votes to take place (it wouldn't make sense to evaluate a merge request once this was already closed). To prevent this from happening, we extend our code, and we raise an exception on the unfortunate event that someone tries to cast a vote on a closed merge request.

After adding two new statuses (OPEN and CLOSED), and a new close() method, we modify the previous methods for the voting to handle this check first:

```python
class MergeRequest:
    def __init__(self):
        self._context = {
            "upvotes": set(),
            "downvotes": set(),
        }
        self._status = MergeRequestStatus.OPEN

    def close(self):
        self._status = MergeRequestStatus.CLOSED


    ...
    def _cannot_vote_if_closed(self):
        if self._status == MergeRequestStatus.CLOSED:
            raise MergeRequestException(
                "can't vote on a closed merge request"
            )

    def upvote(self, by_user):
        self._cannot_vote_if_closed()

        self._context["downvotes"].discard(by_user)
        self._context["upvotes"].add(by_user)

    def downvote(self, by_user):
        self._cannot_vote_if_closed()

        self._context["upvotes"].discard(by_user)
        self._context["downvotes"].add(by_user)
```

Now, we want to check that this validation indeed works. For this, we're going to use the asssertRaises and assertRaisesRegex methods:

```
def test_cannot_upvote_on_closed_merge_request(self):
    self.merge_request.close()
    self.assertRaises(
        MergeRequestException, self.merge_request.upvote, "dev1"
    )

def test_cannot_downvote_on_closed_merge_request(self):
    self.merge_request.close()
    self.assertRaisesRegex(
        MergeRequestException,
        "can't vote on a closed merge request",
        self.merge_request.downvote,
        "dev1",
    )
```

The former will expect that the exception provided is raised when calling the callable in the second argument, with the arguments (*args and **kwargs) on the rest of the function, and if that's not the case it will fail, saying that the exception that was expected to be raised wasn't. The latter does the same, but it also checks that the exception that was raised contains the message matching the regular expression that was provided as a parameter. Even if the exception is raised, but with a different message (not matching the regular expression), the test will fail.

> Try to check for the error message, as not only will the exception, as an extra check, be more accurate and ensure that it is actually the exception we want that is being triggered, it will check whether another one of the same types got there by chance.

Note how these methods can be used as context managers as well. In its first form (the one used in previous examples), the method takes the exception, then the callable, and finally the list of arguments to use in that callable). But we could also pass the exception as a parameter of the method, use it as a context manager, and evaluate our code inside the block of that context manager, in this format:

```
with self.assertRaises(MyException):
    test_logic()
```

This second form is generally more useful (and sometimes, the only option); for example, if the logic we need to test can't be expressed as a single callable.

In some cases, you'll notice that we need to run the same test case, but with different data. Instead of repeating, and generating duplicated tests, we can build a single one and exercise its condition with different values. This is called **parameterized tests**, and we'll start exploring these in the next section. Later on, we'll revisit parameterized tests with `pytest`.

Parameterized tests

Now, we would like to test how the threshold acceptance for the merge request works, just by providing data samples of what the context looks like without needing the entire `MergeRequest` object. We want to test the part of the `status` property that is after the line that checks whether it's closed, but independently.

The best way to achieve this is to separate that component into another class, use composition, and then move on to test this new abstraction with its own test suite:

```python
class AcceptanceThreshold:
    def __init__(self, merge_request_context: dict) -> None:
        self._context = merge_request_context

    def status(self):
        if self._context["downvotes"]:
            return MergeRequestStatus.REJECTED
        elif len(self._context["upvotes"]) >= 2:
            return MergeRequestStatus.APPROVED
        return MergeRequestStatus.PENDING


class MergeRequest:
    ...
    @property
    def status(self):
        if self._status == MergeRequestStatus.CLOSED:
            return self._status

        return AcceptanceThreshold(self._context).status()
```

With these changes, we can run the tests again and verify that they pass, meaning that this small refactor didn't break anything of the current functionality (unit tests ensure regression). With this, we can proceed with our goal to write tests that are specific to the new class:

```python
class TestAcceptanceThreshold(unittest.TestCase):
    def setUp(self):
        self.fixture_data = (
            (
                {"downvotes": set(), "upvotes": set()},
                MergeRequestStatus.PENDING
            ),
            (
                {"downvotes": set(), "upvotes": {"dev1"}},
                MergeRequestStatus.PENDING,
            ),
            (
                {"downvotes": "dev1", "upvotes": set()},
                MergeRequestStatus.REJECTED,
            ),
            (
                {"downvotes": set(), "upvotes": {"dev1", "dev2"}},
                MergeRequestStatus.APPROVED,
            ),
        )

    def test_status_resolution(self):
        for context, expected in self.fixture_data:
            with self.subTest(context=context):
                status = AcceptanceThreshold(context).status()
                self.assertEqual(status, expected)
```

Here, in the setUp() method, we define the data fixture to be used throughout the tests. In this case, it's not actually needed, because we could have put it directly on the method, but if we expect to run some code before any test is executed, this is the place to write it, because this method is called once before every test is run.

In this particular case, we could have defined this tuple as a class attribute, because it's a constant (static) value. If we needed to run some code, and perform some computation (such as building objects or using a factory), then the setUp() method is our only alternative.

By writing this new version of the code, the parameters under the code being tested are clearer and more compact.

To simulate that we're running all of the parameters, the test iterates over all the data, and exercises the code with each instance. One interesting helper here is the use of `subTest`, which in this case we use to mark the test condition being called. If one of these iterations failed, `unittest` would report it with the corresponding value of the variables that were passed to the `subTest` (in this case, it was named `context`, but any series of keyword arguments would work just the same). For example, one error occurrence might look like this:

```
FAIL: (context={'downvotes': set(), 'upvotes': {'dev1', 'dev2'}})
-----------------------------------------------------------------
Traceback (most recent call last):
  File "" test_status_resolution
    self.assertEqual(status, expected)
AssertionError: <MergeRequestStatus.APPROVED: 'approved'> !=
<MergeRequestStatus.REJECTED: 'rejected'>
```

If you choose to parameterize tests, try to provide the context of each instance of the parameters with as much information as possible to make debugging easier.

The idea behind parameterized tests is to run the same test condition over different sets of data. The idea is that you first identify the equivalence classes of the data to test upon, and then you pick the value's representative of each class (more details on this later in the chapter). Then you'd like to know for which equivalence class your test failed, and the context provided by the `subTest` context manager is helpful in this case.

pytest

Pytest is a great testing framework and can be installed via `pip install pytest`. One difference with respect to `unittest` is that, while it's still possible to classify test scenarios in classes and create object-oriented models of our tests, this is not actually mandatory, and it's possible to write unit tests with less boilerplate by just checking the conditions we want to verify in simple functions with the `assert` statement.

By default, making comparisons with an `assert` statement will be enough for `pytest` to identify a unit test and report its result accordingly. More advanced uses, such as those seen in the previous section, are also possible, but they require the use of specific functions from the package.

A nice feature is that the `pytests` command will run all the tests that it can discover, even if they were written with `unittest`. This compatibility makes it easier to transition from `unittest` to `pytest` gradually.

Basic test cases with pytest

The conditions we tested in the previous section can be rewritten in simple functions with pytest.

Some examples with simple assertions are as follows:

```python
def test_simple_rejected():
    merge_request = MergeRequest()
    merge_request.downvote("maintainer")
    assert merge_request.status == MergeRequestStatus.REJECTED


def test_just_created_is_pending():
    assert MergeRequest().status == MergeRequestStatus.PENDING


def test_pending_awaiting_review():
    merge_request = MergeRequest()
    merge_request.upvote("core-dev")
    assert merge_request.status == MergeRequestStatus.PENDING
```

Boolean equality comparisons don't require more than a simple `assert` statement, whereas other kinds of checks, such as the ones for the exceptions, do require that we use some functions:

```python
def test_invalid_types():
    merge_request = MergeRequest()
    pytest.raises(TypeError, merge_request.upvote, {"invalid-object"})


def test_cannot_vote_on_closed_merge_request():
    merge_request = MergeRequest()
    merge_request.close()
    pytest.raises(MergeRequestException, merge_request.upvote, "dev1")
    with pytest.raises(
        MergeRequestException,
        match="can't vote on a closed merge request",
    ):
        merge_request.downvote("dev1")
```

In this case, `pytest.raises` is the equivalent of `unittest.TestCase.assertRaises`, and it also accepts that it be called both as a method and as a context manager. If we want to check the message of the exception, instead of a different method (such as `assertRaisesRegex`), the same function has to be used, but as a context manager, and by providing the `match` parameter with the expression we would like to identify.

pytest will also wrap the original exception into a custom one that can be expected (by checking some of its attributes, such as `.value`, for instance) in case we want to check for more conditions, but this use of the function covers the vast majority of cases.

Parameterized tests

Running parameterized tests with `pytest` is better, not only because it provides a cleaner API, but also because each combination of the test with its parameters generates a new test case (a new function).

To work with this, we have to use the `pytest.mark.parametrize` decorator on our test. The first parameter of the decorator is a string indicating the names of the parameters to pass to the `test` function, and the second has to be iterable with the respective values for those parameters.

Notice how the body of the testing function is reduced to one line (after removing the internal `for` loop, and its nested context manager), and the data for each test case is correctly isolated from the body of the function, making it easier to extend and maintain:

```
@pytest.mark.parametrize("context,expected_status", (
    (
        {"downvotes": set(), "upvotes": set()},
        MergeRequestStatus.PENDING
    ),
    (
        {"downvotes": set(), "upvotes": {"dev1"}},
        MergeRequestStatus.PENDING,
    ),
    (
        {"downvotes": "dev1", "upvotes": set()},
        MergeRequestStatus.REJECTED,
    ),
    (
        {"downvotes": set(), "upvotes": {"dev1", "dev2"}},
        MergeRequestStatus.APPROVED,
    ),
),)
def test_acceptance_threshold_status_resolution(context, expected_
status):
    assert AcceptanceThreshold(context).status() == expected_status
```

Use @pytest.mark.parametrize to eliminate repetition, keep the body of the test as cohesive as possible, and make the parameters (test inputs or scenarios) that the code must support explicitly.

An important recommendation when using parametrization is that each parameter (every iteration) should correspond to only one testing scenario. That means you should not mix different test conditions into the same parameter. If you need to test for the combination of different parameters, then use different parameterizations stacked up. Stacking up this decorator will create as many test conditions as the cartesian product of all the values in the decorators.

For example, a test configured like this:

```
@pytest.mark.parametrize("x", (1, 2))
@pytest.mark.parametrize("y", ("a", "b"))
def my_test(x, y):
    ...
```

Will run for the values (x=1, y=a), (x=1, y=b), (x=2, y=a), and (x=2, y=b).

This is a better approach as each test is smaller, and each parametrization more specific (cohesive). It will allow you to stress the code with the explosion of all the possible combinations in an easier way.

Data parameters work well when you have the data you need to test, or you know how to build it easily, but in some cases, you need specific objects to be constructed for a test, or you find yourself writing or building the same objects repeatedly. To help with this, we can use fixtures, as we will see in the next section.

Fixtures

One of the great things about pytest is how it facilitates creating reusable features so that we can feed our tests with data or objects to test more effectively and without repetition.

For example, we might want to create a MergeRequest object in a particular state and use that object in multiple tests. We define our object as a fixture by creating a function and applying the @pytest.fixture decorator. The tests that want to use that fixture will have to have a parameter with the same name as the function that's defined, and pytest will make sure that it's provided:

```python
@pytest.fixture
def rejected_mr():
    merge_request = MergeRequest()

    merge_request.downvote("dev1")
    merge_request.upvote("dev2")
    merge_request.upvote("dev3")
    merge_request.downvote("dev4")

    return merge_request

def test_simple_rejected(rejected_mr):
    assert rejected_mr.status == MergeRequestStatus.REJECTED

def test_rejected_with_approvals(rejected_mr):
    rejected_mr.upvote("dev2")
    rejected_mr.upvote("dev3")
    assert rejected_mr.status == MergeRequestStatus.REJECTED

def test_rejected_to_pending(rejected_mr):
    rejected_mr.upvote("dev1")
    assert rejected_mr.status == MergeRequestStatus.PENDING

def test_rejected_to_approved(rejected_mr):
    rejected_mr.upvote("dev1")
    rejected_mr.upvote("dev2")
    assert rejected_mr.status == MergeRequestStatus.APPROVED
```

Remember that tests affect the main code as well, so the principles of clean code apply to them as well. In this case, the **Don't Repeat Yourself** (**DRY**) principle that we explored in previous chapters appears once again, and we can achieve it with the help of pytest fixtures.

Besides creating multiple objects or exposing data that will be used throughout the test suite, it's also possible to use them to set up some conditions, for example, to globally patch some functions that we don't want to be called, or when we want patch objects to be used instead.

Code coverage

Tests runners support coverage plugins (to be installed via `pip`) that provide useful information about what lines in the code have been executed as tests ran. This information is of great help so that we know which parts of the code need to be covered by tests, as well identifying improvements to be made (both in the production code and in the tests). What I mean by this is that detecting lines of our production code that are uncovered will force us to write a test for that part of the code (because remember that code that doesn't have tests should be considered broken). In that attempt of covering the code, several things can happen:

- We might realize we were missing a test scenario completely.
- We'll try to come up with more unit tests or unit tests that cover more lines of code.
- We'll try to simplify our production code, removing redundancies, and making it more compact, meaning it's easier to be covered.
- We might even realize that the lines of code we're trying to cover are unreachable (perhaps there was a mistake in the logic) and can be safely removed.

Keep in mind that even though these are positive points, coverage should never be a target, only a metric. This means trying to achieve a high coverage, just to reach 100%, won't be productive or effective. We should understand code coverage as a unit to identify obvious parts of the code that need testing and see how we can improve that. We can, however, set a minimum threshold of say 80% (a generally accepted value) as the minimum level of desired coverage to know that the project has a reasonable number of tests.

Moreover, thinking that a high degree of code coverage is a sign of a healthy code base is also dangerous: keep in mind that most of the coverage tools will report on production lines of code that have been executed. That a line has been called doesn't mean that it has been properly tested (only that it ran). A single statement might encapsulate multiple logical conditions, each of which needs to be tested separately.

 Don't be misguided by a high degree of code coverage, and keep thinking about ways for testing the code, including those lines that are already covered.

One of the most widely used libraries for this is `coverage` (https://pypi.org/project/coverage/). We'll explore how to set up this tool in the next section.

Setting up rest coverage

In the case of pytest, we can install the pytest-cov package. Once installed, when the tests are run, we have to tell the pytest runner that pytest-cov will also run, and which package (or packages) should be covered (among other parameters and configurations).

This package supports multiple configurations, including different sorts of output formats, and it's easy to integrate it with any CI tool, but among all these features, a highly recommended option is to set the flag that will tell us which lines haven't been covered by tests yet, because this is what's going to help us diagnose our code and allow us to start writing more tests.

To show you an example of what this would look like, use the following command:

```
PYTHONPATH=src pytest \
    --cov-report term-missing \
    --cov=coverage_1 \
    tests/test_coverage_1.py
```

This will produce an output similar to the following:

```
test_coverage_1.py ................ [100%]

----------- coverage: platform linux, python 3.6.5-final-0 -----------
Name           Stmts Miss Cover Missing
--------------------------------------------
coverage_1.py 39      1   97%    44
```

Here, it's telling us that there is a line that doesn't have unit tests so that we can take a look and see how to write a unit test for it. This is a common scenario where we realize that to cover those missing lines, we need to refactor the code by creating smaller methods. As a result, our code will look much better, as in the example we saw at the beginning of this chapter.

The problem lies in the inverse situation—can we trust the high coverage? Does this mean our code is correct? Unfortunately, having good test coverage is a necessary but insufficient condition for clean code. Not having tests for parts of the code is clearly something bad. Having tests is actually very good, but we can only say this for the tests that do exist. However, we don't know much about what tests we are missing, and we might be missing lots of conditions even when code coverage is high.

These are some of the caveats of test coverage, which we will mention in the next section.

Caveats of test coverage

Python is interpreted and, at a very high level, coverage tools take advantage of this to identify the lines that were interpreted (run) while the tests were running. It will then report this at the end. The fact that a line was interpreted does not mean that it was properly tested, and this is why we should be careful about reading the final coverage report and trusting what it says.

This is actually true for any language. The fact that a line was exercised does not mean at all that it was stressed with all its possible combinations. The fact that all branches run successfully with the provided data only means that the code supported that combination, but it doesn't tell us anything about any other possible combinations of parameters that would make the program crash (fuzzy testing).

 Use coverage as a tool to find blind spots in the code, but not as a metric or target goal.

To illustrate this with a simple example, consider the following code:

```
def my_function(number: int):
    return "even" if number % 2 == 0 else "odd"
```

Now, let's say we write the following test for it:

```
@pytest.mark.parametrize("number,expected", [(2, "even")])
def test_my_function(number, expected):
    assert my_function(number) == expected
```

If we run the tests with coverage, the report will give us a flashy 100% of coverage. Needless to say, we're missing a test for half of the conditions of the single statement that executed. Even more troubling is the fact that since the else clause of the statement didn't run, we don't know in which ways our code might break (to make this example even more exaggerated, imagine there was an incorrect statement, such as 1/0 instead of the string "odd", or that there's a function call).

Arguably, we might go a step further and think that this is only the "happy path" because we're providing good values to the function. But what about incorrect types? How should the function defend against that?

As you see, even a single and innocent-looking statement might trigger lots of questions and testing conditions that we need to be prepared for.

It's a good idea to check how covered our code is, and even configure code coverage thresholds as part of the CI build, but we have to keep in mind that this is just another tool for us. And just like previous tools that we have explored (linters, code checkers, formatters, and suchlike), it's useful only in the context of more tools and a good environment prepared for a clean code base.

Another tool that will help us in our testing efforts is the use of mock objects. We explore these in the next section.

Mock objects

There are cases where our code is not the only thing that will be present in the context of our tests. After all, the systems we design and build have to do something real, and that usually means connecting to external services (databases, storage services, external APIs, cloud services, and so on). Because they need to have those side effects, they're inevitable. As much as we abstract our code, program toward interfaces, and isolate code from external factors to minimize side effects, they will be present in our tests, and we need an effective way to handle that.

Mock objects are one of the best tactics used to protect our unit tests against undesirable side effects (as seen earlier in this chapter). Our code might need to perform an HTTP request or send a notification email, but we surely don't want that to happen in our unit tests. Unit tests should target the logic of our code, and run quickly, as we want to run them quite often, which means we cannot afford latency. Therefore, real unit tests don't use any actual service—they don't connect to any database, they don't issue HTTP requests, and basically, they do nothing other than exercise the logic of the production code.

We need tests that do such things, but they aren't units. Integration tests are supposed to test functionality with a broader perspective, almost mimicking the behavior of a user. But they aren't fast. Because they connect to external systems and services, they take longer and are more expensive to run. In general, we would like to have lots of unit tests that run quickly in order to run them all the time and have integration tests run less often (for instance, on any new merge request).

While mock objects are useful, abusing them ranges between a code smell or an anti-pattern. This is the first issue we discuss in the next section, before moving into the details of using mocks.

A fair warning about patching and mocks

I said before that unit tests help us write better code, because the moment we start thinking about how to test our code, we'll realize how it can be improved to make it testable. And usually, as the code becomes more testable, it becomes cleaner (more cohesive, granular, divided into smaller, components, and so on).

Another interesting gain is that testing will help us notice code smells in parts where we thought our code was correct. One of the main warnings that our code has code smells is whether we find ourselves trying to monkey patch (or mock) a lot of different things just to cover a simple test case.

The `unittest` module provides a tool for patching our objects at `unittest.mock.patch`.

Patching means that the original code (given by a string denoting its location at import time) will be replaced by something else, other than its original code. If no replacement object is provided, the default is a standard mock object that will simply accept all method calls or attributes is asked about.

The patching function replaces the code at runtime and has the disadvantage that we are losing contact with the original code that was there in the first place, making our tests a little shallower. It also carries performance considerations because of the overhead that imposes modifying objects in the interpreter at runtime, and it's something that might require future changes if we refactor our code and move things around (because the strings declared in the patching function will no longer be valid).

Using monkey patching or mocks in our tests might be acceptable, and by itself it doesn't represent an issue. On the other hand, abuse in monkey patching is indeed a red flag telling us that something has to be improved in our code.

For example, in the same way that encountering difficulties while testing a function might give us the idea that that function is probably too big and should be broken down into smaller pieces, trying to test a piece of code that requires a very invasive monkey patch should tell us that perhaps the code is relying too heavily on hard dependencies, and that dependency injection should be used instead.

Using mock objects

In unit testing terminology, there are several types of object that fall into the category named **test doubles**. A test double is a type of object that will take the place of a real one in our test suite for different kinds of reasons (maybe we don't need the actual production code, but just a dummy object would work, or maybe we can't use it because it requires access to services or it has side effects that we don't want in our unit tests, and so on).

There are different types of test double, such as dummy objects, stubs, spies, or mocks.

Mocks are the most general type of object, and since they're quite flexible and versatile, they are appropriate for all cases without needing to go into much detail about the rest of them. It is for this reason that the standard library also includes an object of this kind, and it is common in most Python programs. That's the one we are going to be using here: `unittest.mock.Mock`.

A **mock** is a type of object created to a specification (usually resembling the object of a production class) and some configured responses (that is, we can tell the mock what it should return upon certain calls, and what its behavior should be). The `Mock` object will then record, as part of its internal status, how it was called (with what parameters, how many times, and so on), and we can use that information to verify the behavior of our application at a later stage.

In the case of Python, the `Mock` object that's available from the standard library provides a nice API to make all sorts of behavioral assertions, such as checking how many times the mock was called, with what parameters, and so on.

Types of mocks

The standard library provides `Mock` and `MagicMock` objects in the `unittest.mock` module. The former is a test double that can be configured to return any value and will keep track of the calls that were made to it. The latter does the same, but it also supports magic methods. This means that, if we have written idiomatic code that uses magic methods (and parts of the code we are testing will rely on that), it's likely that we will have to use a `MagicMock` instance instead of just a `Mock`.

Trying to use `Mock` when our code needs to call magic methods will result in an error. See the following code for an example of this:

```
class GitBranch:
    def __init__(self, commits: List[Dict]):
        self._commits = {c["id"]: c for c in commits}

    def __getitem__(self, commit_id):
        return self._commits[commit_id]

    def __len__(self):
        return len(self._commits)


def author_by_id(commit_id, branch):
    return branch[commit_id]["author"]
```

We want to test this function; however, another test needs to call the `author_by_id` function. For some reason, since we're not testing that function, any value provided to that function (and returned) will be good:

```python
def test_find_commit():
    branch = GitBranch([{"id": "123", "author": "dev1"}])
    assert author_by_id("123", branch) == "dev1"


def test_find_any():
    author = author_by_id("123", Mock()) is not None
    # ... rest of the tests..
```

As anticipated, this will not work:

```python
def author_by_id(commit_id, branch):
>   return branch[commit_id]["author"]
E   TypeError: 'Mock' object is not subscriptable
```

Using `MagicMock` instead will work. We can even configure the magic method of this type of mock to return something we need in order to control the execution of our test:

```python
def test_find_any():
    mbranch = MagicMock()
    mbranch.__getitem__.return_value = {"author": "test"}
    assert author_by_id("123", mbranch) == "test"
```

A use case for test doubles

To see a possible use of mocks, we need to add a new component to our application that will be in charge of notifying the merge request of the `status` of the `build`. When a `build` is finished, this object will be called with the ID of the merge request and the `status` of the `build`, and it will update the `status` of the merge request with this information by sending an HTTP POST request to a particular fixed endpoint:

```python
# mock_2.py

from datetime import datetime
import requests
from constants import STATUS_ENDPOINT


class BuildStatus:
```

```python
    """The CI status of a pull request."""

    @staticmethod
    def build_date() -> str:
        return datetime.utcnow().isoformat()

    @classmethod
    def notify(cls, merge_request_id, status):
        build_status = {
            "id": merge_request_id,
            "status": status,
            "built_at": cls.build_date(),
        }
        response = requests.post(STATUS_ENDPOINT, json=build_status)
        response.raise_for_status()
        return response
```

This class has many side effects, but one of them is an important external dependency that is hard to surmount. If we try to write a test over it without modifying anything, it will fail with a connection error as soon as it tries to perform the HTTP connection.

As a testing goal, we just want to make sure that the information is composed correctly, and that library requests are being called with the appropriate parameters. Since this is an external dependency, we don't want to test the requests module; just checking that it's called correctly will be enough.

Another problem we will face when trying to compare data being sent to the library is that the class is calculating the current timestamp, which is impossible to predict in a unit test. Patching datetime directly is not possible, because the module is written in C. Some external libraries that can do that (freezegun, for example), but they come with a performance penalty, and for this example, this would be overkill. Therefore, we opt to wrap the functionality we want in a static method that we will be able to patch.

Now that we have established the points that need to be replaced in the code, let's write the unit test:

```python
# test_mock_2.py

from unittest import mock

from constants import STATUS_ENDPOINT
from mock_2 import BuildStatus
```

```
@mock.patch("mock_2.requests")
def test_build_notification_sent(mock_requests):
    build_date = "2018-01-01T00:00:01"
    with mock.patch(
        "mock_2.BuildStatus.build_date",
        return_value=build_date
    ):
        BuildStatus.notify(123, "OK")

    expected_payload = {
        "id": 123,
        "status": "OK",
        "built_at": build_date
    }
    mock_requests.post.assert_called_with(
        STATUS_ENDPOINT, json=expected_payload
    )
```

First, we use `mock.patch` as a decorator to replace the `requests` module. The result of this function will create a `mock` object that will be passed as a parameter to the test (named `mock_requests` in this example). Then, we use this function again, but this time as a context manager to change the return value of the method of the class that computes the date of the `build`, replacing the value with one we control, which we will use in the assertion.

Once we have all of this in place, we can call the class method with some parameters, and then we can use the `mock` object to check how it was called. In this case, we are using the method to see whether `requests.post` was indeed called with the parameters as we wanted them to be composed.

This is a nice feature of mocks—not only do they put some boundaries around all external components (in this case to prevent actually sending some notifications or issuing HTTP requests), but they also provide a useful API to verify the calls and their parameters.

While, in this case, we were able to test the code by setting the respective mock objects in place, it's also true that we had to patch quite a lot in proportion to the total lines of code for the main functionality. There is no rule about the ratio of pure productive code being tested versus how many parts of that code we have to mock, but certainly, by using common sense, we can see that, if we had to patch quite a lot of things in the same parts, something is not clearly abstracted, and it looks like a code smell.

The patching of external dependencies can be used in combination with fixtures to apply some global configurations. For example, it's usually a good idea to prevent all the unit tests from performing HTTP calls, so within the subdirectory for unit tests, we can add a fixture in the configuration file of pytest (`tests/unit/conftest.py`):

```
@pytest.fixture(autouse=True)
def no_requests():
    with patch("requests.post"):
        yield
```

This function will be invoked automatically in all unit tests (because of autouse=True), and when it does, it will patch the post function in the requests module. This is just an idea you can adapt to your projects to add some extra safety and make sure your unit tests are free of side effects.

In the next section, we will explore how to refactor code to overcome this issue.

Refactoring

Refactoring means changing the structure of the code by rearranging its internal representation without modifying its external behavior.

One example would be if you identify a class that has lots of responsibilities and very long methods, and then decide to change it by using smaller methods, creating new internal collaborators, and distributing responsibilities into new, smaller objects. As you do that, you're careful not to change the original interface of that class, keep all its public methods as before, and not change any signature. To an external observer of that class, it might look like nothing happened (but we know otherwise).

Refactoring is a critical activity in software maintenance, yet something that can't be done (at least not correctly) without having unit tests. This is because, as each change gets made, we need to know that our code is still correct. In a sense, you can think of our unit tests as the "external observer" for our code, making sure the contract doesn't break.

Every now and then, we need to support a new feature or use our software in unintended ways. The only way to accommodate such requirements is by first refactoring our code, to make it more generic or flexible.

Typically, when refactoring our code, we want to improve its structure and make it better, sometimes more generic, more readable, or more flexible. The challenge is to achieve these goals while at the same time preserving the exact same functionality it had prior to the modifications that were made. This constraint of having to support the same functionalities as before, but with a different version of the code, implies that we need to run regression tests on code that was modified. The only cost-effective way of running regression tests is if those tests are automatic. The most cost-effective version of automatic tests is unit testing.

Evolving our code

In the previous example, we were able to separate out the side effects from our code to make it testable by patching those parts of the code that depended on things we couldn't control on the unit test. This is a good approach since, after all, the mock. patch function comes in handy for these sorts of tasks and replaces the objects we tell it to, giving us back a Mock object.

The downside of that is that we have to provide the path of the object we are going to mock, including the module, as a string. This is a bit fragile, because if we refactor our code (let's say we rename the file or move it to some other location), all the places with the patch will have to be updated, or the test will break.

In the example, the fact that the notify() method directly depends on an implementation detail (the requests module) is a design issue; that is, it is taking its toll on the unit tests as well with the aforementioned fragility that is implied.

We still need to replace those methods with doubles (mocks), but if we refactor the code, we can do it in a better way. Let's separate these methods into smaller ones, and most importantly inject the dependency rather than keep it fixed. The code now applies the dependency inversion principle, and it expects to work with something that supports an interface (in this example, an implicit one), such as the one that the requests module provides:

```python
from datetime import datetime

from constants import STATUS_ENDPOINT


class BuildStatus:

    endpoint = STATUS_ENDPOINT

    def __init__(self, transport):
        self.transport = transport

    @staticmethod
    def build_date() -> str:
        return datetime.utcnow().isoformat()

    def compose_payload(self, merge_request_id, status) -> dict:
        return {
```

```
            "id": merge_request_id,
            "status": status,
            "built_at": self.build_date(),
        }

    def deliver(self, payload):
        response = self.transport.post(self.endpoint, json=payload)
        response.raise_for_status()
        return response

    def notify(self, merge_request_id, status):
        return self.deliver(self.compose_payload(merge_request_id,
    status))
```

We separate the methods (note how notify is now compose + deliver), make compose_
payload() a new method (so that we can replace, without the need to patch the
class), and require the transport dependency to be injected. Now that transport is a
dependency, it is much easier to change that object for any double we want.

It is even possible to expose a fixture of this object, with the doubles replaced as
required:

```
@pytest.fixture
def build_status():
    bstatus = BuildStatus(Mock())
    bstatus.build_date = Mock(return_value="2018-01-01T00:00:01")
    return bstatus


def test_build_notification_sent(build_status):

    build_status.notify(1234, "OK")

    expected_payload = {
        "id": 1234,
        "status": "OK",
        "built_at": build_status.build_date(),
    }
    build_status.transport.post.assert_called_with(
        build_status.endpoint, json=expected_payload
    )
```

As mentioned in the first chapter, the goal of having clean code is to have maintainable code, code that we can refactor so that it can evolve and extend to more requirements. To this end, tests are a great help. But since tests are so important, we also need to refactor them so that they can also maintain their relevance and usefulness as the code evolves. This is the topic of discussion of the next section.

Production code isn't the only one that evolves

We keep saying that unit tests are as important as production code. And if we are careful enough with the production code to create the best possible abstraction, why wouldn't we do the same for unit tests?

If the code for unit tests is as important as the main code, then it's wise to design it with extensibility in mind and make it as maintainable as possible. After all, this is the code that will have to be maintained by an engineer other than its original author, so it has to be readable.

The reason why we pay so much attention to the code's flexibility is that we know requirements change and evolve over time, and eventually, as domain business rules change, our code will have to change as well to support these new requirements. Since the production code changed to support new requirements, in turn, the testing code will have to change as well to support the newer version of the production code.

In one of the first examples we used, we created a series of tests for the merge request object, trying different combinations and checking the status at which the merge request was left. This is a good first approach, but we can do better than that.

Once we understand the problem better, we can start creating better abstractions. With this, the first idea that comes to mind is that we can create a higher-level abstraction that checks for particular conditions. For example, if we have an object that is a test suite that specifically targets the MergeRequest class, we know its functionality will be limited to the behavior of this class (because it should comply to the SRP), and therefore we could create specific testing methods on this testing class. These will only make sense for this class, but that will be helpful in reducing a lot of boilerplate code.

Instead of repeating assertions that follow the exact same structure, we can create a method that encapsulates this and reuse it across all of the tests:

```python
class TestMergeRequestStatus(unittest.TestCase):
    def setUp(self):
```

```
        self.merge_request = MergeRequest()

    def assert_rejected(self):
        self.assertEqual(
            self.merge_request.status, MergeRequestStatus.REJECTED
        )

    def assert_pending(self):
        self.assertEqual(
            self.merge_request.status, MergeRequestStatus.PENDING
        )

    def assert_approved(self):
        self.assertEqual(
            self.merge_request.status, MergeRequestStatus.APPROVED
        )

    def test_simple_rejected(self):
        self.merge_request.downvote("maintainer")
        self.assert_rejected()

    def test_just_created_is_pending(self):
        self.assert_pending()
```

If something changes with how we check the status of a merge request (or let's say we want to add extra checks), there is only one place (the assert_approved() method) that will have to be modified. More importantly, by creating these higher-level abstractions, the code that started as merely unit tests starts to evolve into what could end up being a testing framework with its own API or domain language, making testing more declarative.

More about testing

With the concepts we have revisited so far, we know how to test our code, think about our design in terms of how it is going to be tested, and configure the tools in our project to run the automated tests that will give us some degree of confidence regarding the quality of the software we have written.

If our confidence in the code is determined by the unit tests written on it, how do we know that they are enough? How could we be sure that we have been through enough on the test scenarios and that we are not missing some tests? Who says that these tests are correct? Meaning, who tests the tests?

The first part of the question, about being thorough in terms of the tests we write, is answered by going beyond in our testing efforts through property-based testing.

The second part of the question might have multiple answers from different points of view, but we are going to briefly mention mutation testing as a means of determining that our tests are indeed correct. In this sense, we are thinking that the unit tests check our main productive code, and this works as a control for the unit tests as well.

Property-based testing

Property-based testing consists of generating data for tests cases to find scenarios that will make the code fail, which weren't covered by our previous unit tests.

The main library for this is hypothesis which, configured along with our unit tests, will help us find problematic data that will make our code fail.

We can imagine that what this library does is find counterexamples for our code. We write our production code (and unit tests for it!), and we claim it's correct. Now, with this library, we define a hypothesis that must hold for our code, and if there are some cases where our assertions don't hold, hypothesis will provide a set of data that causes the error.

The best thing about unit tests is that they make us think harder about our production code. The best thing about hypothesis is that it makes us think harder about our unit tests.

Mutation testing

We know that tests are the formal verification method we have to ensure that our code is correct. And what makes sure that the test is correct? The production code, you might think, and yes, in a way this is correct. We can think of the main code as a counterbalance for our tests.

The point in writing unit tests is that we are protecting ourselves against bugs and testing for failure scenarios we don't want to happen in production. It's good that the tests pass, but it would be bad if they pass for the wrong reasons. That is, we can use unit tests as an automatic regression tool—if someone introduces a bug in the code, later on, we expect at least one of our tests to catch it and fail. If this doesn't happen, either there is a test missing, or the ones we had are not doing the right checks.

This is the idea behind mutation testing. With a mutation testing tool, the code will be modified to new versions (called **mutants**) that are variations of the original code, but with some of its logic altered (for example, operators are swapped, conditions are inverted).

A good test suite should catch these mutants and kill them, in which case it means we can rely on the tests. If some mutants survive the experiment, it's usually a bad sign. Of course, this is not entirely precise, so there are intermediate states we might want to ignore.

To quickly show you how this works and to allow you to get a practical idea of this, we are going to use a different version of the code that computes the status of a merge request based on the number of approvals and rejections. This time, we have changed the code for a simple version that, based on these numbers, returns the result. We have moved the enumeration with the constants for the statuses to a separate module so that it now looks more compact:

```
# File mutation_testing_1.py
from mrstatus import MergeRequestStatus as Status


def evaluate_merge_request(upvote_count, downvotes_count):
    if downvotes_count > 0:
        return Status.REJECTED
    if upvote_count >= 2:
        return Status.APPROVED
    return Status.PENDING
```

And now will we add a simple unit test, checking one of the conditions and its expected result:

```
# file: test_mutation_testing_1.py
class TestMergeRequestEvaluation(unittest.TestCase):
    def test_approved(self):
        result = evaluate_merge_request(3, 0)
        self.assertEqual(result, Status.APPROVED)
```

Now, we will install mutpy, a mutation testing tool for Python, with pip install mutpy, and tell it to run the mutation testing for this module with these tests. The following code runs for different cases, which are distinguished by changing the CASE environment variable:

```
$ PYTHONPATH=src mut.py \
    --target src/mutation_testing_${CASE}.py \
    --unit-test tests/test_mutation_testing_${CASE}.py \
    --operator AOD `# delete arithmetic operator`\
    --operator AOR `# replace arithmetic operator` \
    --operator COD `# delete conditional operator` \
    --operator COI `# insert conditional operator` \
    --operator CRP `# replace constant` \
    --operator ROR `# replace relational operator` \
    --show-mutants
```

If you run the previous command for case 2 (which is also possible to run as `make mutation CASE=2`), the result is going to look something similar to this:

```
[*] Mutation score [0.04649 s]: 100.0%
    - all: 4
    - killed: 4 (100.0%)
    - survived: 0 (0.0%)
    - incompetent: 0 (0.0%)
    - timeout: 0 (0.0%)
```

This is a good sign. Let's take a particular instance to analyze what happened. One of the lines on the output shows the following mutant:

```
 - [# 1] ROR mutation_testing_1:11 :
------------------------------------------------------------
   7: from mrstatus import MergeRequestStatus as Status
   8:
   9:
  10: def evaluate_merge_request(upvote_count, downvotes_count):
~11:     if downvotes_count < 0:
  12:         return Status.REJECTED
  13:     if upvote_count >= 2:
  14:         return Status.APPROVED
  15:     return Status.PENDING
------------------------------------------------------------
[0.00401 s] killed by test_approved (test_mutation_testing_1.
TestMergeRequestEvaluation)
```

Notice that this mutant consists of the original version with the operator changed in line 11 (> for <), and the result is telling us that this mutant was killed by the tests. This means that with this version of the code (let's imagine that someone makes this change by mistake), then the result of the function would have been APPROVED, and since the test expects it to be REJECTED, it fails, which is a good sign (the test caught the bug that was introduced).

Mutation testing is a good way to assure the quality of the unit tests, but it requires some effort and careful analysis. By using this tool in complex environments, we will have to take some time analyzing each scenario. It is also true that it is expensive to run these tests because it requires multiple runs of different versions of the code, which might take up too many resources and may take longer to complete. However, it would be even more expensive to have to make these checks manually and will require much more effort. Not doing these checks at all might be even riskier because we would be jeopardizing the quality of the tests.

Common themes in testing

I'd like to briefly touch on some topics that are usually good to keep in mind when thinking of ways of how to test our code because they're recurrent and helpful.

These are points you'll usually want to think about when trying to come up with tests for the code because they lead to ruthless testing. When you're writing unit tests, your mindset has to be all about breaking the code: you want to make sure you find errors so that you can fix them, and that they don't slip into production (which will be much worse).

Boundaries or limit values

Boundary values are usually a great source of trouble in the code, so that's probably a good starting place. Take a look at the code and inspect for conditions set around some values. Then, add tests to make sure you include these values.

For example, in a line of code such as this:

```
if remaining_days > 0: ...
```

Add explicit tests for the zero, because this seems to be a special case in the code.

More generally, in a condition that checks for a range of values, check both ends of the interval. If the code deals with data structures (such as a list or a stack), check for an empty list, or a full stack, and make sure the indexes are always set correctly, even for values on their limits.

Classes of equivalence

An equivalence class is a partition over a set, such that all elements in that partition are equivalent with respect to some function. Because all elements inside this partition are equivalent, we only need one of them as a representative in order to test that condition.

To give a simple example, let's recap our previous code used in the section to demonstrate code coverage:

```
def my_function(number: int):
    return "even" if number % 2 == 0 else "odd"
```

Here, the function has a single `if` statement and is returning different data depending on that condition.

If we wanted to simplify the testing for this function by stipulating that the set of values for input testing, s, is the set of integers, we could argue that it can be partitioned into two: even and odd numbers.

Because this code does something for even numbers, and something else for odd ones, we can say that these are our testing conditions. Namely, we only need one element of each sub-set to test the entire condition, no more than that. In other words, testing with 2 is the same as testing with 4 (the same logic is exercised in both cases), so we don't need both, but only one (any) of them. The same goes for 1, and 3 (or any other odd number).

We can separate these representative elements into different parameters, and run the same test by using the @pytest.mark.parametrize decorator. The important thing is to make sure we cover all the cases, and that we're not repeating elements (that is, that we're not adding two different parametrizations with elements of the same partition, because that doesn't add any value).

Testing by classes of equivalence has two benefits: on the one hand, we test effectively by not repeating new values that don't add anything to our testing scenario, and on the other hand, if we exhaust all classes, then we have good coverage of the scenarios to test for.

Edge cases

Finally, try to add specific tests for all edge cases you can think of. This pretty much depends on the business logic and the peculiarities of the code you're writing, and there's some overlap with the idea of testing around boundary values.

For example, if part of your code deals with dates, make sure you test for leap years, the 29th of February, and in or around the new year.

So far, we have assumed we're writing the tests after the code. This is a typical case. After all, most of the time, you'll find yourself working on an already existing code base, rather than starting it from scratch.

There's an alternative, which is writing the test prior to the code. That might be because you're starting a new project or feature, and you want to see what it will look like before writing the actual production code. Or it might be because there's a defect on the code base, and you first want to write a test to reproduce it, before jumping into the fix. This is called **Test-Driven Design** (**TDD**) and is discussed in the next section.

A brief introduction to test-driven development

There are entire books dedicated only to TDD, so it would not be realistic to try and cover this topic comprehensively in this book. However, it's such an important topic that it has to be mentioned.

The idea behind TDD is that tests should be written before production code in a way that the production code is only written to respond to tests that are failing due to that missing implementation of the functionality.

There are multiple reasons why we would like to write the tests first and then the code. From a pragmatic point of view, we would be covering our production code quite accurately. Since all of the production code was written to respond to a unit test, it would be highly unlikely that there are tests missing for functionality (that doesn't mean that there is 100% coverage of course, but at least all the main functions, methods, or components will have their respective tests, even if they aren't completely covered).

The workflow is simple and, at a high level, consist of three steps:

1. Write a unit test that describes how the code should behave. That can either be new functionality that still doesn't exist or current code that is broken, in which case the test describes the desired scenario. Running this test for the first time must fail.
2. Make the minimal changes in the code to make that test pass. The test should now pass.
3. Improve (refactor) the code and run the test again, making sure it still works.

This cycle has been popularized as the famous **red-green-refactor**, meaning that in the beginning, the tests fail (red), then we make them pass (green), and then we proceed to refactor the code and iterate it.

Summary

Unit testing is a really interesting and deep topic, but more importantly, it is a critical part of the clean code. Ultimately, unit tests are what determine the quality of the code. Unit tests often act as a mirror for the code — when the code is easy to test, it's clear and correctly designed, and this will be reflected in the unit tests.

The code for the unit tests is as important as production code. All principles that apply to production code also apply to unit tests. This means that they should be designed and maintained with the same effort and thoughtfulness. If we don't care about our unit tests, they will start to have problems and become defective (or problematic) and, as a result of that, useless. If this happens, and they are hard to maintain, they become a liability, which makes things even worse, because people will tend to ignore them or disable them entirely. This is the worst scenario because once this happens, the entire production code is in jeopardy. Moving forward blindly (without unit tests) is a recipe for disaster.

Luckily, Python provides many tools for unit testing, both in the standard library and available through `pip`. They are of great help and investing time in configuring them pays off in the long run.

We have seen how unit tests work as the formal specification of the program, and the proof that a piece of software works according to the specification, and we also learned that when it comes to discovering new testing scenarios, there is always room for improvement and we can always create more tests. In this sense, expanding our unit tests with different approaches (such as property-based testing or mutation testing) is a good investment.

In the next chapter, we'll learn about design patterns and their applicability in Python.

References

Here is a list of information you can refer to:

- The `unittest` module of the Python standard library contains comprehensive documentation on how to start building a test suite: `https://docs.python.org/3/library/unittest.html`

- Hypothesis: `https://hypothesis.readthedocs.io/en/latest/`

- `Pytest`'s official documentation: `https://docs.pytest.org/en/latest/`

- *The Cathedral and the Bazaar: Musings on Linux and Open Source by an Accidental Revolutionary (CatB)*, written by Eric S. Raymond (publisher: O'Reilly Media, 1999)

- Refactoring: `https://refactoring.com/`

- *The art of software testing*, written by *Glenford J. Myers* (publisher: Wiley; 3rd edition, November 8, 2011)

- Writing testable code: `https://testing.googleblog.com/2008/08/by-miko-hevery-so-you-decided-to.html`

9
Common Design Patterns

Design patterns have been a widespread topic in software engineering since their original inception in the famous **Gang of Four** (**GoF**) book, *Design Patterns: Elements of Reusable Object-Oriented Software*. Design patterns help to solve common problems with abstractions that work for certain scenarios. When they are implemented properly, the general design of the solution can benefit from them.

In this chapter, we take a look at some of the most common design patterns, but not from the perspective of tools to apply under certain conditions (once the patterns have been devised), but rather we analyze how design patterns contribute to clean code. After presenting a solution that implements a design pattern, we will analyze how the final implementation is comparatively better than if we had chosen a different path.

As part of this analysis, we will see how to concretely implement design patterns in Python. As a result of that, we will see that the dynamic nature of Python implies some differences of implementation, with respect to other static typed languages, for which many of the design patterns were originally thought of. This means that there are some particularities about design patterns that you should bear in mind when it comes to Python, and, in some cases, trying to apply a design pattern where it doesn't really fit is non-Pythonic.

In this chapter, we will cover the following topics:

- Common design patterns
- Design patterns that don't apply in Python, and the idiomatic alternative that should be followed

- The Pythonic way of implementing the most common design patterns
- Understanding how good abstractions evolve naturally into patterns

With the knowledge from previous chapters, we're now in a position to analyze code at a higher level of design and at the same time think in terms of its detailed implementation (how would we write it in a way that uses the features of Python most efficiently?).

In this chapter, we'll analyze how we can use design patterns to achieve cleaner code, starting with analyzing some initial considerations in the following section.

Design pattern considerations in Python

Object-oriented design patterns are ideas of software construction that appear in different scenarios when we deal with models of the problem we're solving. Because they're high-level ideas, it's hard to think of them as being tied to particular programming languages. They are instead more general concepts about how objects will interact in the application. Of course, they will have their implementation details, varying from language to language, but that doesn't form the essence of a design pattern.

That's the theoretical aspect of a design pattern, the fact that it is an abstract idea that expresses concepts about the layout of the objects in the solution. There are plenty of other books and several other resources about object-oriented design, and design patterns in particular, so in this book, we are going to focus on those implementation details for Python.

Given the nature of Python, some of the classical design patterns aren't actually needed. That means that Python already supports features that render those patterns invisible. Some argue that they don't exist in Python, but keep in mind that invisible doesn't mean non-existing. They are there, just embedded in Python itself, so it's likely that we won't even notice them.

Others have a much simpler implementation, again thanks to the dynamic nature of the language, and the rest of them are practically the same as they are in other platforms, with small differences.

In any case, the important goal for achieving clean code in Python is knowing what patterns to implement and how. That means recognizing some of the patterns that Python already abstracts and how we can leverage them. For instance, it would be completely non-Pythonic to try to implement the standard definition of the iterator pattern (as we would do in different languages), because (as we have already covered) iteration is deeply embedded in Python, and the fact that we can create objects that will directly work in a for loop makes this the right way to proceed.

Something similar happens with some of the creational patterns. Classes are regular objects in Python, and so are functions. As we have seen in several examples so far, they can be passed around, decorated, reassigned, and so on. That means that whatever kind of customization we would like to make to our objects, we can most likely do it without needing any particular setup of factory classes. Also, there is no special syntax for creating objects in Python (no new keyword, for example). This is another reason why, most of the time, a simple function call will work just like a factory.

Other patterns are still needed, and we will see how, with some small adaptations, we can make them more Pythonic, taking full advantage of the features that the language provides (magic methods or the standard library).

Out of all the patterns available, not all of them are equally frequent, nor useful, so we will focus on the main ones, those that we would expect to see the most in our applications, and we will do so by following a pragmatic approach.

Design patterns in action

The canonical reference in this subject, as written by the GoF, introduces 23 design patterns, each falling under one of the creational, structural, and behavioral categories. There are even more patterns or variations of existing ones, but rather than learning all of these patterns off by heart, we should focus on keeping two things in mind. Some of the patterns are invisible in Python, and we use them *probably* without even noticing. Secondly, not all patterns are equally common; some of them are tremendously useful, and so they are found very frequently, while others are for more specific cases.

In this section, we will revisit the most common patterns, those that are most likely to emerge from our design. Note the use of the word **emerge** here. We should not force the application of a design pattern to the solution we are building, but rather evolve, refactor, and improve our solution until a pattern emerges.

Design patterns are therefore not invented but discovered. When a situation that occurs repeatedly in our code reveals itself, the general and more abstract layout of classes, objects, and related components appears under a name by which we identify a pattern.

The name of a design pattern wraps up a lot of concepts. This is probably the best thing about design patterns; they provide a language. Through design patterns, it's easier to communicate design ideas effectively. When two or more software engineers share the same vocabulary, and one of them mentions strategy, the rest of the software engineers in the room can immediately think about all the classes, and how they would be related, what their mechanics would be, and so on, without having to repeat this explanation.

The reader will notice that the code shown in this chapter is different from the canonical or original envisioning of the design pattern in question. There is more than one reason for this. The first reason is that the examples take a more pragmatic approach, aimed at solutions for particular scenarios, rather than exploring general design theory. The second reason is that the patterns are implemented with the particularities of Python, which in some cases are very subtle, but in other cases, the differences are noticeable, generally simplifying the code.

Creational patterns

In software engineering, creational patterns are those that deal with object instantiation, trying to abstract away much of the complexity (like determining the parameters to initialize an object, all the related objects that might be needed, and so on), in order to leave the user with a simpler interface that should be safer to use. The basic form of object creation could result in design problems or added complexity to the design. Creational design patterns solve this problem by somehow controlling this object creation.

Out of the five patterns for creating objects, we will discuss mainly the variants that are used to avoid the singleton pattern and replace it with the Borg pattern (most commonly used in Python applications), discussing their differences and advantages.

Factories

As was mentioned in the introduction, one of the core features of Python is that everything is an object, and as such, they can all be treated equally. This means that there are no special distinctions of things that we can or cannot do with classes, functions, or custom objects. They can all be passed by a parameter, assigned, and so on.

It is for this reason that many of the factory patterns are not usually needed. We could just simply define a function that will construct a set of objects, and we can even pass the class that we want to create with a parameter.

We saw an example of a sort of factory in action when we used `pyinject` as a library to help us with dependency injection, and the initialization of complex objects. In cases where we need to deal with a complex setup, and we want to make sure we are using dependency injection to initialize our objects without repeating ourselves, we can use libraries such as `pyinject` or come up with an analogous structure in our code.

Singleton and shared state (monostate)

The singleton pattern, on the other hand, is something not entirely abstracted away by Python. The truth is that most of the time, this pattern is either not really needed or is a bad choice. There are a lot of problems with singletons (after all, they are, in fact, a form of global variables for object-oriented software, and as such are a bad practice). They are hard to unit test, the fact that they might be modified at any time by any object makes them hard to predict, and their side effects can be really problematic.

As a general principle, we should avoid using singletons as much as possible. If in some extreme case they are required, the easiest way of achieving this in Python is by using a module. We can create an object in a module, and once it's there, it will be available from every part of the module that is imported. Python itself makes sure that modules are already singletons, in the sense that no matter how many times they're imported, and from how many places, the same module is *always* the one that is going to be loaded into `sys.modules`. Therefore, an object initialized inside this Python module will be unique.

Note how this is not quite the same as a singleton. The idea of a singleton is to create a class that no matter how many times you invoke it, will always give you the same object. The idea presented in the previous paragraph is about having a unique object. Regardless of how its class is defined, we create an object only once and then use the same object multiple times. These are sometimes called well-known objects; objects that don't need more than one of their kind.

We are familiar with these objects already. Consider `None`. We don't need more than one for the whole Python interpreter. Some developers claim that "`None` is a singleton in Python." I slightly disagree with that. It's a well-known object: something we all know, and we don't need another one. The same goes for `True` and `False`. It wouldn't make sense to try to create a different kind of boolean.

Shared state

Rather than forcing our design to have a singleton in which only one instance is created, no matter how the object is invoked, constructed, or initialized, it is better to replicate the data across multiple instances.

The idea of the monostate pattern (SNGMONO) is that we can have many instances that are just regular objects, without having to care whether they're singletons or not (seeing as they're just objects). The good thing about this pattern is that these objects will have their information synchronized, in a completely transparent way, without us having to worry about how this works internally.

This makes this pattern a much better choice, not only for its convenience, but also because it is less error-prone, and suffers from fewer of the disadvantages of singletons (regarding their testability, creating derived classes, and so on).

We can use this pattern on many levels, depending on how much information we need to synchronize.

In its simplest form, we can assume that we only need to have one attribute to be reflected across all instances. If that is the case, the implementation is as trivial as using a class variable, and we just need to take care of providing a correct interface to update and retrieve the value of the attribute.

Let's say we have an object that has to pull a version of some code in a Git repository by the latest tag. There might be multiple instances of this object, and when every client calls the method for fetching the code, this object will use the tag version from its attribute. At any point, this tag can be updated for a newer version, and we want any other instance (new or already created) to use this new branch when the fetch operation is being called, as shown in the following code:

```python
class GitFetcher:
    _current_tag = None

    def __init__(self, tag):
        self.current_tag = tag

    @property
    def current_tag(self):
        if self._current_tag is None:
            raise AttributeError("tag was never set")
        return self._current_tag

    @current_tag.setter
    def current_tag(self, new_tag):
        self.__class__._current_tag = new_tag

    def pull(self):
        logger.info("pulling from %s", self.current_tag)
        return self.current_tag
```

The reader can simply verify that creating multiple objects of the `GitFetcher` type with different versions will result in all objects being set with the latest version at any time, as shown in the following code:

```
>>> f1 = GitFetcher(0.1)
>>> f2 = GitFetcher(0.2)
>>> f1.current_tag = 0.3
>>> f2.pull()
0.3
>>> f1.pull()
0.3
```

In the case that we need more attributes, or that we wish to encapsulate the shared attribute a bit more, to make the design cleaner, we can use a descriptor.

A descriptor, like the one shown in the following code, solves the problem, and while it's true that it requires more code, it also encapsulates a more concrete responsibility, and part of the code is actually moved away from our original class, making it more cohesive and compliant with the single responsibility principle:

```python
class SharedAttribute:
    def __init__(self, initial_value=None):
        self.value = initial_value
        self._name = None

    def __get__(self, instance, owner):
        if instance is None:
            return self
        if self.value is None:
            raise AttributeError(f"{self._name} was never set")
        return self.value

    def __set__(self, instance, new_value):
        self.value = new_value

    def __set_name__(self, owner, name):
        self._name = name
```

Apart from these considerations, it's also true that the pattern is now more reusable. If we want to repeat this logic, we just have to create a new descriptor object that would work (complying with the DRY principle).

If we *now* want to do the same but for the current branch, we create this new class attribute, and the rest of the class is kept intact, while still having the desired logic in place, as shown in the following code:

```
class GitFetcher:
    current_tag = SharedAttribute()
    current_branch = SharedAttribute()

    def __init__(self, tag, branch=None):
        self.current_tag = tag
        self.current_branch = branch

    def pull(self):
        logger.info("pulling from %s", self.current_tag)
        return self.current_tag
```

The balance and trade-off of this new approach should be clear by now. This new implementation uses a bit more code, but it's reusable, so it saves lines of code (and duplicated logic) in the long run. Once again, refer to the three or more instances rule to decide if you should create such an abstraction.

Another important benefit of this solution is that it also reduces the repetition of unit tests (because we only need to test the `SharedAttribute` class, and not all uses of it).

Reusing code here will give us more confidence in the overall quality of the solution, because now we just have to write unit tests for the descriptor object, not for all the classes that use it (we can safely assume that they're correct as long as the unit tests prove the descriptor to be correct).

The Borg pattern

The previous solutions should work for most cases, but if we really have to go for a singleton (and this has to be a really good exception), then there is one last better alternative to it, only this is a riskier one.

This is the actual mono-state pattern, referred to as the Borg pattern in Python. The idea is to create an object that is capable of replicating all of its attributes among all instances of the same class. The fact that absolutely every attribute is being replicated has to be a warning to keep in mind undesired side effects. Still, this pattern has many advantages over the singleton.

In this case, we are going to split the previous object into two—one that works over Git tags, and the other over branches. And we are using the code that will make the Borg pattern work:

```
class BaseFetcher:
    def __init__(self, source):
        self.source = source


class TagFetcher(BaseFetcher):
    _attributes = {}

    def __init__(self, source):
        self.__dict__ = self.__class__._attributes
        super().__init__(source)

    def pull(self):
        logger.info("pulling from tag %s", self.source)
        return f"Tag = {self.source}"


class BranchFetcher(BaseFetcher):
    _attributes = {}

    def __init__(self, source):
        self.__dict__ = self.__class__._attributes
        super().__init__(source)

    def pull(self):
        logger.info("pulling from branch %s", self.source)
        return f"Branch = {self.source}"
```

Both objects have a base class, sharing their initialization method. But then they have to implement it again in order to make the *Borg logic* work. The idea is that we use a class attribute that is a dictionary to store the attributes, and then we make the dictionary of each object (at the time it's being initialized) use this very same dictionary. This means that any update on the dictionary of an object will be reflected in the class, which will be the same for the rest of the objects because their class is the same, and dictionaries are mutable objects that are passed as a reference. In other words, when we create new objects of this type, they will all use the same dictionary, and this dictionary is constantly being updated.

Note that we cannot put the logic of the dictionary on the base class, because this will mix the values among the objects of different classes, which is not what we want. This boilerplate solution is what would make many think it's actually an idiom rather than a pattern.

A possible way of abstracting this in a way that achieves the DRY principle would be to create a `mixin` class, as shown in the following code:

```python
class SharedAllMixin:
    def __init__(self, *args, **kwargs):
        try:
            self.__class__._attributes
        except AttributeError:
            self.__class__._attributes = {}

        self.__dict__ = self.__class__._attributes
        super().__init__(*args, **kwargs)


class BaseFetcher:
    def __init__(self, source):
        self.source = source


class TagFetcher(SharedAllMixin, BaseFetcher):
    def pull(self):
        logger.info("pulling from tag %s", self.source)
        return f"Tag = {self.source}"


class BranchFetcher(SharedAllMixin, BaseFetcher):
    def pull(self):
        logger.info("pulling from branch %s", self.source)
        return f"Branch = {self.source}"
```

This time, we are using the `mixin` class to create the dictionary with the attributes in each class in case it doesn't already exist, and then continuing with the same logic.

This implementation should not have any major problems with inheritance, so it's a more viable alternative.

Builder

The builder pattern is an interesting pattern that abstracts away all the complex initialization of an object. This pattern does not rely on any particularity of the language, so it's as equally applicable in Python as it would be in any other language.

While it solves a valid case, it's usually also a complicated case that is more likely to appear in the design of a framework, library, or API. Similar to the recommendations given for descriptors, we should reserve this implementation for cases where we expect to expose an API that is going to be consumed by multiple users.

The high-level idea of this pattern is that we need to create a complex object, that is, an object that also requires many others to work with. Rather than letting the user create all those auxiliary objects, and then assign them to the main one, we would like to create an abstraction that allows all of that to be done in a single step. In order to achieve this, we will have a `builder` object that knows how to create all the parts and link them together, giving the user an interface (which could be a class method) to parametrize all the information about what the resulting object should look like.

Structural patterns

Structural patterns are useful for situations where we need to create simpler interfaces or objects that are more powerful by extending their functionality without adding complexity to their interfaces.

The best thing about these patterns is that we can create more interesting objects, with enhanced functionality, and we can achieve this in a clean way; that is, by composing multiple single objects (the clearest example of this being the composite pattern), or by gathering many simple and cohesive interfaces.

Adapter

The adapter pattern is probably one of the simplest design patterns there are, and one of the most useful ones at the same time.

Also known as a *wrapper*, this pattern solves the problem of adapting interfaces of two or more objects that are not compatible.

We typically encounter a situation where part of our code works with a model or set of classes that were polymorphic with respect to a method. For example, if there were multiple objects for retrieving data with a `fetch()` method, then we want to maintain this interface so we don't have to make major changes to our code.

But then we come to a point where we need to add a new data source, and alas, this one won't have a `fetch()` method. To make things worse, not only is this type of object not compatible, but it is also not something we control (perhaps a different team decided on the API, and we cannot modify the code, or it is an object coming from an external library).

Instead of using this object directly, we adapt its interface to the one we need. There are two ways of doing this.

The first way would be to create a class that inherits from the one we need and create an alias for the method (if required, it will also have to adapt the parameters and the signature), which internally will adapt the call to make it compatible with the method we need.

By means of inheritance, we import the external class and create a new one that will define the new method, calling the one that has a different name. In this example, let's say the external dependency has a method named search(), which takes only one parameter for the search because it queries in a different fashion, so our adapter method not only calls the external one, but it also translates the parameters accordingly, as shown in the following code:

```
from _adapter_base import UsernameLookup


class UserSource(UsernameLookup):
    def fetch(self, user_id, username):
        user_namespace = self._adapt_arguments(user_id, username)
        return self.search(user_namespace)

    @staticmethod
    def _adapt_arguments(user_id, username):
        return f"{user_id}:{username}"
```

Taking advantage of the fact that Python supports multiple inheritance, we can use it to create our adapters (and even create a mixin class that's an adapter, as we have seen in previous chapters).

However, as we have seen many times before, inheritance comes with more coupling (who knows how many other methods are being carried from the external library?), and it's inflexible. Conceptually, it also wouldn't be the right choice because we reserve inheritance for situations of specification (an inheritance IS-A kind of relationship), and in this case, it's not clear at all that our object has to be one of the kinds that are provided by a third-party library (especially since we don't fully comprehend that object).

Therefore, a better approach would be to use composition instead. Assuming that we can provide our object with an instance of UsernameLookup, the code would be as simple as just redirecting the petition prior to adopting the parameters, as shown in the following code:

```
class UserSource:
    ...
    def fetch(self, user_id, username):
        user_namespace = self._adapt_arguments(user_id, username)
        return self.username_lookup.search(user_namespace)
```

If we need to adapt multiple methods, and we can devise a generic way of adapting their signature as well, it might be worth using the __getattr__() magic method to redirect requests toward the wrapped object, but as always with generic implementations, we should be careful of not adding more complexity to the solution.

The use of __getattr__() might enable us to have a sort of "generic adapter"; something that can wrap another object and adapt all its methods by redirecting calls in a generic way. But we should really be careful with this because this method will create something so generic that it might be even riskier and have unanticipated side effects. If we want to perform transformations or extra functionality over an object, while keeping its original interface, the decorator pattern is a much better option, as we'll see later in this chapter.

Composite

There will be parts of our programs that require us to work with objects that are made out of other objects. We have base objects that have a well-defined logic, and then we will have other container objects that will group a bunch of base objects, and the challenge is that we want to treat both of them (the base and container objects) without noticing any differences.

The objects are structured in a tree hierarchy, where the basic objects would be the leaves of the tree, and the composed objects intermediate nodes. A client might want to call any of them to get the result of a method that is called. The composite object, however, will act as a client; this will also pass this request along with all the objects it contains, whether they are leaves or other intermediate notes, until they are all processed.

Imagine a simplified version of an online store in which we have products. Say that we offer the possibility of grouping those products, and we give customers a discount per group of products. A product has a price, and this value will be asked for when the customers come to pay. But a set of grouped products also has a price that has to be computed. We will have an object that represents this group that contains the products, and that delegates the responsibility of asking the price to each particular product (which might be another group of products as well), and so on, until there is nothing else to compute.

The implementation of this is shown in the following code:

```
class Product:
    def __init__(self, name: str, price: float) -> None:
        self._name = name
        self._price = price

    @property
    def price(self):
        return self._price


class ProductBundle:
    def __init__(
        self,
        name: str,
        perc_discount: float,
        *products: Iterable[Union[Product, "ProductBundle"]]
    ) -> None:
        self._name = name
        self._perc_discount = perc_discount
        self._products = products

    @property
    def price(self) -> float:
        total = sum(p.price for p in self._products)
        return total * (1 - self._perc_discount)
```

We expose the `public` interface through a property and leave `price` as a `private` attribute. The `ProductBundle` class uses this property to compute the value with the discount applied by first adding all the prices of all the products it contains.

The only discrepancy between these objects is that they are created with different parameters. To be fully compatible, we should have tried to mimic the same interface and then added extra methods for adding products to the bundle but using an interface that allows the creation of complete objects. Not needing these extra steps is an advantage that justifies this small difference.

Decorator

Don't confuse the decorator pattern with the concept of a Python decorator, which we have gone through in *Chapter 5, Using Decorators to Improve Our Code*. There is some resemblance, but the idea of the design pattern is quite different.

This pattern allows us to dynamically extend the functionality of some objects, without needing inheritance. It's a good alternative to multiple inheritance in creating more flexible objects.

We are going to create a structure that lets a user define a set of operations (decorations) to be applied over an object, and we'll see how each step takes place in the specified order.

The following code example is a simplified version of an object that constructs a query in the form of a dictionary from parameters that are passed to it (it might be an object that we would use for running queries to Elasticsearch, for instance, but the code leaves out distracting implementation details to focus on the concepts of the pattern).

In its most basic form, the query just returns the dictionary with the data it was provided when it was created. Clients expect to use the render() method of this object:

```python
class DictQuery:
    def __init__(self, **kwargs):
        self._raw_query = kwargs

    def render(self) -> dict:
        return self._raw_query
```

Now we want to render the query in different ways by applying transformations to the data (filtering values, normalizing them, and so on). We could create decorators and apply them to the render method, but that wouldn't be flexible enough—what if we want to change them at runtime? Or if we want to select some of them, but not others?

The design is to create another object, with the same interface and the capability of enhancing (decorating) the original result through many steps, but that can be combined. These objects are chained, and each one of them does what it was originally supposed to do, plus something else. This something else is the particular decoration step.

Since Python has duck typing, we don't need to create a new base class and make these new objects part of that hierarchy, along with DictQuery. Simply creating a new class that has a render() method will be enough (again, polymorphism should not require inheritance). This process is shown in the following code:

```python
class QueryEnhancer:
    def __init__(self, query: DictQuery):
        self.decorated = query
```

```
    def render(self):
        return self.decorated.render()


class RemoveEmpty(QueryEnhancer):
    def render(self):
        original = super().render()
        return {k: v for k, v in original.items() if v}


class CaseInsensitive(QueryEnhancer):
    def render(self):
        original = super().render()
        return {k: v.lower() for k, v in original.items()}
```

The `QueryEnhancer` phrase has an interface that is compatible with what the clients of `DictQuery` are expecting, so they are interchangeable. This object is designed to receive a decorated one. It's going to take the values from this and convert them, returning the modified version of the code.

If we want to remove all values that evaluate to `False` and normalize them to form our original query, we have to use the following schema:

```
>>> original = DictQuery(key="value", empty="", none=None,
upper="UPPERCASE", title="Title")
>>> new_query = CaseInsensitive(RemoveEmpty(original))
>>> original.render()
{'key': 'value', 'empty': '', 'none': None, 'upper': 'UPPERCASE',
'title': 'Title'}
>>> new_query.render()
{'key': 'value', 'upper': 'uppercase', 'title': 'title'}
```

This is a pattern that we can also implement in different ways, taking advantage of the dynamic nature of Python, and the fact that functions are objects. We could implement this pattern with functions that are provided to the base decorator object (`QueryEnhancer`), and define each decoration step as a function, as shown in the following code:

```
class QueryEnhancer:
    def __init__(
        self,
        query: DictQuery,
        *decorators: Iterable[Callable[[Dict[str, str]], Dict[str,
```

```
str]]]
    ) -> None:
        self._decorated = query
        self._decorators = decorators


    def render(self):
        current_result = self._decorated.render()
        for deco in self._decorators:
            current_result = deco(current_result)
        return current_result
```

With respect to the client, nothing has changed because this class maintains the compatibility through its `render()` method. Internally, however, this object is used in a slightly different fashion, as shown in the following code:

```
>>> query = DictQuery(foo="bar", empty="", none=None,
upper="UPPERCASE", title="Title")
>>> QueryEnhancer(query, remove_empty, case_insensitive).render()
{'foo': 'bar', 'upper': 'uppercase', 'title': 'title'}
```

In the preceding code, `remove_empty` and `case_insensitive` are just regular functions that transform a dictionary.

In this example, the function-based approach seems easier to understand. There might be cases with more complex rules that rely on data from the object being decorated (not only its result), and in those cases, it might be worth going for the object-oriented approach, especially if we really want to create a hierarchy of objects where each class actually represents some knowledge we want to make explicit in our design.

Facade

Facade is an excellent pattern. It's useful in many situations where we want to simplify the interaction between objects. The pattern is applied where there is a relation of many-to-many among several objects, and we want them to interact. Instead of creating all of these connections, we place an intermediate object in front of many of them that act as a facade.

The facade works as a hub or a single point of reference in this layout. Every time a new object wants to connect to another one, instead of having to have **N** interfaces for all **N** possible objects it needs to connect to (requiring $O(N^2)$ total connections), it will instead just talk to the facade, and this will redirect the request accordingly. Everything that's behind the facade is completely opaque to the rest of the external objects.

Apart from the main and obvious benefit (the decoupling of objects), this pattern also encourages a simpler design with fewer interfaces and better encapsulation.

This is a pattern that we can use not only for improving the code of our domain problem but also to create better APIs. If we use this pattern and provide a single interface, acting as a single point of truth or entry point for our code, it will be much easier for our users to interact with the functionality exposed. Not only that, but by exposing a functionality and hiding everything behind an interface, we are free to change or refactor that underlying code as much as we want, because as long as it is behind the facade, it will not break backward compatibility, and our users will not be affected.

Note how this idea of using facades is not even limited to objects and classes, but also applies to packages (technically, packages are objects in Python, but still). We can use this idea of the facade to decide the layout of a package; that is, what is visible to the user and importable, and what is internal and should not be imported directly.

When we create a directory to build a package, we place the __init__.py file along with the rest of the files. This is the root of the module, a sort of facade. The rest of the files define the objects to export, but they shouldn't be directly imported by clients. The __init__.py file should import them and then clients should get them from there. This creates a better interface because users only need to know a single entry point from which to get the objects, and more importantly, the package (the rest of the files) can be refactored or rearranged as many times as needed, and this will not affect clients as long as the main API on the init file is maintained. It is of utmost importance to keep principles like this one in mind in order to build maintainable software.

There is an example of this in Python itself, with the os module. This module groups an operating system's functionality, but underneath it, uses the posix module for **Portable Operating System Interface (POSIX)** operating systems (this is called **nt** on Windows platforms). The idea is that, for portability reasons, we shouldn't ever really import the posix module directly, but always the os module. It is up to this module to determine from which platform it is being called and expose the corresponding functionality.

Behavioral patterns

Behavioral patterns aim to solve the problem of how objects should cooperate, how they should communicate, and what their interfaces should be at runtime.

We mainly discuss the following behavioral patterns:

- Chain of responsibility
- Template method
- Command
- State

This can be accomplished statically by means of inheritance or dynamically by using composition. Regardless of what the pattern uses, what we will see throughout the following examples is that what these patterns have in common is the fact that the resulting code is better in some significant way, whether this is because it avoids duplication or creates good abstractions that encapsulate behavior accordingly and decouple our models.

Chain of responsibility

Now we are going to take another look at our event systems. We want to parse information about the events that happened on the system from the log lines (text files, dumped from our HTTP application server, for example), and we want to extract this information in a convenient way.

In our previous implementation, we achieved an interesting solution that was compliant with the open/closed principle and relied on the use of the __subclasses__() magic method to discover all possible event types and process the data with the right event, resolving the responsibility through a method encapsulated on each class.

This solution worked for our purposes, and it was quite extensible, but as we'll see, this design pattern will bring additional benefits.

The idea here is that we are going to create the events in a slightly different way. Each event still has the logic to determine whether or not it can process a particular log line, but it will also have a successor. This successor is a new event, the next one in the line, that will continue processing the text line in case the first one was not able to do so. The logic is simple — we chain the events, and each one of them tries to process the data. If it can, then it just returns the result. If it can't, it will pass it to its successor and repeat, as shown in the following code:

```
import re
from typing import Optional, Pattern

class Event:
```

```python
    pattern: Optional[Pattern[str]] = None

    def __init__(self, next_event=None):
        self.successor = next_event

    def process(self, logline: str):
        if self.can_process(logline):
            return self._process(logline)

        if self.successor is not None:
            return self.successor.process(logline)

    def _process(self, logline: str) -> dict:
        parsed_data = self._parse_data(logline)
        return {
            "type": self.__class__.__name__,
            "id": parsed_data["id"],
            "value": parsed_data["value"],
        }

    @classmethod
    def can_process(cls, logline: str) -> bool:
        return (
            cls.pattern is not None and cls.pattern.match(logline) is
not None
        )

    @classmethod
    def _parse_data(cls, logline: str) -> dict:
        if not cls.pattern:
            return {}
        if (parsed := cls.pattern.match(logline)) is not None:
            return parsed.groupdict()
        return {}

class LoginEvent(Event):
    pattern = re.compile(r"(?P<id>\d+):\s+login\s+(?P<value>\S+)")

class LogoutEvent(Event):
    pattern = re.compile(r"(?P<id>\d+):\s+logout\s+(?P<value>\S+)")
```

With this implementation, we create the event objects, and arrange them in the particular order in which they are going to be processed. Since they all have a `process()` method, they are polymorphic for this message, so the order in which they are aligned is completely transparent to the client, and either one of them would be transparent too. Not only that, but the `process()` method has the same logic; it tries to extract the information if the data provided is correct for the type of object handling it, and if not, it moves on to the next one in the line.

This way, we could process a login event in the following way:

```
>>> chain = LogoutEvent(LoginEvent())
>>> chain.process("567: login User")
{'type': 'LoginEvent', 'id': '567', 'value': 'User'}
```

Note how `LogoutEvent` received `LoginEvent` as its successor, and when it was asked to process something that it couldn't handle, it redirected to the correct object. As we can see from the type key on the dictionary, `LoginEvent` was the one that actually created that dictionary.

This solution is flexible enough and shares an interesting trait with our previous one—all conditions are mutually exclusive. As long as there are no collisions, and no piece of data has more than one handler, processing the events in any order will not be an issue.

But what if we cannot make such an assumption? With the previous implementation, we could still change the __subclasses__() call for a list that we made according to our criteria, and that would have worked just fine. And what if we wanted that order of precedence to be determined at runtime (by the user or client, for example)? That would be a shortcoming.

With the new solution, it's possible to accomplish such requirements because we assemble the chain at runtime so we can manipulate it dynamically as we need to.

For example, now we add a generic type that groups both the login and logout session events, as shown in the following code:

```
class SessionEvent(Event):
    pattern = re.compile(r"(?P<id>\d+):\s+log(in|out)\s+(?P<value>\
S+)")
```

If for some reason, and in some part of the application, we want to capture this before the login event, this can be done by the following chain:

```
chain = SessionEvent(LoginEvent(LogoutEvent()))
```

By changing the order, we can, for instance, say that a generic session event has a higher priority than the login, but not the logout, and so on.

The fact that this pattern works with objects makes it more flexible with respect to our previous implementation, which relied on classes (and while they are still objects in Python, they aren't excluded from some degree of rigidity).

The template method

The template method is a pattern that yields important benefits when implemented properly. Mainly, it allows us to reuse code, and it also makes our objects more flexible and easier to change while preserving polymorphism.

The idea is that there is a class hierarchy that defines some behavior, let's say an important method of its public interface. All of the classes of the hierarchy share a common template and might need to change only certain elements of it. The idea, then, is to place this generic logic in the public method of the parent class that will internally call all other (private) methods, and these methods are the ones that the derived classes are going to modify; therefore, all the logic in the template is reused.

Astute readers might have noticed that we already implemented this pattern in the previous section (as part of the chain of responsibility example). Note that the classes derived from Event implement only one thing in their particular pattern. For the rest of the logic, the template is in the Event class. The process event is generic, and relies on two auxiliary methods: can_process() and process() (which in turn calls _parse_data()).

These extra methods rely on a class attribute pattern. Therefore, in order to extend this with a new type of object, we just have to create a new derived class and place the regular expression. After that, the rest of the logic will be inherited with this new attribute changed. This reuses a lot of code because the logic for processing the log lines is defined once and only once in the parent class.

This makes the design flexible because preserving the polymorphism is also easily achievable. If we need a new event type that for some reason needs a different way of parsing data, we only override this private method in that subclass, and the compatibility will be kept, as long as it returns something of the same type as the original one (complying with the Liskov's substitution and open/closed principles). This is because it is the parent class that is calling the method from the derived classes.

This pattern is also useful if we are designing our own library or framework. By arranging the logic this way, we give users the ability to change the behavior of one of the classes quite easily. They would have to create a subclass and override the particular private method, and the result will be a new object with the new behavior that is guaranteed to be compatible with previous callers of the original object.

Command

The command pattern provides us with the ability to separate an action that needs to be done from the moment that it is requested to its actual execution. More than that, it can also separate the original request issued by a client from its recipient, which might be a different object. In this section, we are going to focus mainly on the first aspect of the patterns: the fact that we can separate how an order has to be run from when it actually executes.

We know we can create callable objects by implementing the __call__() magic method, so we could just initialize the object and then call it later on. In fact, if this is the only requirement, we might even achieve this through a nested function that, by means of a closure, creates another function to achieve the effect of delayed execution. But this pattern can be extended to ends that aren't so easily achievable.

The idea is that the command might also be modified after its definition. This means that the client specifies a command to run, and then some of its parameters might be changed, more options added, and so on, until someone finally decides to perform the action.

Examples of this can be found in libraries that interact with databases. For instance, in psycopg2 (a PostgreSQL client library), we establish a connection. From this, we get a cursor, and to that cursor, we can pass a SQL statement to run. When we call the execute method, the internal representation of the object changes, but nothing is actually run in the database. It is when we call fetchall() (or a similar method) that the data is actually queried and is available in the cursor.

The same happens in the popular **Object Relational Mapper SQLAlchemy (ORM SQLAlchemy)**. A query is defined through several steps, and once we have the query object, we can still interact with it (add or remove filters, change the conditions, apply for an order, and so on), until we decide we want the results of the query. After calling each method, the query object changes its internal properties and returns self (itself).

These are examples that resemble the behavior that we would like to achieve. A very simple way of creating this structure would be to have an object that stores the parameters of the commands that are to be run. After that, it has to also provide methods for interacting with those parameters (adding or removing filters, and so on). Optionally, we can add tracing or logging capabilities to that object to audit the operations that have been taking place. Finally, we need to provide a method that will actually perform the action. This one can be just __call__() or a custom one. Let's call it do().

This pattern can be useful when we're dealing with asynchronous programming. As we have seen, asynchronous programming has syntax nuances. By separating the preparation of a command from its execution, we can make the former still have the synchronous form, and the latter the asynchronous syntax (assuming this is the part that needs to run asynchronously, if, for example, we're using a library to connect to a database).

State

The state pattern is a clear example of reification in software design, making the concept of our domain problem an explicit object rather than just a side value (for example, using strings or integer flags to represent values or managing state).

In *Chapter 8, Unit Testing and Refactoring*, we had an object that represented a merge request, and it had a state associated with it (open, closed, and so on). We used an enumeration to represent those states because, at that point, they were just data holding a value (the string representation of that particular state). If they had to have some behavior, or the entire merge request had to perform some actions depending on its state and transitions, this would not have been enough.

The fact that we are adding behavior, a runtime structure, to a part of the code has to make us think in terms of objects, because that's what objects are supposed to do, after all. And here comes the reification—now the state cannot just simply be an enumeration with a string; it needs to be an object.

Imagine that we have to add some rules to the merge request, say that when it moves from open to closed, all approvals are removed (they will have to review the code again)—and that when a merge request is just opened, the number of approvals is set to zero (regardless of whether it's a reopened or brand-new merge request). Another rule could be that when a merge request is merged, we want to delete the source branch, and of course, we want to forbid users from performing invalid transitions (for example, a closed merge request cannot be merged, and so on).

If we put all that logic into a single place, namely in the MergeRequest class, we will end up with a class that has lots of responsibilities (a sign of a poor design), probably many methods, and a very large number of if statements. It would be hard to follow the code and to understand which part is supposed to represent which business rule.

It's better to distribute this into smaller objects, each one with fewer responsibilities, and the state objects are a good place for this. We create an object for each kind of state we want to represent, and, in their methods, we place the logic for the transitions with the aforementioned rules. The MergeRequest object will then have a state collaborator, and this, in turn, will also know about MergeRequest (the double-dispatching mechanism is needed to run the appropriate actions on MergeRequest and handle the transitions).

We define a base abstract class with the set of methods to be implemented, and then a subclass for each particular state we want to represent. Then the MergeRequest object delegates all the actions to state, as shown in the following code:

```python
class InvalidTransitionError(Exception):
    """Raised when trying to move to a target state from an unreachable
    Source
    state.
    """


class MergeRequestState(abc.ABC):
    def __init__(self, merge_request):
        self._merge_request = merge_request

    @abc.abstractmethod
    def open(self):
        ...

    @abc.abstractmethod
    def close(self):
        ...

    @abc.abstractmethod
    def merge(self):
        ...

    def __str__(self):
        return self.__class__.__name__


class Open(MergeRequestState):
    def open(self):
        self._merge_request.approvals = 0

    def close(self):
        self._merge_request.approvals = 0
        self._merge_request.state = Closed

    def merge(self):
        logger.info("merging %s", self._merge_request)
        logger.info(
```

```
                "deleting branch %s",
                self._merge_request.source_branch
            )
            self._merge_request.state = Merged


class Closed(MergeRequestState):
    def open(self):
        logger.info(
            "reopening closed merge request %s",
            self._merge_request
        )
        self._merge_request.state = Open

    def close(self):
        """Current state."""

    def merge(self):
        raise InvalidTransitionError("can't merge a closed request")


class Merged(MergeRequestState):
    def open(self):
        raise InvalidTransitionError("already merged request")

    def close(self):
        raise InvalidTransitionError("already merged request")

    def merge(self):
        """Current state."""


class MergeRequest:
    def __init__(self, source_branch: str, target_branch: str) -> None:
        self.source_branch = source_branch
        self.target_branch = target_branch
        self._state = None
        self.approvals = 0
        self.state = Open

    @property
    def state(self):
```

```
        return self._state

    @state.setter
    def state(self, new_state_cls):
        self._state = new_state_cls(self)

    def open(self):
        return self.state.open()

    def close(self):
        return self.state.close()

    def merge(self):
        return self.state.merge()

    def __str__(self):
        return f"{self.target_branch}:{self.source_branch}"
```

The following list outlines some clarifications about implementation details and the design decisions that should be made:

- The state is a property, so not only is it public, but there is also a single place with the definitions of how states are created for a merge request, passing self as a parameter.

- The abstract base class is not strictly needed, but there are benefits to having it. First, it makes the kind of object we are dealing with more explicit. Second, it forces every substate to implement all the methods of the interface. There are two alternatives to this:

    - We could have not written the methods and let AttributeError raise when trying to perform an invalid action, but this is not correct, and it doesn't express what happened.

    - Related to this point is the fact that we could have just used a simple base class and left those methods empty, but then the default behavior of not doing anything doesn't make it any clearer what should happen. If one of the methods in the subclass should do nothing (as in the case of merge), then it's better to let the empty method just sit there and make it explicit that for that particular case, nothing should be done, as opposed to forcing that logic to all objects.

- MergeRequest and MergeRequestState have links to each other. The moment a transition is made, the former object will not have extra references and should be garbage-collected, so this relationship should be always 1:1. With some small and more detailed considerations, a weak reference might be used.

The following code shows some examples of how the object is used:

```
>>> mr = MergeRequest("develop", "mainline")
>>> mr.open()
>>> mr.approvals
0
>>> mr.approvals = 3
>>> mr.close()
>>> mr.approvals
0
>>> mr.open()
INFO:log:reopening closed merge request mainline:develop
>>> mr.merge()
INFO:log:merging mainline:develop
INFO:log:deleting branch develop
>>> mr.close()
Traceback (most recent call last):
...
InvalidTransitionError: already merged request
```

The actions for transitioning states are delegated to the state object, which
MergeRequest holds at all times (this can be any of the subclasses of ABC). They all
know how to respond to the same messages (in different ways), so these objects will
take the appropriate actions corresponding to each transition (deleting branches,
raising exceptions, and so on), and will then move MergeRequest to the next state.

Since MergeRequest delegates all actions to its state object, we will find that this
typically happens every time the actions that it needs to do are in the form self.
state.open(), and so on. Can we remove some of that boilerplate?

We could, by means of __getattr__(), as it is portrayed in the following code:

```
class MergeRequest:
    def __init__(self, source_branch: str, target_branch: str) -> None:
        self.source_branch = source_branch
        self.target_branch = target_branch
        self._state: MergeRequestState
        self.approvals = 0
        self.state = Open

    @property
    def state(self) -> MergeRequestState:
        return self._state
```

```python
@state.setter
def state(self, new_state_cls: Type[MergeRequestState]):
    self._state = new_state_cls(self)

@property
def status(self):
    return str(self.state)

def __getattr__(self, method):
    return getattr(self.state, method)

def __str__(self):
    return f"{self.target_branch}:{self.source_branch}"
```

 Be careful with implementing these types of generic redirections in the code, because it might harm readability. Sometimes, it's better to have some small boilerplate, but be explicit about what our code does.

On the one hand, it is good that we reuse some code and remove repetitive lines. This gives the abstract base class even more sense. Somewhere, we want to have all possible actions documented, listed in a single place. That place used to be the MergeRequest class, but now those methods are gone, so the only remaining source of that truth is in MergeRequestState. Luckily, the type annotation on the state attribute is really helpful for users to know where to look for the interface definition.

A user can simply take a look and see that everything that MergeRequest doesn't have will be asked of its state attribute. From the init definition, the annotation will tell us that this is an object of the MergeRequestState type, and by looking at this interface, we will see that we can safely ask for the open(), close(), and merge() methods on it.

The null object pattern

The null object pattern is an idea that relates to the good practices that were mentioned in previous chapters of this book. Here, we are formalizing them, and giving more context and analysis to this idea.

The principle is rather simple—functions or methods must return objects of a consistent type. If this is guaranteed, then clients of our code can use the objects that are returned with polymorphism, without having to run extra checks on them.

In the previous examples, we explored how the dynamic nature of Python made things easier for most design patterns. In some cases, they disappear entirely, and in others, they are much easier to implement. The main goal of design patterns as they were originally thought of is that methods or functions should not explicitly name the class of the object that they need in order to work. For this reason, they propose the creation of interfaces and a way of rearranging the objects to make them fit these interfaces in order to modify the design. But most of the time, this is not needed in Python, and we can just pass different objects, and as long as they respect the methods they must have, then the solution will work.

On the other hand, the fact that objects don't necessarily have to comply with an interface requires us to be more careful as to the things that are returning from such methods and functions. In the same way that our functions didn't make any assumptions about what they were receiving, it's fair to assume that clients of our code will not make any assumptions either (it is our responsibility to provide objects that are compatible). This can be enforced or validated with design by contract. Here, we will explore a simple pattern that will help us avoid these kinds of problems.

Consider the chain of responsibility design pattern explored in the previous section. We saw how flexible it is and its many advantages, such as decoupling responsibilities into smaller objects. One of the problems it has is that we never actually know what object will end up processing the message, if any. In particular, in our example, if there was no suitable object to process the log line, then the method would simply return None.

We don't know how users will use the data we passed, but we do know that they are expecting a dictionary. Therefore, the following error might occur:

```
AttributeError: 'NoneType' object has no attribute 'keys'
```

In this case, the fix is rather simple—the default value of the process() method should be an empty dictionary rather than None.

 Ensure that you return objects of a consistent type.

But what if the method didn't return a dictionary, but a custom object of our domain?

To solve this problem, we should have a class that represents the empty state for that object and return it. If we have a class that represents users in our system, and a function that queries users by their ID, then in the case that a user is not found, it should do one of the following two things:

- Raise an exception
- Return an object of the UserUnknown type

But in no case should it return None. The phrase None doesn't represent what just happened, and the caller might legitimately try to ask methods to it, and it will fail with AttributeError.

We have discussed exceptions and their pros and cons earlier on, so we should mention that this null object should just have the same methods as the original user and do nothing for each one of them.

The advantage of using this structure is that not only are *we* avoiding an error at runtime but also that this object might be useful. It could make the code easier to test, and it can even, for instance, help in debugging (maybe we could put logging into the methods to understand why that state was reached, what data was provided to it, and so on).

By exploiting almost all of the magic methods of Python, it would be possible to create a generic null object that does absolutely nothing, no matter how it is called, but that can be called from almost any client. Such an object would slightly resemble a Mock object. It is not advisable to go down that path because of the following reasons:

- It loses meaning with the domain problem. Back in our example, having an object of the UnknownUser type makes sense, and gives the caller a clear idea that something went wrong with the query.

- It doesn't respect the original interface. This is problematic. Remember that the point is that an UnknownUser is a user, and therefore it must have the same methods. If the caller accidentally asks for a method that is not there, then, in that case, it should raise an AttributeError exception, and that would be good. With the generic null object that can do anything and respond to anything, we would be losing this information, and bugs might creep in. If we opt for creating a Mock object with spec=User, then this anomaly would be caught, but again, using a Mock object to represent what is actually an empty state doesn't match our intention of providing clear, understandable code.

This pattern is a good practice that allows us to maintain polymorphism in our objects.

Final thoughts about design patterns

We have seen the world of design patterns in Python, and in doing so, we have found solutions to common problems, as well as more techniques that will help us achieve a clean design.

All of this sounds good, but it begs the question: how good are design patterns? Some people argue that they do more harm than good, that they were created for languages whose limited type system (and lack of first-class functions) makes it impossible to accomplish things we would normally do in Python. Others claim that design patterns force a design solution, creating some bias that limits a design that would have otherwise emerged, and that would have been better. Let's look at each of these points in turn.

The influence of patterns over the design

A design pattern cannot be good or bad by itself, but rather by how it's implemented, or used. In some cases, there is no need for a design pattern when a simpler solution would do. Trying to force a pattern where it doesn't fit is a case of over-engineering, and that's clearly bad, but it doesn't mean that there is a problem with the design pattern, and most likely in these scenarios, the problem is not even related to patterns at all. Some people try to over-engineer everything because they don't understand what flexible and adaptable software really means.

As we mentioned before in this book, making good software is not about anticipating future requirements (there is no point in doing futurology), but just solving the problem that we have at hand right now, in a way that doesn't prevent us from making changes to it in the future. It doesn't have to handle those changes now; it just needs to be flexible enough so that it can be modified in the future. And when that future comes, we will still have to remember the rule of three or more instances of the same problem before coming up with a generic solution or a proper abstraction.

This is typically the point where the design patterns should emerge, once we have identified the problem correctly and can recognize the pattern and abstract accordingly.

Let's come back to the topic of the suitability of the patterns to the language. As we said in the introduction of the chapter, design patterns are high-level ideas. They typically refer to the relation of objects and their interactions. It's hard to think that such things might disappear from one language to another.

It's true that some patterns would require less work in Python, as is the case of the iterator pattern (which, as it was heavily discussed earlier in the book, is built in Python), or a strategy (because, instead, we would just pass functions like any other regular object; we don't need to encapsulate the strategy method into an object, as the function itself would be that object).

But other patterns are actually needed, and they indeed solve problems, as in the case of the decorator and composite patterns. In other cases, there are design patterns that Python itself implements, and we just don't always see them, as in the case of the facade pattern that we discussed earlier in the chapter.

As to our design patterns leading our solution in the wrong direction, we have to be careful here. Once again, it's better if we start designing our solution by thinking in terms of the domain problem and creating the right abstractions, and then later see whether there is a design pattern that emerges from that design. Let's say that it does. Is that a bad thing? The fact that there is already a solution to the problem we're trying to solve cannot be a bad thing. It would be bad to reinvent the wheel, as happens many times in our field. Moreover, the fact that we are applying a pattern, something already proven and validated, should give us greater confidence in the quality of what we are building.

Design patterns as theory

One interesting way I see design patterns is as software engineering theory. While I agree with the idea that the more naturally the code evolves, the better, that doesn't mean we should ignore design patterns completely.

Design patterns exist because there's no point in reinventing the wheel. If there's a solution that has already been devised for a particular kind of problem, it will save us some time to ponder that idea as we plan our design. In this sense (and to re-invoke an analogy from the first chapter), I like to think about design patterns as analogous to chess openings: professional chess players don't think about every combination in the early stages of a game. That's the theory. It's already been studied. It's the same as with a math or physics formula. You should understand it deeply the first time, know how to infer it, and incorporate its meaning, but after that, there's no need to develop that theory over and over again.

As practitioners of software engineering, we should use the theory of design patterns to save mental energy and come up with solutions faster. More than that, design patterns should become not only language but building blocks as well.

Names in our models

Should we mention that we are using a design pattern in our code?

If the design is good and the code is clean, it should speak for itself. It is not recommended that you name things after the design patterns you are using for a couple of reasons:

- Users of our code and other developers don't need to know the design pattern behind the code, as long as it works as intended.

- Stating the design pattern ruins the intention revealing principle. Adding the name of the design pattern to a class makes it lose part of its original meaning. If a class represents a query, it should be named Query or EnhancedQuery, something that reveals the intention of what that object is supposed to do. EnhancedQueryDecorator doesn't mean anything meaningful, and the Decorator suffix creates more confusion than clarity.

Mentioning the design patterns in docstrings might be acceptable because they work as documentation, and expressing the design ideas (again, communicating) in our design is a good thing. However, this should not be needed. Most of the time, though, we do not need to know that a design pattern is there.

The best designs are those in which design patterns are completely transparent to the users. An example of this is how the facade pattern appears in the standard library, making it completely transparent to users as to how to access the os module. An even more elegant example is how the iterator design pattern is so completely abstracted by the language that we don't even have to think about it.

Summary

Design patterns have always been seen as proven solutions to common problems. This is a correct assessment, but in this chapter, we explored them from the point of view of good design techniques, patterns that leverage clean code. In most of the cases, we looked at how they provide a good solution to preserve polymorphism, reduce coupling, and create the right abstractions that encapsulate details as needed—all traits that relate to the concepts explored in *Chapter 8, Unit Testing and Refactoring*.

Still, the best thing about design patterns is not the clean design we can obtain from applying them, but the extended vocabulary. Used as a communication tool, we can use their names to express the intention of our design. And sometimes, it's not the entire pattern that we need to apply, but we might need to take a particular idea (a substructure, for example) of a pattern from our solution, and here, too, they prove to be a way of communicating more effectively.

When we create solutions by thinking in terms of patterns, we are solving problems at a more general level. Thinking in terms of design patterns brings us closer to higher-level design. We can slowly "zoom-out" and think more in terms of architecture. And now that we are solving more general problems, it's time to start thinking about how the system is going to evolve and be maintained in the long run (how it's going to scale, change, adapt, and so on).

For a software project to be successful in these goals, it requires clean code at its core, but the architecture also has to be clean as well, which is what we are going to look at in the next chapter.

References

Here is a list of information you can refer to:

- *GoF*: The book written by *Erich Gamma, Richard Helm, Ralph Johnson,* and *John Vlissides* named *Design Patterns: Elements of Reusable Object-Oriented Software*

- *SNGMONO*: An article written by *Robert C. Martin,* 2002, named *SINGLETON and MONOSTATE*: `http://staff.cs.utu.fi/~jounsmed/doos_06/material/SingletonAndMonostate.pdf`

- *The Null Object Pattern,* written by *Bobby Woolf*

10

Clean Architecture

In this final chapter, we focus on how everything fits together in the design of a whole system. This is more of a theoretical chapter. Given the nature of the topic, it would be too complex to delve down into the more low-level details. Besides, the point is precisely to escape from those details, assume that all the principles explored in previous chapters are assimilated, and focus on the design of a system at scale.

The main goals of this chapter are as follows:

- Designing software systems that can be maintained in the long run
- Working effectively on a software project by maintaining quality attributes
- Studying how all concepts applied to code relate to systems in general

This chapter explores how clean code evolves into a clean architecture, and conversely how clean code is also the cornerstone of good architecture. A software solution is effective if it has quality. The architecture needs to enable this by achieving quality attributes (performance, testability, maintainability, and so on). But then the code needs to also enable this on every component.

The first section starts by exploring the relationship between the code and the architecture.

From clean code to clean architecture

This section is a discussion of how concepts that were emphasized in previous chapters reappear in a slightly different shape when we consider aspects of large systems. There is an interesting resemblance to how concepts that apply to more detailed design, as well as code, also apply to large systems and architectures.

The concepts explored in previous chapters were related to single applications, generally, a project, which might be a single repository (or a few), of a source control version system (Git). This is not to say that those design ideas are only applicable to code, or that they are of no use when thinking of an architecture, for two reasons: the code is the foundation of the architecture, and, if it's not written carefully, the system will fail regardless of how well thought-out the architecture is.

Second, some principles that were covered in previous chapters do not apply only to code but are design ideas instead. The clearest example comes from design patterns. They are high-level abstractions. With them, we can get a quick picture of how a component in our architecture might appear, without going into the details of the code.

But large enterprise systems typically consist of many of these applications, and now it's time to start thinking in terms of a larger design, in the form of a distributed system.

In the following sections, we discuss the main topics that have been discussed throughout the book, but now from the perspective of a whole system.

Software architecture is good if it's effective. The most common aspects to look at in a good architecture are the so-called quality attributes (traits like scalability, security, performance, and endurance are the most common ones). This makes sense; after all, you want your system to handle an increase of load without collapsing, and to be able to work continuously for indefinite periods of time without requiring maintenance, and also to be extensible to support new requirements.

But the operational aspects of an architecture also make it clean. Traits like operability, continuous integration, and how easy it is to release changes also influence the overall quality of the system.

Separation of concerns

Inside an application, there are multiple components. Their code is divided into other subcomponents, such as modules or packages, and the modules into classes or functions, and the classes into methods. Throughout the book, the emphasis has been on keeping these components as small as possible, particularly in the case of functions—functions should do one thing and be small.

Several reasons were presented to justify this rationale. Small functions are easier to understand, follow, and debug. They are also easier to test. The smaller the pieces in our code, the easier it will be to write unit tests for it.

For the components of each application, we wanted different traits, mainly high cohesion and low coupling. By dividing components into smaller units, each one with a single and well-defined responsibility, we achieve a better structure where changes are easier to manage. In the face of new requirements, there will be a single correct place to make the changes, and the rest of the code should probably be unaffected.

When we talk about code, we say *component* to refer to one of these cohesive units (it might be a class, for example). When speaking in terms of architecture, a component means anything in the system that can be treated as a working unit. The term component itself is quite vague, so there is no universally accepted definition in software architecture of what this means more concretely. The concept of a working unit is something that can vary from project to project. A component should be able to be released or deployed with its own cycles, independently from the rest of the system.

For Python projects, a component could be a package, but a service can also be a component. Notice how two different concepts, with different levels of granularity, can be considered under the same category. To give an example, the event systems we used in previous chapters could be considered a component. They are a working unit with a clearly defined purpose (to enrich events identified from logs). They can be deployed independently from the rest (whether as a Python package, or, if we expose their functionality, as a service; more on that later), and they're a part of the entire system, but not the whole application itself.

In the examples in previous chapters, we saw idiomatic code, and we also highlighted the importance of good design for our code, with objects that have single, well-defined responsibilities being isolated, orthogonal, and easier to maintain. This very same criteria, which applies to a detailed design (functions, classes, methods), also applies to the components of software architecture.

 Keep in mind good design principles when looking at the big picture.

It's probably undesirable for a large system to be just one component. A monolithic application will act as the single source of truth, responsible for everything in the system, and that will carry a lot of undesired consequences (harder to isolate and identify changes, to test effectively, and so on).

In the same way, our code will be harder to maintain if we are not careful and place everything in one place, the application will suffer from similar problems if its components aren't treated with the same level of attention.

The idea of creating cohesive components in a system can have more than one implementation, depending on the level of abstraction we require.

One option would be to identify common logic that is likely to be reused multiple times and place it in a Python package (we will discuss the details later in the chapter).

Another alternative would be to break the application down into multiple smaller services, in a microservice architecture. The idea is to have components with a single and well-defined responsibility and achieve the same functionality as a monolithic application by making those services cooperate and exchange information.

Monolithic applications and microservices

The most important idea from the previous section is the concept of separating concerns: different responsibilities should be distributed across diverse components. Just as in our code (a more detailed level of design) it wouldn't be good to have a giant object that knows everything, in our architecture, there shouldn't be a single component owning everything.

There is, however, an important distinction. Different components don't necessarily mean different services. It's possible to divide the application into smaller Python packages (we'll look at packaging later in the chapter) and create a single service composed of many dependencies.

Separating responsibilities into different services is a good idea that has some benefits, but it also comes at a cost.

In the case that there's code that needs to be reused across several other services, a typical response is to encapsulate that into a microservice to be called by many other services in the company. This isn't the only way to reuse code. Consider the possibility of packaging that logic as a library to be imported by other components. Of course, this is only viable as long as all other components are written in the same language; otherwise, yes, the microservices pattern is the only option left.

Microservices architecture has the advantage of total decoupling: different services can be written in different languages or frameworks, and even be deployed independently. They can also be tested in isolation. This comes at a cost. They also need a strong contract for clients to know how to interact with this service, and they're also subject to **service-level agreements** (SLAs) and **service-level objectives** (SLOs), respectively.

They also incur increased latency: having to call external services to get data (whether via HTTP or gRPC) takes a toll on the overall performance.

An application composed of fewer services is more rigid and can't be deployed independently. It could even be more fragile as it might become a single point of failure. On the other hand, it could be more efficient (since we're avoiding expensive I/O calls), and we could still achieve a good separation of components by using Python packages.

The food for thought of this section is to ponder the right architectural style between creating a new service or using Python packages.

Abstractions

This is where encapsulation appears again. When it comes to our systems (as we do in relation to code), we want to speak in terms of the domain problem and leave the implementation details as hidden as possible.

In the same way that code has to be expressive (almost to the point of being self-documenting) and have the right abstractions that reveal the solution to the essential problem (minimizing accidental complexity), the architecture should tell us what the system is about. Details such as the solution used to persist data on disk, the web framework of choice, the libraries used to connect to external agents, and interaction between systems are not relevant. What is relevant is what the system does. A concept such as a screaming architecture (SCREAM) reflects this idea.

The **Dependency Inversion Principle** (**DIP**), explained in *Chapter 4, The SOLID Principles*, is of great help in this regard; we don't want to depend upon concrete implementations but rather abstractions. In the code, we place abstractions (or interfaces) on the boundaries, the dependencies, those parts of the application that we don't control and might change in the future. We do this because we want to invert the dependencies and let them have to adapt to our code (by having to comply with an interface), not the other way round.

Creating abstractions and inverting dependencies are good practices, but they're not enough. We want our entire application to be independent and isolated from things that are out of our control. And this goes even further than just abstracting with objects—we need layers of abstraction.

This is a subtle yet important difference with respect to the detailed design. In the DIP, it is recommended to create an interface that could be implemented with the abc module from the standard library, for instance. Because Python works with duck typing, while using an abstract class might be helpful, it's not mandatory, as we can easily achieve the same effect with regular objects as long as they comply with the required interface.

The dynamic typing nature of Python allows us to have these alternatives. When thinking in terms of architecture, there is no such thing. As it will become clearer with the following example, we need to abstract dependencies entirely, and there is no feature of Python that can do that for us.

Some might argue: "Well, the **Object-Relational Mapper (ORM)** is a good abstraction for a database, isn't it?" No. The ORM itself is a dependency and, as such, is out of our control. It would be even better to create an intermediate layer, an adapter, between the API of the ORM and our application.

This means that we don't abstract the database just with an ORM; we use the abstraction layer we create on top of it to define objects of our own that belong to our domain. If that abstraction just happens to use an ORM underneath, that's a coincidence; the domain layer (where our business logic lies) shouldn't be concerned with it.

Having abstractions of our own gives us more flexibility and control over the application. We might even later decide that we don't want an ORM at all (let's say because we want more control over the database engine we're using), and if we coupled our application with a specific ORM (or any library in general), it'll be harder to change that in the future. The idea is to insulate the core of our application from external dependencies we don't have control over.

The application then imports this component, and uses the entities provided by this layer, but not the other way round. The abstraction layer should not know about the logic of our application; it's even truer that the database should know nothing about the application itself. If that were the case, the database would be coupled to our application. The goal is to invert the dependency—this layer provides an API, and every storage component that wants to connect has to conform to this API. This is the concept of a *hexagonal architecture* (HEX).

In the next section, we analyze concrete tools that will help us create components to use in our architecture.

Software components

We have a large system now, and we need to scale it. It also has to be maintainable. At this point, the concerns aren't only technical but also organizational. This means it's not just about managing software repositories; each repository will most likely belong to an application, and it will be maintained by a team who owns that part of the system.

This demands that we keep in mind how a large system is divided into different components. This can have many phases, from a very simple approach about, say, creating Python packages, to more complex scenarios in a microservice architecture.

The situation could be even more complex when different languages are involved, but in this chapter, we will assume they are all Python projects.

These components need to interact, as do the teams. The only way this can work at scale is if all the parts agree on an interface, a contract.

Packages

A Python package is a convenient way to distribute software and reuse code in a more general way. Packages that have been built can be published to an artifact repository (such as an internal PyPi server for the company), from where they will be downloaded by the rest of the applications that require them.

The motivation behind this approach has many elements to it—it's about reusing code at large, and also achieving conceptual integrity.

Here, we discuss the basics of packaging a Python project that can be published in a repository. The default repository might be PyPi (the *Python Package Index*, at https://pypi.org/), but also could be internal; or custom setups will work with the same basics.

We are going to simulate that we have created a small library, and we will use that as an example to review the main points to take into consideration.

Aside from all the open-source libraries available, sometimes we might need some extra functionality—perhaps our application uses a particular idiom repeatedly or relies on a function or mechanism quite heavily and the team has devised a better function for these particular needs. In order to work more effectively, we can place this abstraction into a library, and encourage all team members to use the idioms as provided by it, because doing so will help avoid mistakes and reduce bugs.

That's typically the case when you own a service and a client library for that service. You don't want clients calling your API directly, so instead, you provide them with a client library. The code for this library will be wrapped into a Python package and distributed through the internal package management systems.

Potentially, there are infinite examples that could suit this scenario. Maybe the application needs to extract a lot of .tar.gz files (in a particular format) and has faced security problems in the past with malicious files that ended up with path traversal attacks.

As a mitigation measure, the functionality for abstracting custom file formats securely was put in a library that wraps the default one and adds some extra checks. This sounds like a good idea.

Or maybe there is a configuration file that has to be written, or parsed in a particular format, and this requires many steps to be followed in order; again, creating a helper function to wrap this, and using it in all the projects that need it, constitutes a good investment, not only because it saves a lot of code repetition, but also because it makes it harder to make mistakes.

The gain is not only complying with the DRY principle (avoiding code duplication, encouraging reuse) but also that the abstracted functionality represents a single point of reference of how things should be done, hence contributing to the attainment of conceptual integrity.

In general, the minimum layout for a library would look like this:

```
├── Makefile
├── README.rst
├── setup.py
├── src
│   └── apptool
│       ├── common.py
│       ├── __init__.py
│       └── parse.py
└── tests
    ├── integration
    └── unit
```

The important part is the `setup.py` file, which contains the definition for the package. In this file, all the important definitions of the project (its requirements, dependencies, name, description, and so on) are specified.

The `apptool` directory under `src` is the name of the library we're working on. This is a typical Python project, so we place here all the files we need.

An example of the `setup.py` file could be:

```python
from setuptools import find_packages, setup

with open("README.rst", "r") as longdesc:
    long_description = longdesc.read()


setup(
```

```
    name="apptool",
    description="Description of the intention of the package",
    long_description=long_description,
    author="Dev team",
    version="0.1.0",
    packages=find_packages(where="src/"),
    package_dir={"": "src"},
)
```

This minimal example contains the key elements of the project. The name argument in the setup function is used to give the name that the package will have in the repository (under this name, we run the command to install it; in this case, it's pip install apptool). It's not strictly required that it matches the name of the project directory (src/apptool), but it's highly recommended, so it's easier for users.

In this case, since both names match, it's easier to see the relationship between pip install apptool and then, in our code, from apptool import myutil. But the latter corresponds to the name under the src/ directory and the former to the one specified in the setup.py file.

The version is important to keep different releases going on, and then the packages are specified. By using the find_packages() function, we automatically discover everything that's a package, in this case under the src/ directory. Searching under this directory helps to avoid mixing up files beyond the scope of the project and, for instance, accidentally releasing tests or a broken structure of the project.

A package is built by running the following commands, assuming its run inside a virtual environment with the dependencies installed:

```
python -m venv env
source env/bin/activate
$VIRTUAL_ENV/bin/pip install -U pip wheel
$VIRTUAL_ENV/bin/python setup.py sdist bdist_wheel
```

This will place the artifacts in the dist/ directory, from where they can later be published either to PyPi or to the internal package repository of the company.

The key points in packaging a Python project are:

- Test and verify that the installation is platform-independent and that it doesn't rely on any local setup (this can be achieved by placing the source files under an src/ directory). This means that the package that is constructed should not depend upon files that are on your local machine and won't be available when shipped (nor in a custom directory structure).

- Make sure that unit tests aren't shipped as part of the package being built. This is meant for production. In the Docker image that will run in production, you don't need extra files (for example, the fixtures) that aren't strictly needed.

- Separate dependencies — what the project strictly needs to run is not the same as what developers require.

- It's a good idea to create entry points for the commands that are going to be required the most.

The `setup.py` file supports multiple other parameters and configurations and can be affected in a much more complicated manner. If our package requires several operating system libraries to be installed, it's a good idea to write some logic in the `setup.py` file to compile and build the extensions that are required. This way, if something is amiss, it will fail early on in the installation process, and if the package provides a helpful error message, the user will be able to fix the dependencies more quickly and continue.

Installing such dependencies represents another difficult step in making the application ubiquitous and easy to run by any developer regardless of their platform of choice. The best way to surmount this obstacle is to abstract the platform by creating a Docker image, as we will discuss in the next section.

Managing dependencies

Before describing how we'll leverage Docker containers to deliver our application, it's important to take a look at a **Software Configuration Management (SCM)** issue, namely: how do we list the dependencies for our applications, so that they're repeatable?

Keep in mind that issues in software might not only come from our code. External dependencies also impact the final delivery. At all times, you'd want to know the full list of packages and their versions that were delivered. This is called a baseline.

The idea is that if at any time a dependency introduced an issue with our software, you'd want to be able to pinpoint it quickly. More importantly, you'd also want your builds to be repeatable: given everything else is unchanged, a new build should produce the exact same artifacts as the last one.

The software is delivered to production by following a development pipeline. This starts in a first environment, then the tests run on it (integration, acceptance, and so on), and then through continuous integration and continuous deployment, it moves through the different stages of the pipeline (for example, if you have a beta-testing environment, or pre-production before it ultimately reaches production).

Docker is great at ensuring the exact same image is moved along the pipeline, but there's no guarantee that if you run the same version of the code (the same git commit, let's say) again through the pipeline, you'll get the same results. That work is on us, and it's what we're exploring in this section.

Let's say the setup.py file of our web package looks like this:

```
from setuptools import find_packages, setup

with open("README.rst", "r") as longdesc:
    long_description = longdesc.read()

install_requires = ["sanic>=20,<21"]

setup(
    name="web",
    description="Library with helpers for the web-related
functionality",
    long_description=long_description,
    author="Dev team",
    version="0.1.0",
    packages=find_packages(where="src/"),
    package_dir={"": "src"},
    install_requires=install_requires,
)
```

In this case, there's only one dependency (declared in the install_requires parameter), and it's controlling a version interval. This is usually a good practice: we want to at least work with a specific version of a package, but we are also interested in not going beyond the next major version (as major versions can carry backward-incompatible changes).

We set the versions like this because we're interested in getting updates for our dependencies (there are tools like Dependabot — https://dependabot.com/ — that automatically detect when there are new releases for our dependencies and can open a new pull request), but we still want to know the exact version that was installed at any given time.

Not only that, but we also want to track the full tree of dependencies, meaning transitive dependencies should also be listed.

One way of doing that is by using pip-tools (https://github.com/jazzband/pip-tools) and compiling the requirements.txt file.

The idea is to use this tool to generate the requirements file from the setup.py file, like so:

```
pip-compile setup.py
```

This will generate a requirements.txt file that we are going to use in our Dockerfile to install the dependencies.

 Always install the dependencies in your Dockerfile from the requirements.txt file, in order to have builds that are deterministic from the point of view of version control.

The file that lists the requirements should be placed under version control, and whenever we want to upgrade a dependency, we run the command again with the -U flag and track the new version of the requirements file.

Having all dependencies listed is not only good for repeatability, but it also adds clarity. If you are using many dependencies, it can happen that there are some conflicts with versions, and this will be easier to spot if we know which package imports which library (and on what version). But once again, this is only part of the problem. There are more considerations we need to take into account when dealing with dependencies.

Other considerations when managing dependencies

By default, when installing dependencies, pip will use the public repository from the internet (https://pypi.org/). It's also possible to install from other indexes, or even version control systems.

This has some problems and limitations. For starters, you will depend on the availability of those services. There's also the caveat that you won't be able to publish your internal packages (which contain your company's intellectual property) on a public repository. And finally, there's the problem that we don't really know for sure how reliable or trustworthy some of the authors are in terms of keeping the versions of the artifacts accurate and secure (for example, some authors might want to republish a different version of the code with the same version number, something that's obviously wrong and not allowed, but all systems have flaws). I don't recall a particular issue like this in Python, but I do remember a few years ago this happened in the JavaScript community when someone deleted a package from the NPM registry (REGISTER01), and by unpublishing this library, lots of other builds broke. Even if PyPi doesn't allow this, we don't want to be at the mercy of someone else's good (or bad) faith.

The solution is simple: your company must have an internal server for dependencies, and all builds must target this internal repository. Regardless of how this is implemented (on-premises, on the cloud, by using an open-source tool, or by outsourcing to a provider) the idea is that new, needed dependencies have to be added to this repository, and this is also where the internal packages are published as well.

Make sure this internal repository gets updated and configure all repositories to receive upgrades when new versions of your dependencies are made available. Keep in mind that this is also another form of technical debt. There are several reasons for this. As we've discussed in previous chapters, technical debt is not just about poorly written code. When new technology is made available, you're missing out on those features, which means you could probably be making better use of the technology available. More importantly, packages might have security vulnerabilities that are discovered over time, so you'd want to upgrade to make sure your software is patched.

 Having outdated versions of dependencies is another form of technical debt. Make the habit of using the latest versions available of your dependencies.

Don't let too much time pass before upgrading dependencies because the more you wait, the harder it will be to catch up. After all, that's the whole point of continuous integration: you'd want to integrate changes (including new dependencies) continuously, in an incremental way, provided you have automated tests that run as part of the build and act as a safety net for regressions.

 Configure a tool that automatically sends pull requests for new versions of your dependencies, and also configure automatic security checks on them.

This workflow should require minimal work. The idea is that you configure the setup.py file of your project with a range of versions and have the requirements file. When there are new versions available, the tool you've configured for your repository will rebuild the requirements file, which will list all packages and their new versions (which will show up in the difference of the pull request the tool opens). If the build is green, and there's nothing suspicious in the difference the pull request shows, you can go ahead and merge, trusting the continuous integration would have caught the issues. If, on the other hand, the build fails, that will require your intervention to adjust.

Artifact versions

There's a trade-off between stability and cutting-edge software. Having the latest versions is usually positive, because it means we get the latest features and bug fixes just by upgrading. That's when the new version doesn't bring incompatible changes (the downside). For that reason, software is managed in versions with a clear meaning.

When we establish a range of desired versions, we want to get upgrades, but at the same time not be too aggressive and break the application.

If we only upgrade the dependencies and write the new version of the requirements file, we should be publishing a new version of our artifact (after all, we're delivering something new, hence different). This can be a minor or micro version, but the important part is that we have to abide by the same rules we expect from third-party libraries when we're publishing our own custom artifacts.

A good reference for this in Python is PEP-440 (`https://www.python.org/dev/peps/pep-0440/`), which describes how to set the version numbers in the `setup.py` file for our libraries.

In the next section, we take a look at a different technology that will also help us create components to deliver our code.

Docker containers

This chapter is dedicated to architecture, so the term container refers to something completely different from a Python container (an object with a __contains__ method), explored in *Chapter 2*, *Pythonic Code*. A container is a process that runs in the operating system under a group with certain restrictions and isolation considerations. Concretely, we refer to `Docker` containers, which allow managing applications (services or processes) as independent components.

Containers represent another way of delivering software. Creating Python packages that take into account the considerations in the previous section is more suitable for libraries, or frameworks, where the goal is to reuse code and take advantage of using a single place where specific logic is gathered.

In the case of containers, the objective will not be creating libraries but applications (most of the time). However, an application or platform does not necessarily mean an entire service. The idea of building containers is to create small components that represent a service with a small and clear purpose.

In this section, we will mention Docker when we talk about containers, and we will explore the basics of how to create Docker images and containers for Python projects. Keep in mind that this is not the only technology for launching applications into containers, and also that it's completely independent of Python.

A Docker container needs an image to run on, and this image is created from other base images. But the images we create can themselves serve as base images for other containers. We will want to do that in cases where there is a common base in our application that can be shared across many containers. A potential use would be creating a base image that installs a package (or many) in the way we described in the previous section, and also all of its dependencies, including those at the operating system level. As discussed in *Chapter 9*, *Common Design Patterns*, a package we create can depend not only on other Python libraries, but also on a particular platform (a specific operating system), and particular libraries preinstalled in that operating system, without which the package will simply not install and will fail.

Containers are a great portability tool for this. They can help us ensure that our application will have a canonical way of running, and they will also ease the development process a lot (reproducing scenarios across environments, replicating tests, on-boarding new team members, and so on).

Docker helps avoid platform-dependent issues. The idea is that we package our Python application as a Docker container image, and this will be useful for developing and testing locally, as well as for launching our software in production.

Typically, in the past, Python was hard to deploy because of its nature. Since it's an interpreted language, the code you write will be run by the Python virtual machine on the host on production. So, you need to make sure the target platform will have the version of the interpreter you're expecting it to have. Moreover, the packaging of the dependencies was also hard: this was done by packaging everything into a virtual environment and running it. Things got harder if you had platform-dependent specifics, and some of your dependencies used C extensions. And here I'm not even talking about Windows or Linux; sometimes, even different versions of Linux (Debian-based versus Red Hat-based) had different versions of the C libraries needed for the code to run, so the only true way to test your application and make sure it'd run properly was to use a virtual machine, and compile everything against the right architecture. In modern applications, most of those pains should go away. Now you'll have a `Dockerfile` in your root directory, with the instructions to build that application. And your application is delivered in production also by running it in Docker.

Just as packages are the way we reuse code and unify criteria, containers represent the way we create the different services of the application. They meet the criteria behind the principle of **Separation of Concerns (SoC)** of the architecture. Each service is another kind of component that will encapsulate a set of functionalities independently of the rest of the application. These containers ought to be designed in such a way that they favor maintainability—if the responsibilities are clearly divided, a change in a service should not impact any other part of the application whatsoever.

We cover the basics of how to create a Docker container from a Python project in the next section.

Use case

As an example of how we might organize the components of our application, and how the previous concepts might work in practice, we present the following simple example.

The use case is that there is an application for delivering food, and this application has a specific service for tracking the status of each delivery at its different stages. We are going to focus only on this particular service, regardless of how the rest of the application might appear. The service has to be really simple—a REST API that, when asked about the status of a particular order, will return a JSON response with a descriptive message.

We are going to assume that the information about each particular order is stored in a database, but this detail should not matter at all.

Our service has two main concerns for now: getting the information about a particular order (from wherever this might be stored), and presenting this information in a useful way to the clients (in this case, delivering the results in JSON format, exposed as a web service).

As the application has to be maintainable and extensible, we want to keep these two concerns as hidden as possible and focus on the main logic. Therefore, these two details are abstracted and encapsulated into Python packages that the main application with the core logic will use, as shown in *Figure 10.1*:

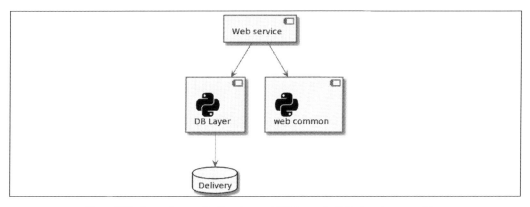

Figure 10.1: A service application (named "Web service") that makes use of two
Python packages, one of which connects to a database.

In the following sections, we briefly demonstrate how the code might appear, in
terms of the packages mainly, and how to create services from these, in order to
finally see what conclusions we can infer.

The code

The idea of creating Python packages in this example is to illustrate how abstracted
and isolated components can be made, in order to work effectively. In reality, there
is no actual need for these to be Python packages; we could just create the right
abstractions as part of the "delivery service" project, and, while the correct isolation
is preserved, it will work without any issues.

Creating packages makes more sense when there is logic that is going to be repeated
and is expected to be used across many other applications (that will import from
those packages) because we want to favor code reuse. In this particular case, there
are no such requirements, so it might be beyond the scope of the design, but such
distinction still makes clearer the idea of a "pluggable architecture" or component,
something that is really a wrapper abstracting technical details we don't really want
to deal with, much less depend upon.

The storage package is in charge of retrieving the data that is required and
presenting this to the next layer (the delivery service) in a convenient format,
something that is suitable for the business rules. The main application should now
know where this data came from, what its format is, and so on. This is the entire
reason why we have such an abstraction in between, so the application doesn't
use a row or an ORM entity directly, but rather something workable.

Domain models

The following definitions apply to classes for business rules. Notice that they are meant to be pure business objects, not bound to anything in particular. They aren't models of an ORM, or objects of an external framework, and so on. The application should work with these objects (or objects with the same criteria).

In each case, the docstring documents the purpose of each class, according to the business rule:

```python
from typing import Union

class DispatchedOrder:
    """An order that was just created and notified to start its
delivery."""

    status = "dispatched"

    def __init__(self, when):
        self._when = when

    def message(self) -> dict:
        return {
            "status": self.status,
            "msg": "Order was dispatched on {0}".format(
                self._when.isoformat()
            ),
        }


class OrderInTransit:
    """An order that is currently being sent to the customer."""

    status = "in transit"

    def __init__(self, current_location):
        self._current_location = current_location

    def message(self) -> dict:
        return {
            "status": self.status,
            "msg": "The order is in progress (current location: {})".
format(
```

```
                    self._current_location
            ),
        }


class OrderDelivered:
    """An order that was already delivered to the customer."""

    status = "delivered"

    def __init__(self, delivered_at):
        self._delivered_at = delivered_at

    def message(self) -> dict:
        return {
            "status": self.status,
            "msg": "Order delivered on {0}".format(
                self._delivered_at.isoformat()
            ),
        }


class DeliveryOrder:
    def __init__(
        self,
        delivery_id: str,
        status: Union[DispatchedOrder, OrderInTransit, OrderDelivered],
    ) -> None:
        self._delivery_id = delivery_id
        self._status = status

    def message(self) -> dict:
        return {"id": self._delivery_id, **self._status.message()}
```

From this code, we can already get an idea of what the application will look like — we want to have a `DeliveryOrder` object, which will have its own status (as an internal collaborator), and once we have that, we will call its `message()` method to return this information to the user.

Calling from the application

This is how these objects are going to be used in the application. Notice how this depends on the previous packages (`web` and `storage`), but not the other way round:

```python
from storage import DBClient, DeliveryStatusQuery, OrderNotFoundError
from web import NotFound, View, app, register_route


class DeliveryView(View):
    async def _get(self, request, delivery_id: int):
        dsq = DeliveryStatusQuery(int(delivery_id), await DBClient())
        try:
            result = await dsq.get()
        except OrderNotFoundError as e:
            raise NotFound(str(e)) from e

        return result.message()


register_route(DeliveryView, "/status/<delivery_id:int>")
```

In the previous section, the `domain` objects were shown and here the code for the application is displayed. Aren't we missing something? Sure, but is it something we really need to know now? Not necessarily.

The code inside the `storage` and `web` packages was deliberately left out (although the reader is more than encouraged to look at it—the repository for the book contains the full example). Also, and this was done on purpose, the names of such packages were chosen so as not to reveal any technical details—`storage` and `web`.

Look again at the code in the previous listing. Can you tell which frameworks are being used? Does it say whether the data comes from a text file, a database (if so, of what type? SQL? NoSQL?), or another service (the web, for instance)? Assume that it comes from a relational database. Is there any clue as to how this information is retrieved (manual SQL queries? Through an ORM?)?

What about the web? Can we guess what frameworks are used?

The fact that we cannot answer any of these questions is probably a good sign. Those are details, and details ought to be encapsulated. We can't answer these questions unless we take a look at what's inside those packages.

There is another way of answering the previous questions, and it comes in the form of a question itself: why do we need to know that? Looking at the code, we can see that there is a DeliveryOrder, created with an identifier of a delivery, and that it has a get() method, which returns an object representing the status of the delivery. If all of this information is correct, that's all we should care about. What difference does it make how it is done?

The abstractions we created make our code declarative. In declarative programming, we declare the problem we want to solve, not how we want to solve it. It's the opposite of imperative, in which we have to make all the steps required explicit in order to get something (for instance, connect to the database, run this query, parse the result, load it into this object, and so on). In this case, we are declaring that we just want to know the status of the delivery given by some identifier.

These packages are in charge of dealing with the details and presenting what the application needs in a convenient format, namely objects of the kind presented in the previous section. We just have to know that the storage package contains an object that, given an ID for a delivery and a storage client (this dependency is being injected into this example for simplicity, but other alternatives are also possible), it will retrieve DeliveryOrder, which we can then ask to compose the message.

This architecture provides convenience and makes it easier to adapt to changes, as it protects the kernel of the business logic from the external factors that can change.

Imagine we want to change how the information is retrieved. How hard would that be? The application relies on an API, like the following one:

```
dsq = DeliveryStatusQuery(int(delivery_id), await DBClient())
```

So, it would just be about changing how the get() method works, adapting it to the new implementation detail. All we need is for this new object to return DeliveryOrder on its get() method and that would be all. We can change the query, the ORM, the database, and so on, and, in all cases, the code in the application does not need to change!

Adapters

Still, without looking at the code in the packages, we can conclude that they work as interfaces for the technical details of the application.

In fact, since we are seeing the application from a high-level perspective, without needing to look at the code, we can imagine that inside those packages there must be an implementation of the adapter design pattern (introduced in *Chapter 9, Common Design Patterns*). One or more of these objects is adapting an external implementation to the API defined by the application. This way, dependencies that want to work with the application must conform to the API, and an adapter will have to be made.

There is one clue pertaining to this adapter in the code for the application though. Notice how the view is constructed. It inherits from a class named `View` that comes from our `web` package. We can deduce that this `View` is, in turn, a class derived from one of the web frameworks that might be being used, creating an adapter by inheritance. The important thing to note is that once this is done, the only object that matters is our `View` class, because, in a way, we are creating our own framework, which is based on adapting an existing one (but again, changing the framework will mean just changing the adapters, not the entire application).

Starting from the next section, we'll take a look at what the services look like internally.

The services

To create the service, we are going to launch the Python application inside a Docker container. Starting from a base image, the container will have to install the dependencies for the application to run, which also has dependencies at the operating system level.

This is actually a choice because it depends on how the dependencies are used. If a package we use requires other libraries on the operating system to compile at installation time, we can avoid this simply by building a wheel for our platform of the library and installing this directly. If the libraries are needed at runtime, then there is no choice but to make them part of the image of the container.

Now, we will discuss one of the many ways of preparing a Python application to be run inside a Docker container. This is one of the numerous alternatives for packaging a Python project into a container. First, we take a look at what the structure of the directories looks like:

```
├── Dockerfile
├── libs
│   ├── README.rst
│   ├── storage
│   └── web
├── Makefile
├── README.rst
```

```
├── setup.py
└── statusweb
    ├── __init__.py
    └── service.py
```

The libs directory can be ignored since it's just the place where the dependencies are placed (it's displayed here to keep them in mind when they are referenced in the setup.py file, but they could be placed in a different repository and installed remotely via pip).

We have Makefile with some helper commands, then the setup.py file, and the application itself inside the statusweb directory. A common difference between packaging applications and libraries is that while the latter specify their dependencies in the setup.py file, the former have a requirements.txt file from where dependencies are installed via pip install -r requirements.txt. Normally, we would do this in the Dockerfile, but in order to keep things simpler, in this particular example, we will assume that taking the dependencies from the setup.py file is enough. This is because besides this consideration, there are a lot more considerations to be taken into account when dealing with dependencies, such as freezing the version of the packages, tracking indirect dependencies, using extra tools such as pipenv, and more topics that are beyond the scope of the chapter. In addition, it is also customary to make the setup.py file read from requirements.txt for consistency.

Now we have the content of the setup.py file, which states some details of the application:

```
from setuptools import find_packages, setup

with open("README.rst", "r") as longdesc:
    long_description = longdesc.read()


install_requires = ["web==0.1.0", "storage==0.1.0"]

setup(
    name="delistatus",
    description="Check the status of a delivery order",
    long_description=long_description,
    author="Dev team",
    version="0.1.0",
    packages=find_packages(),
    install_requires=install_requires,
```

```
    entry_points={
        "console_scripts": [
            "status-service = statusweb.service:main",
        ],
    },
)
```

The first thing we notice is that the application declares its dependencies, which are the packages we created and placed under `libs/`, namely `web` and `storage`, abstracting and adapting to some external components. These packages, in turn, will have dependencies, so we will have to make sure the container installs all the required libraries when the image is being created so that they can install successfully, and then this package afterward.

The second thing we notice is the definition of the `entry_points` keyword argument passed to the `setup` function. This is not strictly mandatory, but it's a good idea to create an entry point. When the package is installed in a virtual environment, it shares this directory along with all its dependencies. A virtual environment is a structure of directories with the dependencies of a given project. It has many subdirectories, but the most important ones are:

- `<virtual-env-root>/lib/<python-version>/site-packages`
- `<virtual-env-root>/bin`

The first one contains all the libraries installed in that virtual environment. If we were to create a virtual environment with this project, that directory would contain the `web` and `storage` packages, along with all its dependencies, plus some extra basic ones and the current project itself.

The second, `/bin/`, contains the binary files and commands available when that virtual environment is active. By default, it would just be the version of Python, `pip`, and some other basic commands. When we create a console entry point, a binary with that declared name is placed there, and, as a result, we have that command available to run when the environment is active. When this command is called, it will run the function that is specified with all the context of the virtual environment. That means it is a binary we can call directly without having to worry about whether the virtual environment is active, or whether the dependencies are installed in the path that is currently running.

The definition is the following one:

```
"status-service = statusweb.service:main"
```

The left-hand side of the equals sign declares the name of the entry point. In this case, we will have a command named `status-service` available. The right-hand side declares how that command should be run. It requires the package where the function is defined, followed by the function name after `:`. In this case, it will run the `main` function declared in `statusweb/service.py`.

This is followed by a definition of the `Dockerfile`:

```
FROM python:3.9-slim-buster

RUN apt-get update && \
    apt-get install -y --no-install-recommends \
        python-dev \
        gcc \
        musl-dev \
        make \
    && rm -rf /var/lib/apt/lists/*
WORKDIR /app
ADD . /app

RUN pip install /app/libs/web /app/libs/storage
RUN pip install /app

EXPOSE 8080
CMD ["/usr/local/bin/status-service"]
```

The image is built based on a lightweight Linux image with Python installed, and then the operating system dependencies are installed so that our libraries can be deployed. Following the previous consideration, this `Dockerfile` simply copies the libraries, but this might as well be installed from a `requirements.txt` file accordingly. After all the `pip install` commands are ready, it copies the application in the working directory, and the entry point from Docker (the `CMD` command, not to be confused with the Python one) calls the entry point of the package where we placed the function that launches the process. For local development, we'd still use the `Dockerfile`, in conjunction with a `docker-compose.yml` file with the definitions of all the services (including dependencies such as databases), base images, and how they are linked and interconnected.

Now that we have the container running, we can launch it and run a small test on it to get an idea of how it works:

```
$ curl http://localhost:5000/status/1
{"id":1,"status":"dispatched","msg":"Order was dispatched on 2018-08-01T22:25:12+00:00"}
```

Let's analyze the architectural traits for the code we've seen so far, starting in the next section.

Analysis

There are many conclusions to be drawn from the previous implementation. While it might seem like a good approach, there are cons that come with the benefits; after all, no architecture or implementation is perfect. This means that a solution such as this one cannot be good for all cases, so it will pretty much depend on the circumstances of the project, the team, the organization, and more.

While it's true that the main idea of the solution is to abstract details as much as possible, as we shall see, some parts cannot be fully abstracted away, and also the contracts between the layers imply an abstraction leak.

After all, technology always creeps in. For example, if we were to change our implementation from a REST service to serve our data through GraphQL, we would have to adapt how the application server is configured and built, but still, we should be able to have a structure very similar to the preceding one. Even if we want to make a more radical change so as to transform our service into a gRPC server, we would of course be forced to adapt some glue code, but we should still be able to use our packages as much as possible. The changes needed should be kept to a minimum.

The dependency flow

Notice that dependencies flow in only one direction, as they move closer to the kernel, where the business rules lie. This can be traced by looking at the `import` statements. The application imports everything it needs from storage, for example, and in no part is this inverted.

Breaking this rule would create coupling. The way the code is arranged now means that there is a weak dependency between the application and storage. The API is such that we need an object with a `get()` method, and any storage that wants to connect to the application needs to implement this object according to this specification. The dependencies are therefore inverted—it's up to every storage to implement this interface, in order to create an object according to what the application is expecting.

Limitations

Not everything can be abstracted away. In some cases, it's simply not possible, and in others, it might not be convenient. Let's start with the convenience aspect.

In this example, there is an adapter of the web framework of choice to a clean API to be presented to the application. In a more complex scenario, such a change might not be possible. Even with this abstraction, parts of the library are still visible to the application. It's not entirely a problem to be completely isolated from the web framework because, sooner or later, we will need some of its features or technical details.

The important takeaway here is not the adapter, but the idea of hiding technical details as much as possible. That means that the best thing that is displayed on the listing for the code of the application is not the fact that there is an adapter between our version of the web framework and the actual one, but instead, the fact that the latter is not mentioned by name in any part of the visible code. The service has made clear that `web` is just a dependency (a detail being imported) and revealed the intention behind what it was supposed to do. The goal is to reveal the intention (as in the code) and to defer details as much as possible.

As to what things cannot be isolated, those are the elements that are closest to the code. In this case, the web application is using the objects operating within them in an asynchronous fashion. That is a hard constraint we cannot circumvent. It's true that whatever is inside the `storage` package can be changed, refactored, and modified, but whatever these modifications might be, it still needs to preserve the interface, and that includes the asynchronous interface.

Testability

Again, much like with the code, the architecture can benefit from separating pieces into smaller components. The fact that dependencies are now isolated and controlled by separate components leaves us with a cleaner design for the main application, and now it's easier to ignore the boundaries to focus on testing the core of the application.

We could create a patch for the dependencies and write unit tests that are simpler (they won't need a database), or launch an entire web service, for instance. Working with pure `domain` objects means it will be easier to understand the code and the unit tests. Even the adapters will not need that much testing because their logic should be very simple.

Keep in mind the software testing pyramid mentioned in *Chapter 8, Unit Testing and Refactoring*. We want to have a large number of unit tests, followed by fewer component tests, and finally even fewer integration tests. Separating our architecture into different components goes a long way for component testing: we can mock up our dependencies and test some components in isolation.

This is both cheaper and faster, but it doesn't mean that we shouldn't have integration tests at all. To make sure our final application works as expected, we need integration tests that will exercise all components of our architecture (be that microservices or packages), working together.

Intention revealing

Intention revealing is a critical concept for our code—every name has to be wisely chosen, clearly communicating what it's supposed to do. Every function should tell a story. We should keep functions short, concerns separated, and dependencies isolated and assign the right meaning to abstractions in every part of the code.

Good architecture should reveal the intent of the system it entails. It should not mention the tools it's built with; those are details, and as we discussed at length, details should be hidden and encapsulated.

Summary

The principles of good software design apply to all levels. In the same way that we want to write readable code, and for that we need to keep in mind the intention-revealing aspects of the code, the architecture also has to express the intent of the problem it is trying to solve.

All these ideas are interconnected. The same intention revealing that ensures our architecture is defined in terms of the domain problem also leads us to abstract details as much as possible, create layers of abstraction, invert dependencies, and separate concerns.

When it comes to reusing code, Python packages are a great and flexible option. Criteria such as cohesion and the single responsibility principle are the most important considerations when deciding to create a package. In line with having components with cohesion and few responsibilities, the concept of microservices comes into play, and for that, we have seen how a service can be deployed in a Docker container starting from a packaged Python application.

As with everything in software engineering, there are limitations and there are exceptions. It will not always be possible to abstract things as much as we would like to or to completely isolate dependencies. Sometimes, it will just not be possible (or practical) to comply with the principles explained here in the book. But that is probably the best piece of advice the reader should take from the book—they are just principles, not laws. If it's not possible, or practical, to abstract from a framework, it should not be a problem. Remember what has been quoted from the *Zen of Python* itself throughout the book—*practicality beats purity*.

References

Here is a list of information you can refer to:

- *SCREAM*: *Screaming Architecture* (`https://8thlight.com/blog/uncle-bob/2011/09/30/Screaming-Architecture.html`)
- *CLEAN-01*: *The Clean Architecture* (`https://8thlight.com/blog/uncle-bob/2012/08/13/the-clean-architecture.html`)
- *HEX*: *Hexagonal Architecture* (`https://staging.cockburn.us/hexagonal-architecture/`)
- *PEP-508*: Dependency specification for Python software packages (`https://www.python.org/dev/peps/pep-0508/`)
- Packaging and distributing projects in Python: `https://python-packaging-user-guide.readthedocs.io/guides/distributing-packages-using-setuptools/#distributing-packages`
- *PEP-440*: `https://www.python.org/dev/peps/pep-0440/`
- *REGISTER01*: `https://www.theregister.com/2016/03/23/npm_left_pad_chaos/`
- Python packaging user guide: `https://packaging.python.org/`
- AWS builder's library: *Going faster with continuous delivery* (`https://aws.amazon.com/builders-library/going-faster-with-continuous-delivery/`)

Summing it all up

The content of this book is a reference, a possible way of implementing a software solution by following the mentioned criteria. These criteria are explained through examples, and the rationale for every decision is presented. The reader might very well disagree with the approaches taken in the examples.

In fact, I encourage you to disagree: the more viewpoints there are, the richer the debate. But regardless of opinions, it's important to make clear that what is presented here is by no means a strong directive, something that must be followed imperatively. Quite the opposite; it's a way of presenting a solution and a set of ideas that you might find helpful.

As introduced at the beginning, the goal of this book was not to give you recipes or formulas that you can apply directly, but rather to develop your critical thinking. Idioms and syntax features come and go; they change over time. But ideas and core software concepts remain. With these tools and the examples provided, you should have a better understanding of what clean code means.

I sincerely hope this book has helped you become a better developer than you were before you started it, and I wish you much success in your projects.

Share your experience

Thank you for taking the time to read this book. If you enjoyed this book, help others to find it. Leave a review at: https://www.amazon.com/dp/1800560214

Other Books You May Enjoy

If you enjoyed this book, you may be interested in these books by Packt:

Modern Python Cookbook

Steven F. Lott

ISBN: 978-1-80020-745-5

- See the intricate details of the Python syntax and how to use it to your advantage
- Improve your coding with Python readability through functions
- Manipulate data effectively using built-in data structures
- Get acquainted with advanced programming techniques in Python
- Equip yourself with functional and statistical programming features
- Write proper tests to be sure a program works as advertised
- Integrate application software using Python

Python Machine Learning by Example

Yuxi (Hayden) Liu

ISBN: 978-1-80020-971-8

- Understand the important concepts in ML and data science
- Use Python to explore the world of data mining and analytics
- Scale up model training using varied data complexities with Apache Spark
- Delve deep into text analysis and NLP using Python libraries such NLTK and Gensim
- Select and build an ML model and evaluate and optimize its performance
- Implement ML algorithms from scratch in Python, TensorFlow 2, PyTorch, and scikit-learn

Index

get method 203, 204
idiomatic implementation 219-221
implementing 222
implementing, in decorators 237
interface 237
issue of shared state 222, 223
methods 230-233
non-data descriptors 212-214
object-oriented design 238
set method 205, 207
set name method 210, 211
slots 235, 236
type annotations, applying on 238
types 211, 212
using 230
weak references, using 224
working 217
Design by Contract (DbC) 74, 178
design patterns 358
as theory 359
behavioral patterns 344
considerations, in Python 328, 329
creational patterns 330
names, in models 360
null object pattern 355, 357
structural patterns 337
working 329, 330
design principles 286
Docker containers 376, 377
docstring 10-13
documentation 9
domain models 380, 381
Don't Repeat Yourself (DRY)
principle 92, 192, 305
with decorators 193
duck typing 145
dynamic attributes
for objects 59, 61

E

Easier to Ask Forgiveness than Permission
(EAFP) 98
edge cases 324
empty except blocks
avoiding 85, 87

equivalence class 323
error handling 78, 79
events system
extending 135-137
refactoring, for extensibility 133-135
exception handling 80, 81
exceptions
handling, at right level of abstraction 81-85

F

facade pattern 343
factory pattern 330
flake8 23
function arguments
and coupling 117
working 107
function decorators 159, 160
functions
arguments, copying to 107, 108
number of arguments 117
function signatures
adapting 176, 178
functools.partial
reference link 227

G

generator interface, methods 260
close() 260, 261
send(value) 263-266
throw(ex_type[, ex_value[, ex_traceback]])
261-263
generators
creating 242
example 242-245
expressions 246, 247
using 250, 251
generic validations
in code 22, 23
God objects 126
Graphene
URL 61
GraphQL
URL 61

H

hexagonal architecture (HEX) 368
hint 13

I

idioms
  for iteration 247-249
incompatible signatures
  detecting, with pylint 140
incorrect method signatures
  detecting, with mypy 138, 139
indexes 30, 31
inheritance 189
  anti-patterns 100-103
  good case 99, 100
  in Python 99
  multiple inheritance 103, 104
integration test 287
intention revealing 390
interface 145
interface segregation principle (ISP) 144-149
IPython
  URL 11
iterable 256
iterable objects 52
  creating 53-55
iteration
  interface 256, 257
iterator pattern
  in Python 255
iterators 256
  code, simplifying 252
itertools module 251-253

K

keyword-only arguments 115, 116
KIS (Keep It Simple) 95-97

L

limit values 323
Liskov's substitution principle
    (LSP) 137, 138, 144
Look Before You Leap (LBYL) 98

LSP issues, detecting with tools 138
  mypy, used for detecting incorrect method
    signatures 138, 139
  pylint, used for detecting incompatible
    signatures 140
LSP violations
  subtle cases 141-144

M

magic asynchronous methods 275
magic methods 63, 64, 277
maintainability perils
  examples 130-132
Method Resolution Order (MRO) 104, 105
microservices architecture 366
mixin 106
mocking 287
mock objects 309
  using 310
mocks 310, 311
  types 311, 312
monolithic applications 367
monostate pattern 331
multiple inheritance 103, 104
mutable default arguments 64, 65
mutants 320
mutation testing 320-322
mypy
  reference link 9, 20
  used, for detecting incorrect method
    signatures 138, 139

N

nested loops 253, 254
next() function 249, 250
non-data descriptor 212-214
null object pattern 355, 357

O

object-oriented design
  of descriptors 238
Object-Relational Mapper (ORM) 368
Object Relational Mapper SQLAlchemy
    (ORM SQLAlchemy) 349

Printed in Great Britain
by Amazon

60498285R00240